"This is an invaluable resource on the recently developed latent variable method of scoring and analyzing test data. It includes very clear explanations of terminology and excellent illustrations of concepts. It is a must read for anyone interested in measurement theory and practice."
—**George A. Marcoulides**, *Distinguished Professor, University of California, Santa Barbara*

D-scoring Method of Measurement

D-scoring Method of Measurement presents a unified framework of classical and latent measurement referred to as *D*-scoring method of measurement (DSM). Provided are detailed descriptions of DSM procedures and illustrative examples of how to apply the DSM in various scenarios of measurement.

The DSM is designed to combine merits of the traditional CTT and IRT for the purpose of transparency, ease of interpretations, computational simplicity of test scoring and scaling, and practical efficiency, particularly in large-scale assessments. Through detailed descriptions of DSM procedures, this book shows how practical applications of such procedures are facilitated by the inclusion of operationalized guidance for their execution using the computer program DELTA for DSM-based scoring, equating, and item analysis of test data. In doing so, the book shows how DSM procedures can be readily translated into computer source codes for other popular software packages such as R. *D-scoring Method of Measurement* equips researchers and practitioners in the field of educational and psychological measurement with a comprehensive understanding of the DSM as a unified framework of classical and latent scoring, equating, and psychometric analysis.

Dimiter M. Dimitrov is Professor Emeritus at George Mason University, USA, and Senior Psychometrician at the National Center for Assessment in Riyadh, Saudi Arabia. His areas of expertise include assessment, psychometrics, and advanced quantitative research methods in education, psychology, and related fields. Dr. Dimitrov earned a PhD in mathematics education from the University of Sofia, Bulgaria (1984) and a PhD in educational measurement and statistics from Southern Illinois University, Carbondale, USA (1995). His professional work and publications have received international recognition. Dr. Dimitrov has served as president of the Mid-Western Educational Research Association in the USA, program chair of the SIG Rasch Measurement of the American Educational Research Association (AERA), editor of *Measurement and Evaluation in Counseling and Development*, and member of the editorial board of numerous other professional journals in the field of educational and psychological measurement. His most recent research efforts resulted in the development of the *D*-scoring method of measurement (DSM) as a unified framework of classical and latent scoring and analysis of test data. Dr. Dimitrov is multilingual and has lectured and published professional work in English, Bulgarian, Russian, and French.

Quantitative Methodology Series
George A. Marcoulides, Series Editor

This series presents methodological techniques to investigators and students. The goal is to provide an understanding and working knowledge of each method with a minimum of mathematical derivations. Each volume focuses on a specific method (e.g. Factor Analysis, Multilevel Analysis, Structural Equation Modeling).

Proposals are invited from interested authors. Each proposal should consist of: a brief description of the volume's focus and intended market; a table of contents with an outline of each chapter; and a curriculum vita. Materials may be sent to Dr. George A. Marcoulides, University of California – Santa Barbara, gmarcoulides@education.ucsb.edu.

Marcoulides • *Modern Methods for Business Research*
Marcoulides/Moustaki • *Latent Variable and Latent Structure Models*
Heck • *Studying Educational and Social Policy: Theoretical Concepts and Research Methods*
Van der Ark/Croon/Sijtsma • *New Developments in Categorical Data Analysis for the Social and Behavioral Sciences*
Duncan/Duncan/Strycker • *An Introduction to Latent Variable Growth Curve Modeling: Concepts, Issues, and Applications, Second Edition*
Cardinet/Johnson/Pini • *Applying Generalizability Theory Using EduG*
Creemers/Kyriakides/Sammons • *Methodological Advances in Educational Effectiveness Research*
Heck/Thomas/Tabata • *Multilevel Modeling of Categorical Outcomes Using IBM SPSS*
Heck/Thomas/Tabata • *Multilevel and Longitudinal Modeling with IBM SPSS, Second Edition*
McArdle/Ritschard • *Contemporary Issues in Exploratory Data Mining in the Behavioral Sciences*
Heck/Thomas • *An Introduction to Multilevel Modeling Techniques: MLM and SEM Approaches Using Mplus, Third Edition*
Hox/Moerbeek/van de Schoot • *Multilevel Analysis: Techniques and Applications, Third Edition*
Lamprianou • *Applying the Rasch Model in Social Sciences using R and BlueSky Statistics*
Heck/Thomas • *An Introduction to Multilevel Modeling Techniques: MLM and SEM Approaches, Fourth Edition*
Heck/Thomas/Tabata • *Multilevel and Longitudinal Modeling with IBM SPSS, Third Edition*
Dimitrov/Dimiter • *D-scoring Method of Measurement: Classical and Latent Frameworks*

D-scoring Method of Measurement
Classical and Latent Frameworks

Dimiter M. Dimitrov

LONDON AND NEW YORK

Designed cover image: © Getty images

First published 2024
by Routledge
4 Park Square, Milton Park, Abingdon, Oxon OX14 4RN

and by Routledge
605 Third Avenue, New York, NY 10158

Routledge is an imprint of the Taylor & Francis Group, an informa business

© 2024 Dimiter M. Dimitrov

The right of Dimiter M. Dimitrov to be identified as author of this work has been asserted in accordance with sections 77 and 78 of the Copyright, Designs and Patents Act 1988.

All rights reserved. No part of this book may be reprinted or reproduced or utilised in any form or by any electronic, mechanical, or other means, now known or hereafter invented, including photocopying and recording, or in any information storage or retrieval system, without permission in writing from the publishers.

Trademark notice: Product or corporate names may be trademarks or registered trademarks, and are used only for identification and explanation without intent to infringe.

British Library Cataloguing-in-Publication Data
A catalogue record for this book is available from the British Library

ISBN: 9781032380049 (hbk)
ISBN: 9781032380063 (pbk)
ISBN: 9781003343004 (ebk)

DOI: 10.4324/9781003343004

Typeset in Bembo
by codeMantra

To those with whom I share mutual love (observable and latent)

—*D.M.D.*

Contents

Preface xiv
Acknowledgment xvi
List of abbreviations xvii

1 Classical Test Theory: Basic Concepts and Features 1
   Introduction 1
   What Is Measurement? 1
   Levels of Measurement 1
      Nominal Scale 1
      Ordinal Scale 1
      Interval Scale 2
      Ratio Scale 2
   CTT Assumptions 2
      Parallel Tests 2
      Essentially Tau-Equivalent Tests 3
   CTT Scoring 3
      Raw Scores 3
      Percentiles 3
      Standard Scores 3
      Standardized Scores 4
      Normalized Scores 4
      Equal-Interval Scales 4
   CTT Item Analysis 4
      Item Difficulty 4
      Item Discrimination 4
      Item/Total Score Correlation 5
      Item Characteristic Curves 5
   Reliability 6
      Internal Consistency Reliability 7
      Test-retest Reliability 7
      Alternate Form Reliability 7
   Standard Error of Measurement 8
      Confidence Interval for SEM 8
   Standard Error of Estimation 9
   Reliability of Composite Scores 9
   Equating Test Scores 9
      Linear Equating 10
      Equipercentile Equating 10
   CTT Strengths 10
   CTT Limitations 10
   Summary Points 11
   References 12

2 Item Response Theory: Basic Concepts and Features — 13

Introduction 13
IRT Assumptions 13
    Unidimensionality 13
    Local Independence 14
    ICC Specification 15
Basic IRT Models 16
    Two-Parameter Logistic Model 16
    One-Parameter Logistic Model 16
    Three-Parameter Logistic Model 17
Ability Scale 18
    IRT Logit Scale 18
    Scale Indeterminacy 19
    True Domain Scores 20
Ability Estimation 20
Information Functions 22
    Test Information Function 22
    Item Information Function 22
Testing for Model-Data Fit 24
    Log-Likelihood Ratio Test 24
    $G^2(\text{dif})$ Test 25
    Item Fit 25
    Person Fit 27
Differential Item Functioning 28
    Differential Test Functioning 30
    A Compensatory DIF Index 30
    A Noncompensatory DIF Index 30
Test Equating 31
    True-Score Equating 32
Summary Points 33
Appendix 2.1: Rasch Model 34
    Rasch Ratio Scale Property 34
References 35

3 CTT-IRT: Comparison and Connections — 39

Introduction 39
CTT-IRT Comparison 39
    CTT and IRT Models and Assumptions 39
    CTT Advantages 40
    CTT Disadvantages 40
    IRT Advantages 40
    IRT Disadvantages 40
    Comparing CTT-IRT Performance 41
CTT-IRT Connections 42
Summary Points 43
References 43

4 Classical *D*-scoring Method — 45

Introduction 45
Expected Item Difficulty 45
    Bootstrap Estimation of δ_i 45
    Estimation of δ_i via IRT Item Parameters 46
Computation of Classical D-scores 46
Intervalness of the D-Scale 47

Item Response Function Models 47
  Two-Parameter RFM (RFM2) 47
  One-Parameter RFM (RFM1) 47
  Three-Parameter RFM (RFM3) 48
True Values and Standard Errors of D_w Scores 50
Item-Person Map on the D-scale 51
"Odds for Success" Properties 52
Features and Practical Applications of D_w Scores 53
Summary Points 54
Appendix 4.1: R Code for Classical D-scores and Item Parameters 54
References 55

5 Latent *D*-scoring Method   57

Introduction 57
Latent Rational Function Models of IRFs 57
  Two-Parameter Rational Function Model (RFM2) 57
  One-Parameter Rational Function Model (RFM1) 57
  Three-Parameter Rational Function Model (RFM3) 58
Item and Test Information Functions 58
  Item Information Function (IIF) 58
  Test Information Function (TIF) 59
  Standard Error of Estimation 59
RFM-Based Estimations 60
  JML-CNO Estimation 61
  Base *D*-scale 61
  Rescaling *D*-scores to the Base *D*-scale 62
Summary Points 64
Appendix 5.1: DSM-L Estimations via the JML-CNO Method 64
Appendix 5.2: R Code for the Estimation of Latent D-scores and Item Parameters 65
Appendix 5.3: Rescaling of D-scores Obtained via Different Methods for the Same Data 66
  Syntax Code in SPSS and R 66
  SPSS Code 66
  R Code 67
References 67

6 DSM Test Equating   68

Introduction 68
Rescaling of Item Parameters 68
  DSM-C: Rescaling of Expected Item Difficulty 68
  DSM-L: Rescaling of Item Parameters b_i and s_i 69
Equating of D-scores 70
  Equating of Classical *D*-scores 70
  Equating of Latent *D*-scores 70
Summary Points 71
Appendix 6.1: R Code for Rescaling of Expected Item Difficulties 72
References 73

7 Item and Person Fit   74

Testing for Item Fit 74
Testing for Person Fit 75
  Zd Person-Fit Statistic 75
  Deterministic Guttman Model 75
  U3 Person-Fit Statistic 76

Ud Person-Fit Statistic 76
Zd and Ud Cutoff Values 76
Summary Points 77
References 77

8 DSM Testing for Differential Item/Test Functioning — 78
Introduction 78
P–Z Method of Testing for DIF 78
    Differential Test Functioning 82
    Effect Size for DIF and DTF 82
    Some Practical Notes 82
Summary Points 84
Appendix 8.1: R Code for DIF Testing 85
References 85

9 DSM for Polytomous Items — 87
Introduction 87
Graded Response Model 87
D-scoring of Polytomous Items 88
Summary Points 92
References 92

10 DSM for Standard Setting — 93
Introduction 93
Some Popular Standard Setting Methods 93
    Angoff Method 93
    Bookmark Method 93
    ID Matching Method 94
Response Vector for Mastery (RVM) Method 95
    Motivation 95
    Response Vector Units 95
    RVM Cut-Scores 95
    The Choice of RVUs 98
    Computation of Cut-Scores 98
Summary Points 99
Appendix 10.1: R Code for the Computation of a Latent Cut-Score, D_c, Corresponding to a Given RVM 99
References 100

11 DSM for Multistage Testing — 102
Introduction 102
Multistage Tests 102
    MST Structure 102
    Routing Rules 102
    Scoring and Equating 103
    Test Assembly 104
MST Using D-scoring 104
    MST-D Routing and Scoring 105
    MST-D Test Assembly 106
Summary Points 108
References 108

12 DSM-IRT Connections   110

Introduction 110
Derivation of IRF Models on the D-scale 110
   One-Parameter RFM 110
   Two-Parameter RFM 111
   Three-Parameter RFM 111
Connecting the RFM2 and 2PL Models 111
   Logit-Normal Distribution 113
   Conditional Standard Errors 114
   Multidimensional Latent D-scoring 114
Rescaling of Latent D-scores 115
Summary Points 119
Appendix 12.1: CFA-Based Computation of Latent Factor Scores and Expected Item Difficulties for Unidimensional Data of Binary Scores: Procedure and Syntax Code in Mplus 119
   Relating CFA and IRT Parameters 119
   Mplus Syntax Code 120
References 121

13 Summary Notes   122

Motivation 122
DSM-C and CTT 122
DSM-C and DSM-L 122
DSM-L and IRT 123
DSM Software 124
References 125

Index   127

Preface

Classical test theory (CTT) and item response theory (IRT) are the two main frameworks of measurement in education, psychology, and related fields, each with its own advantages and disadvantages. The CTT, which has been the foundation of measurement theory for over a century, is valued for its simplicity, transparency, and easy-to-meet assumptions in real-data assessments. The main drawback of the CTT is the lack of invariance, in the sense that the examinees' scores depend on the set of test items, and conversely, the item parameters (e.g., difficulty) depend on the sample of examinees. Another drawback of the CTT is the lack of models for the relationship between test scores and chances of success on individual test items. Drawbacks of CTT are avoided in IRT but at the price of stronger assumptions, complexity of modeling and computations, and difficulty of interpretations. There are ongoing efforts in the field of measurement to study CTT-IRT connections and problems from both methodological and practical perspectives. Some researchers emphasize problems with using unweighted sum scores in CTT, as well as problems with IRT score estimations over the whole real numeric line $(-\infty, +\infty)$, calling for "optimal" scoring on a bounded metric. Other researchers emphasize the (often neglected) role of scaling in drawing inferences about test scores as an important aspect of test validation.

The *D-scoring method of measurement* (DSM) is designed to combine merits of the traditional CTT and IRT, *not* to replace them, in a unified framework of classical and latent scoring of test data and their psychometric analysis. The DSM is developed in classical and latent versions, denoted as DSM-C and DSM-L, respectively. The DSM-C (Chapter 4) and DSM-L (Chapter 5) share the same scale on a bounded metric for person scores and item difficulties, same analytic models for item response functions, and other psychometric features, but differ in approaches (classical vs. latent) used for the estimation of person ability and item parameters. The DSM is developed for dichotomously scored items, but it is readily applicable to polytomous items upon a simple recoding of their ordered categories (Chapter 9). To date (2016–2022), key articles on DSM have been published mainly in two journals, *Educational and Psychological Measurement* and *Measurement: Interdisciplinary Research and Perspectives*. The DSM was first piloted and implemented in large-scale assessments at the National Center for Assessment of the Education & Training Evaluation Commission (ETEC) in Saudi Arabia (https://etec.gov.sa/en). There is a rising interest in DSM by testing companies and academic programs in other countries as well.

DSM-C provides important extensions of the traditional CTT such as (a) scoring based on the examinee's response pattern and expected item difficulties, (b) interval scoring scale, (c) person scores and item difficulties presented on the same scale, (d) classical modeling of item response functions, and (e) conditional standard error of test scores. Under DSM-C, the test score of a person is a weighted sum of binary scores on the test items, where the item "weight" depends on the expected item difficulty, δ ("*delta*"), hence the name "*Delta*-scoring" (or "*D*-scoring," for short). The *D*-scores form an interval scale [0, 1], and they are usually multiplied by 100 to place them on a scale from 0 to 100 in reports of test results.

DSM-L is a latent "mirror" of the classical DSM-C, with some advantages in the accuracy of estimation, additive test information function (as a sum of item information functions), and other psychometric features based on the use of latent (e.g., maximum likelihood) estimation of person and item parameters. Furthermore, the DSM-L analytic models of item response functions are mathematically equivalent to their counterparts in IRT upon logistic transformations of the model parameters for person ability and item difficulty (Chapter 12). In this sense, DSM-L can be seen as IRT modeling on a bounded scale (0, 1). One of the advantages of using DSM-L is that the conditional standard errors of person scores decrease towards the ends of the *D*-scale, whereas their IRT-based counterparts increase for large and small values on the logit scale. Thus, compared to IRT, DSM-L provides higher discrimination and more accurate estimation of ability (trait) levels for low- and high-performing examinees.

Organization of the Book

This book is organized into 13 chapters. The first three chapters introduce basic concepts and features of the traditional CTT and IRT to prepare the ground for the presentation of DSM-C as an extension of CTT, and

DSM-L as IRT-like modeling on a bounded scale. Chapter 1 focuses on CTT assumptions, scoring, item analysis, reliability, equating, strengths, and limitations. Chapter 2 presents IRT assumptions, basic logistic models, ability scale, information functions, testing for model-data fit, differential item functioning, and test equating. Chapter 3 presents some aspects of CTT-IRT comparison and connections, as well as the advantages and disadvantages of these two measurement frameworks. Chapter 4 introduces DSM-C (classical DSM)—key concepts, scoring, classical nonlinear regression models of item response functions, conditional standard error of score estimates, and some properties. Chapter 5 introduces DSM-L (latent DSM)—latent item response function models, item and test information functions, conditional standard error, and estimation. Chapter 6 deals with rescaling of item parameters and equating of D-scores under DSM-C and DSM-L. Chapter 7 describes approaches to testing for item and person fit under DSM. Chapter 8 presents an approach to testing for differential item functioning and differential test functioning under DSM. Chapter 9 presents an approach to D-scoring of polytomous items with ordered response categories and provides an illustration with a comparison to the graded response model in IRT. Chapter 10 introduces an approach to standard setting, referred to as "response vector for mastery" (RVM) method, which is designed for DSM applications, but it can be used in the context of IRT as well. Chapter 11 deals with multistage testing using DSM-C scoring. Chapter 12 presents some DSM-IRT connections—the derivation of item response function (IRF) models in DSM from the Rasch model, mathematical equivalence of the two-parameter IRF models in DSM-L and IRT, and rescaling of D-scores obtained *via* different estimation approaches (e.g., transformations of IRT-based ability scores). Chapter 13 provides summary notes on key aspects of DSM-C and DSM-L, their connections to the traditional CTT and IRT, and some practical suggestions.

From a pedagogical perspective, the presentation of topics was guided by the intent to provide the reader with an understandable treatment of the classical and latent DSM methodology as bridging, *not* replacing, CTT and IRT scaling and psychometric features on a bounded metric. The attainment of this goal is facilitated by the use of numerous explanatory notes, illustrative examples, tables, and graphical depictions throughout the text. Key procedures for scoring, rescaling, equating, and testing for model-data fit are presented in a stepwise format to facilitate related computations and their computer-based implementations. Provided also are syntax codes (mainly in R) for some procedures and website references to software available to DSM users (e.g., researchers, assessment practitioners, and educators). Each chapter ends with a list of "summary points" that highlight key concepts, procedures, and methodological issues.

Intended Audience

This book is intended for a large audience of researchers, practitioners, faculty, and graduate students. For example, this book can be of great interest to psychometricians, test developers, and practitioners in testing companies and assessment centers who want to combine the merits of CTT and IRT in large-scale assessments. DSM features of transparency, computational simplicity, clarity of interpretations, and psychometric dependability can be appealing to the practice of assessment worldwide. This book can be used also as a supplementary text for graduate-level courses on measurement in education, psychology, health, and other fields. Students in such courses can benefit from this book for a better understanding of CTT and IRT issues addressed in DSM. Furthermore, the DSM methodology and procedures presented in this book provide an excellent framework for further research and dissertation topics.

Acknowledgment

I would like to thank all my colleagues who have provided their help at various stages of my work on this book: Dr. Faisal AlMashary, Dr. Abdullah Qataee, and Dr. Abdullah Sadaawi from the National Center for Assessment at the Education & Training Evaluation Commission (ETEC) in Saudi Arabia—for their support on my work on the D-scoring method of measurement (DSM) and its implementation in the assessment practice at ETEC; Dr. Dimitar Atanasov from the New Bulgarian University—for his outstanding work on the development of DSM software; Prof. George Marcoulides—for his encouragement on writing this book; Adam Woods, Editor at Routledge and Nivedita Menon (editorial assistant)—for their help throughout the publication process.

Abbreviations

CCRF	Cumulative category response function
CNO	Constraint nonlinear optimization
CTT	Classical test theory
DIF	Differential item functioning
DSM	*D*-scoring method of measurement
DSM-C	Classical DSM
DSM-L	Latent DSM
GP	Guttman pattern
GRM	Graded response model
ICC	Item characteristic curve
IIF	Item information function
IRF	Item response function
IRT	Item response theory
JML	Joint-maximum likelihood
MAD	Mean absolute difference
MAE	Mean absolute error
MIRT	Multidimensional item response theory
MLE	Maximum-likelihood estimation
MST	Multistage test
NEAT	Nonequivalent groups with anchor tests
OIB	Ordered item booklet
PLD	Performance level descriptors
RFM	Rational function model
DTF	Differential test functioning
TIF	Test information function
RGP	Reversed Guttman pattern
RMSE	Root-mean-square error
RVM	Response vector for mastery
RVU	Response vector unit
SCRF	Score category response function
SEE	Standard error of estimation
SEM	Standard error of measurement

1 Classical Test Theory

Basic Concepts and Features

Introduction

Classical test theory (CTT) has been the foundation for measurement theory for over a century. The first book in measurement theory by E.L. Thorndike (1904) was followed by ongoing research, publications, and practical applications of CTT and modern measurement. For comprehensive presentations of CTT, the reader may refer to seminal books on this topic (e.g., Allen & Yen, 1979; Crocker & Algina, 1986; Lord & Novick, 1968; Wainer & Thissen, 2001). The traditional CTT is identified as a measurement framework called a *classical* (or *weak*) *true-score theory*. There is also a *strong true-score theory* which involves stronger assumptions (e.g., Lord, 1965; see also Allen & Yen, 1979). This chapter outlines concepts of the traditional CTT and highlights its strengths and limitations.

What Is Measurement?

One can think of measurement as a process that involves three components—an *object of measurement*, a *set of numbers*, and a *system of rules* that serve to assign numbers to the magnitudes of the variable being measured. Typically, objects of measurement are characteristics of persons that represent observable or latent variables (e.g., age, ability, and trait). In this context, a latent variable can be viewed as a "hidden" continuum with magnitudes increasing in a given direction, say, from left to right if the continuum is represented with a straight line. A latent variable of interest is usually defined with a set of observable indicators (e.g., responses on test items). The person's score on such indicators, derived under a scoring procedure, is assigned to the magnitude (*location*) of the person on the continuum of the latent variable.

Levels of Measurement

Measurement of variables can take place at four different levels—nominal, ordinal, interval, and ratio—depending on the presence/absence of four characteristics of the relationship between the magnitudes of the variable being measured and the scores assigned to these magnitudes—distinctiveness, ordering, equal intervals, and equal ratios. The scales produced at these four levels of measurement are referred to as *nominal*, *ordinal*, *interval*, and *ratio scales*, respectively.

Nominal Scale

A *nominal scale* is used to classify persons (or objects) into mutually exclusive categories, say, by gender, ethnicity, etc. The numbers on a nominal scale serve only as "names" of such categories, hence the name of this scale (in Latin, "nome" means "name"). Thus, the nominal scale possesses *distinctiveness*, but it is *not* a true measurement scale because we cannot place individuals in (increasing or decreasing) order based on their nominal classification.

Ordinal Scale

An *ordinal scale* is one in which the magnitudes of the variable being measured are ordered in the same way as the numbers assigned to these magnitudes. Thus, an ordinal scale possesses *distinctiveness* and *ordering*. However, equal differences between ordinal measures (e.g., ranks) do not necessarily represent equal distances between the corresponding magnitudes of the variable being measured.

Interval Scale

An *interval scale* provides information about the order and distances between the actual magnitudes of the variable being measured. Specifically, equal distances between the magnitudes of the variable being measured will result in equal differences between the scores assigned to these magnitudes. The interval scale has the characteristics of *distinctiveness*, *ordering*, and *equal intervals*. It is important to note that the interval scale has an arbitrary *zero* point. For example, the measurement of temperature is an interval scale, but a temperature of "zero degrees" (in Fahrenheit or Celsius) does not mean that there is no temperature at all at this moment. The *zero* (origin) of an interval scale is conventional and can be "moved" (up or down) using a linear transformation. For example, the linear transformation "F = 1.8C + 32" is used to convert temperature degrees from Celsius to Fahrenheit.

Unlike the nominal and ordinal scales, the interval scale allows for arithmetic operations over its numerical values; that is, one can add, subtract, multiply, and divide numerical values (scores) obtained with an interval scale. Interval scales allow for linear transformation and algebraic operations with their scale values. However, the ratio of two numbers on an interval scale does not provide information about the *ratio* of the trait magnitudes corresponding to these two numbers. For example, if the temperature readings in two consecutive days were, say, 60°F on Tuesday and 30°F on Wednesday, we cannot say that "on Tuesday was twice as hot as on Wednesday."

Ratio Scale

A *ratio scale* possesses the characteristics of *distinctiveness*, *ordering*, *equal intervals*, and *equal ratios*. The zero (origin) of a ratio scale is naturally "fixed"; that is, "zero" indicates the absence of the property being measured. For example, "zero distance" between two points on a straight line indicates that there is no distance between these two points—that is, the two points perfectly coincide. If we multiply the numbers on a ratio scale by a (non-zero) constant, the resulting new numbers will also be on a ratio scale. To illustrate, "inch = 2.54 cm" is the formula for converting inches to centimeters, both measuring distance on a ratio scale. Arithmetic operations with ratio scale numbers are permissible.

CTT Assumptions

CTT uses a set of relatively "relaxed" (*weak*) assumptions to describe how errors of measurement influence observed scores on a test (e.g., Allen & Yen, 1979; pp. 56–70).

- The *main assumption* is that each observed score, X, is a sum of two parts, T = true score and E = random error score, that is:

$$X = T + E \tag{1.1}$$

- The *second assumption* states that the true score of a person, T, is the expected value (population mean) of the observed scores, X, that this person can obtain under an infinite number of administrations of the same test under the same conditions, that is, $T = \varepsilon(X)$.
- The *third assumption* states that true scores and error scores are uncorrelated: $\rho_{TE} = 0$. That is, it is not reasonable to expect that persons with high true scores on a test will have more positive (or negative) error scores compared to persons with low scores on the same test.
- The *fourth assumption* states that error scores on two different tests are *not* correlated: $\rho_{E_1 E_2} = 0$. Indeed, as the error scores are random, it is not reasonable to expect that persons with positive errors on one test will have positive (or negative) errors on the other test.
- The *fifth assumption* states that if persons take two different tests, their true scores on one test are uncorrelated with their error scores on the other test: $\rho_{T_1 E_2} = 0$.

Parallel Tests

Two tests are called *parallel tests* if (a) their scores satisfy the above five assumptions and (b) their true scores and error variances are equal: $T_1 = T_2$ and $\sigma^2_{E_1} = \sigma^2_{E_2}$. At item level, using the assumption that the score on each test item, X_i, has a true part, T_i, and random error part, E_i (i.e., $X_i = T_i + E_i$), two items i and j are *parallel* if $T_i = T_j$ and $\sigma^2_{E_i} = \sigma^2_{E_j}$.

Essentially Tau-Equivalent Tests

Two tests are *essentially tau-equivalent* if (a) their observed scores satisfy the above five assumptions and (b) the difference between their true scores is a constant ($T_1 - T_2$ = const) for every population of examinees.

Numerous important relationships are derived from the above assumptions, given as follows:

- The expected value (population mean) of the error scores equals zero: $\varepsilon(E) = 0$.
- The expected value of the product of true and error scores equals zero: $\varepsilon(TE) = 0$.
- The covariance between true and error scores equals zero: $\sigma_{TE} = 0$. This follows from the known relationship $\sigma_{TE} = \varepsilon(TE) - \varepsilon(T)\varepsilon(E)$, taking into account that $\varepsilon(TE) = 0$ and $\varepsilon(E) = 0$.

Thus, the correlation between true and error scores also equals zero: $\rho_{TE} = 0$.

- The variance of observed scores equals the sum of the variances of their true scores and error scores: $\sigma_X^2 = \sigma_T^2 + \sigma_E^2$.
- The squared correlation between observed and true scores equals the ratio of the true score variance to observed score variance: $\rho_{XT}^2 = \sigma_T^2 / \sigma_X^2$. As shown in the following, this ratio is an alternative form of the definition of *internal consistency reliability* of observed scores, X.

CTT Scoring

Raw Scores

The *raw score* on a test of n items is obtained as the sum of all item scores, that is, $X = \sum X_i$; ($i = 1, \ldots, n$). If the items are dichotomously scored (1 = correct and 0 = incorrect), the raw score X is referred to as the *number of correct responses* (NCR) score. For example, NCR scores are used with tests that consist of *multiple-choice* items (MCI), where one of several response options is a correct response and the other options are incorrect responses (*distractors*). An examinee's raw score on a test does not provide information about how well the examinee performed relative to the other examinees who took the test or relative to a specific criterion performance (e.g., for pass/fail decisions). To allow for such interpretations, raw scores are transformed via (linear or nonlinear) monotonic transformations. Typically, the resulting scores are percentiles, standard scores, standardized scores, normalized scores, or equal-interval scores.

Percentiles

Given the distribution of raw scores for a *norm* group of examinees, the *percentile rank* (or *percentile score*) corresponding to a raw score X is the percentage of scores in the norm distribution that fall at or below X. For example, a raw score of 32 is transformed into a percentile score of 75 if 75% of the distribution scores fall at or below 32. In other words, one can say that (a) 32 is the 75th percentile ($P_{75} = 32$) and, conversely, (b) the percentile rank of 32 is 75 ($PR_{32} = 75$). That is, an examinee with a raw score of 32 has performed better than 75% of the examinees in the norm sample.

Standard Scores

The standard score, Z, corresponding to a raw score, X, shows how many standard deviations is X above (or below) the *mean* of the raw scores in the population (or sample) of examinees under consideration, that is, $Z = (X - \mu)/\sigma$, where μ and σ are the *mean* and *standard deviation*, respectively, for the population of examinees. If the population μ and σ are unknown, they can be replaced with their sample estimates ($\bar{X}$ and s). For example, $Z = 2$ shows that the raw score is two standard deviations above the mean, whereas $Z = -1$ shows that the raw score is one standard deviation below the mean. The Z-scores always have a mean of 0 and a standard deviation of 1. Also, the shape of the distribution of Z-scores is the same as the shape of the distribution of raw scores. If the distribution of raw scores is normal, then the distribution of Z scores is also normal and referred to as *standard normal distribution*, $N(0,1)$.

Standardized Scores

Standardized scores are linear transformations of raw scores that produce scores with a desired mean and standard deviation. Specifically, the transformation of raw scores X (mean μ_X and standard deviation σ_X) into standardized scores Y, with a desired mean μ_Y and standard deviation σ_Y, is performed as follows: $Y = \sigma_Y Z_X + \mu_Y$, where Z_X is the standard score of X. For example, raw scores are often standardized to T-scale scores ($\mu_T = 50$, $\sigma_T = 10$) using the transformation: $T = 10 Z_X + 50$.

Normalized Scores

When it is reasonable to expect that the ability (trait) measured by a test is normally distributed, but the raw score distribution is not normal, the raw scores can be "normalized" by transforming their distribution to become as close as possible to a normal distribution. This can be done in steps as follows (e.g., Allen & Yen, 1979, p. 164):

Step 1. Transform the raw scores to percentiles.
Step 2. Find the Z-score in the standard normal distribution, $N(0,1)$, that corresponds to each percentile. The resulting Z-scores are normalized scores.
Step 3. The Z-scores obtained in Step 2 can be transformed to standardized scores with a desired mean and standard deviation (e.g., T-scores). The resulting standardized scores are also normalized (i.e., their distribution is close to normal).

Equal-Interval Scales

Typically, the raw scores on a test form an ordinal scale, which jeopardizes the validity of algebraic operations (e.g., computation of means and standard deviations). Under certain conditions, the raw scores can be transformed to form an interval scale which allows for algebraic operations. One commonly used approach to transforming raw scores into an interval scale is the *Thurstone's absolute scaling method* (e.g., Gulliksen, 1950; see also Allen & Yen, 1979, pp. 168–170). This method works under the assumptions that (a) the latent variable measured by the test has a normal distribution in the target population and (b) the raw scores are monotonically related to the magnitudes of that latent variable. If these two assumptions are met, the normalized raw score forms an interval scale.

CTT Item Analysis

Item Difficulty

In CTT, the *difficulty* of item i, p_i, is defined as the sample proportion of examinees who answered the item correctly: ($0 \leq p_i \leq 1$). It should be clarified that p_i actually indicates item "easiness" as high p_i values reflect easy items (e.g., the highest value, $p_i = 1$, indicates that all examinees have answered the item correctly). If maximum discrimination among examinees over all levels of the ability measured by the test is targeted, the p_i values of the items should range from about 0.3 to 0.7 (Lord, 1953). Random samples of the same size produce different p_i values, each of which represents an *unbiased estimate* of the population parameter π_i; that is, the population proportion of correct responses on the item, π_i, is the *mean* of the sampling distribution of p_i values. In fact, the distribution of p_i values, produced by random samples of size n, is normal and its variance equals $p_i(1-p_i)/n$. Thus, one can construct confidence intervals for π_i, given the p_i value and its sample size, n. For example, a 95% confidence interval for π_i is $p_i \pm 1.96\sqrt{p_i(1-p_i)/n}$.

Item Discrimination

An *item discrimination index*, d_i, is used to indicate how well an item is discriminating between high-scoring examinees and low-scoring examinees on the test. Specifically, d_i is computed as the difference between the proportion of high-scoring examinees who answered the item correctly and the proportion of low-scoring examinees who answered the item correctly. The analytic formula for the computation of d_i is:

$$d_i = \frac{U_i}{n_U} - \frac{L_i}{n_L}, \tag{1.2}$$

where:
U_i = the number of high-scoring examinees who answered the item correctly and scored in the upper range of total test scores (e.g., top 30%),
L_i = the number of low-scoring examinees who answered the item correctly and scored in the lower range of total test scores (e.g., bottom 30%),
n_U = the number of high-scoring examinees who scored in the upper range of total test scores, regardless of their response on item i,
n_L = the number of low-scoring examinees who scored in the lower range of total test scores, regardless of their response on item i.

Item/Total Score Correlation

An alternative measure of *item discrimination* is the Pearson correlation coefficient between the examinees' scores on item i and their total test scores, X: r_{iX}. If the item is dichotomously scored (1/0), the Pearson r_{iX} formula is reduced to a simpler form, referred to as *point-biserial correlation coefficient*:

$$r_{pbis} = \left(\frac{\bar{X}_1 - \bar{X}}{s_X}\right)\sqrt{\frac{p_i}{1-p_i}}, \quad (1.3)$$

where:
$\bar{X}_1$ = the mean of total scores, X, for examinees who answered item i correctly,
$\bar{X}$ = the overall mean of total scores, X, for all examinees,
p_i = the proportion of examinees who answered item i correctly, and
s_X = the standard deviation of the total scores, X, for all examinees.

The binary (1/0) score on item i is based on an artificial dichotomization of a continuous latent variable underlying the examinees' responses on the item, η_i. The Pearson correlation between η_i and the total test score, X, cannot be computed directly, but it is approximated well by the *biserial correlation coefficient* between the binary item score and the total test score, X:

$$r_{bis} = \left(\frac{\bar{X}_1 - \bar{X}}{s_X}\right)\left[\frac{p_i}{f(z_i)}\right], \quad (1.4)$$

where $\bar{X}_1$, $\bar{X}$, p_i, and s_X are the same as in Equation 1.3, and $f(z_i)$ is the standard normal density at the z_i value above which the proportion of cases under the $N(0,1)$ distribution equals p_i; that is, z_i is the percentile corresponding to a percentile rank of $(1 - p_i)$. The values of z_i and $f(z_i)$ can be obtained, for example, using statistical tables or via online available calculators. Biserial correlations are preferred over point-biserial correlations in estimating the discrimination of items because they are more invariant over examinee samples (Lord & Novick, 1968).

Item Characteristic Curves

Item characteristic curve (ICC) is a graphical depiction of the relationship between the probability of correct response on an item and the examinee's location on the scale of ability measured by the test. The ICCs provide more fine-grained information about the psychometric characteristics of an item, such as *difficulty, discrimination*, and *monotonicity* (the probability of correct item response increases with the increase of ability scores). As the traditional CTT does not model the probability of correct item response, classical ICCs are constructed by replacing (a) ability scores with observed scores and (b) model-based probability of correct item response with the proportion of correct responses on the item at each observed score.

The ICCs of two items from a hypothetical test of 12 dichotomously scored items are depicted in Figure 1.1. As the ICC of Item 1 is consistently above the ICC of Item 2, this shows that Item 1 is easier than Item 2 at any level of the total score scale. The steepness of the ICC shows how well the item discriminates among examinees who do not differ much in their total scores. Let us compare the discrimination power of the two items over three intervals on the total score scale: (a) from 1 to 4, both items provide similar (yet poor) discrimination, with parallel

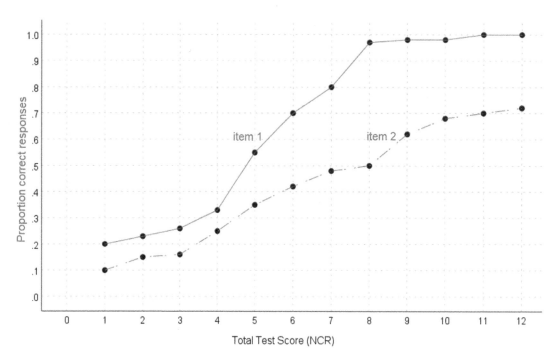

Figure 1.1. Item characteristic curves of two items from a test of 12 dichotomously scored items.

> **NOTE [1.1]** Ability scores are more fundamental because they are *test independent*, whereas observed scores and true scores are *test dependent* (Lord, 1953). As stated by Hambleton and Jones (1999):
>
> "over time, abilities may change because of instruction and other factors, but at the time of an assessment, each examinee will have an ability score that is defined in relation to the construct, and it remains invariant (i.e., independent) over various samples of assessment tasks that might be used in the assessment."
>
> (p. 38)

(yet not quite steep) ICCs; (b) from 4 to 8, Item 1 is a much stronger discriminator than Item 2; and (c) from 8 to 12, Item 2 is a better discriminator than Item 1, the latter being a very poor discriminator with a "ceiling effect" over this interval of the scale.

Reliability

The *reliability* of test scores is defined and interpreted in different ways in the theory of measurement. To clarify, *reliability* is a property of scores, not the test itself, so "test reliability" should be understood as a "reliability of test scores." Under one definition, the reliability of a test X is the correlation between the observed scores on X and a parallel test X', hence the notation $\rho_{XX'}$ for test reliability (or, just ρ_{XX}). Equivalently, $\rho_{XX'}$ can be represented as the "ratio of true score variance to observed score variance" (e.g., Allen & Yen, 1979):

$$\rho_{XX} = \frac{\sigma_T^2}{\sigma_X^2}. \tag{1.5}$$

Thus, ρ_{XX} shows what proportion of the observed-score variance is true-score variance. This yields an alternative expression for reliability as the "squared correlation between observed scores and true scores": $\rho_{XX} = \rho_{XT}^2$.

As true scores cannot be directly determined, the reliability is typically estimated by coefficients of internal consistency, test-retest, alternate forms, and other reliability methods (e.g., Allen & Yen, 1979; Crocker & Algina, 1986; Feldt & Brennan, 1989). It should be noted that reliability is estimated under the assumption of unidimensionality; that is, the test measures one dominating ability (or trait).

Internal Consistency Reliability

One of the most frequently used methods of estimating internal consistency reliability is the Cronbach's coefficient α (Cronbach, 1951). Assuming that the test is divided into N components (set of items or individual items), α is computed as follows:

$$\alpha = \left(\frac{N}{N-1}\right)\left(\frac{\sigma_X^2 - \sum_{k=1}^{N}\sigma_{X_k}^2}{\sigma_X^2}\right), \tag{1.6}$$

where X = observed test score, X_k = observed score on test component k, σ_X^2 = population variance of X, and $\sigma_{X_k}^2$ = population variance of X_k.

It should be noted that (even at population level) Cronbach's α is an accurate estimate of reliability only under the assumptions that (a) the test components are *essentially tau-equivalent* and (b) there is *no* correlation among errors associated with the test components. If there are no correlated errors, but the test components are not essentially tau-equivalent, Cronbach's α will underestimate the reliability ($\alpha < \rho_{XX}$). If there are correlated errors, Cronbach's α may substantially overestimate ρ_{XX} (e.g., Raykov, 2001; Zimmerman, Zumbo, & Lalonde, 1993). Correlated errors may occur, for example, with adjacent items in a multicomponent instrument, with items related to a common stimulus (e.g., same paragraph or graph), or with tests presented in a speeded fashion.

Test-retest Reliability

Test-retest reliability is estimated by the correlation between observed scores of the same people taking the same test twice (or parallel test forms). However, this procedure may run into problems such as carry-over effects due to memory and/or practice (Lord & Novick, 1968). Test-retest reliability estimates are most appropriate for measuring traits that are stable across a time period between the two test administrations (e.g., work values, visual or auditory acuity, and personality). It is important to note that test-retest reliability and internal consistency reliability are independent concepts. They are affected by different sources of error, and therefore, it may happen that measures with low internal consistency have high temporal stability and vice versa (e.g., Nunnally & Bernstein, 1994). Research on stability in reliability showed that the test-retest correlation coefficient can serve reasonably well as a surrogate for the classical reliability coefficient if an essentially tau-equivalent model with equal error variances or a parallel model is in place (Tisak & Tisak, 1996).

Alternate Form Reliability

Alternate form reliability is a measure of the consistency of scores across comparable forms of a test administered to the same group of individuals. Ideally, the alternate forms should be parallel, but this is difficult to achieve, especially with personality measures. The correlation between observed scores on two alternate test forms is usually referred to as the *coefficient of equivalence*. Basically, the alternate form reliability and internal consistency reliability are affected by different sources of error. If the correlation between alternate forms is much lower than the internal consistency coefficient (e.g., by 0.20 or more), this might be due to (a) differences in content, (b) subjectivity of scoring, and (c) changes in the trait being measured during the time between the two administrations of alternate forms. To determine the relative contribution of these sources of error, it is recommendable to administer the two alternate forms (a) on the same day for some respondents and (b) within a 2-week time interval for others (e.g., Nunnally & Bernstein, 1994).

NOTE [1.2] The use of difference (gain) scores in the measurement of pretest to posttest change has been criticized because of the (generally false) assertion that the difference between scores is less reliable than the scores themselves (Cronbach & Furby, 1970). However, this assertion is true *only if* the pretest scores and the posttest scores have equal variances and equal reliability. When this is not the case, the reliability of the gain score is reasonably high (Zimmerman & Williams, 1982). Also, the reliability of gain scores can be interpreted as a context-specific, between-examinees precision index (Kane, 1996).

8   Classical Test Theory: Basic Concepts and Features

Standard Error of Measurement

The CTT assumes that (a) the distribution of observed scores that a person may have under repeated independent administrations of the same test (or parallel testes) is normal, and (b) the standard deviation of this normal distribution, referred to as *standard error of measurement* (*SEM*), is the same for all persons taking the test. Under these assumptions, Figure 1.2 shows a hypothetical normal distribution of observed scores for repeated independent measurements of one person with the same test. The mean of this distribution is the person's *true score* ($T = 20$), and the standard deviation is the standard error of measurement ($SEM = 2$).

Confidence Interval for SEM

Based on statistical properties of the normal distribution, about 95% of the scores fall in the interval between two standard deviations below the mean, $T - 2(SEM)$, and two standard deviations above the mean, $T + 2(SEM)$. In Figure 1.2, for example, this is the interval from 16 to 24. This property can be used to construct a 95% *confidence interval* of a person's true score, T, given the person's observed score, X. Smaller *SEM* values produce smaller confidence intervals for the person's true score, thus improving the accuracy of measurement.

As the *SEM* is inversely related to the accuracy of measurement, low *SEM* indicates high reliability. If the reliability, ρ_{XX}, and the standard deviation of the observed scores, σ_X, are given, the *SEM* can be computed as follows (e.g., Lord & Novick, 1968; Allen & Yen, 1979):

$$SEM = \sigma_X \sqrt{1 - \rho_{XX}} \tag{1.7}$$

[*Check*: If $\rho_{XX} = 0.80$ and $\sigma_X = 10$, then $SEM = 10\sqrt{1 - 0.80} = 4.47$.]

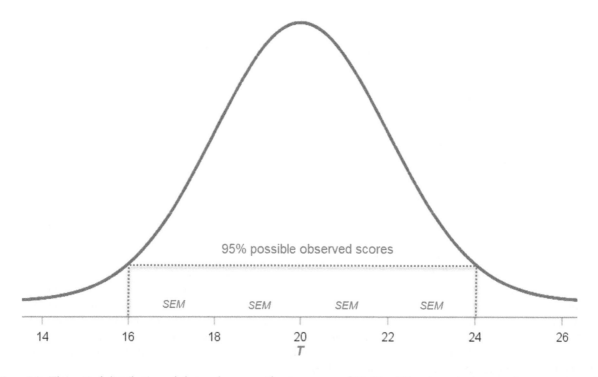

Figure 1.2. Theoretical distribution of observed scores with a true score of 20 ($T = 20$) and standard error of measurement of 2 ($SEM = 2$).

NOTE [1.3] It has been proven in CTT that, instead of taking the same test many times to get an estimate of the standard error for one person, the test can be given once to a large sample of people (e.g., 1,000) and get the same *SEM* that will generalize to the population (e.g., Allen & Yen, 1979).

Standard Error of Estimation

In CTT, an estimate of a person's true score, T, from his/her observed score, X, can be obtained by simply regressing T on X as follows (Lord & Novick, 1968, p. 65):

$$\hat{T} = \rho_{XX} X + (1 - \rho_{XX}) \mu, \tag{1.8}$$

where μ is the population mean of test scores and ρ_{XX} is their reliability.

Equation 1.8 shows that the estimated (predicted) true score, $\hat{T}$, is closer to the observed score, X, when the reliability, ρ_{XX}, is high, and conversely, it is closer to the mean, μ, when the reliability is low. In the extreme cases, (a) $\hat{T} = X$, with perfectly reliable scores ($\rho_{XX} = 1$), and (b) $\hat{T} = \mu$, with totally unreliable scores ($\rho_{XX} = 0$).

Under Equation 1.8, all persons with the same observed score, X, will have the same predicted true score, $\hat{T}$, but not necessarily the same actual true score, T. The standard deviation of the estimation error ($\varepsilon = T - \hat{T}$), referred to as *standard error of estimation* (SEE), is obtained as follows:

$$SEE = \sigma_X \sqrt{\rho_{XX}(1 - \rho_{XX})}, \tag{1.9}$$

where σ_X is the standard deviation of the observed scores, X, and ρ_{XX} is their reliability.

The *SEE*, obtained via Equation 1.9, is always smaller than the *SEM*, obtained via Equation 1.7, that is, *SEE* < *SEM*. Thus, the *SEE* provides a more accurate estimation of a person's true score, T, compared to confidence intervals for T based on *SEM*.

Reliability of Composite Scores

The composite score may be the sum of several scale scores, but its reliability is usually not simply the mean of the reliabilities for the scales being combined. For example, if Y is a composite score obtained by adding together the scores of two scales, X_1 and X_2 ($Y = X_1 + X_2$), the reliability of the composite score, ρ_{YY}, can be estimated as follows:

$$\rho_{YY} = 1 - \frac{(1 - \rho_{11})\sigma_1^2 + (1 - \rho_{22})\sigma_2^2}{\sigma_Y^2}, \tag{1.10}$$

where ρ_{11} and ρ_{22} are the reliability of the scores X_1 and X_2, respectively; σ_1^2 and σ_2^2 are their variances; and σ_Y^2 is the variance of Y. Equation 1.10 can be extended for three or more variables.

Although not explicitly shown in Equation 1.10, the correlation between X_1 and X_2 affects the reliability of the composite score. When X_1 and X_2 do not correlate ($r_{12} = 0$), the reliability of the composite score is the average of their reliabilities: $\rho_{YY} = (\rho_{11} + \rho_{22})/2$.

Consider a more general case where the composite score is a weighted sum of, say, three scales, X_1, X_2, and X_3, that is, $Y = w_1 X_1 + w_2 X_2 + w_3 X_3$. Also, if Z_1, Z_2, and Z_3 are the standard scores of X_1, X_2, and X_3, their composite score is $Y_Z = w_1 Z_1 + w_2 Z_2 + w_3 Z_3$. With this, the reliability of the composite score Y_Z (or Y) can be estimated as follows:

$$\rho_{YY} = 1 - \frac{(1 - \rho_{11})w_1^2 + (1 - \rho_{22})w_2^2 + (1 - \rho_{33})w_3^2}{\sigma_{Y_Z}^2}, \tag{1.11}$$

where ρ_{11}, ρ_{22}, and ρ_{33} are the reliabilities of X_1, X_2, and X_3, respectively, and $\sigma_{Y_Z}^2$ is the variance of Y_Z.

Equating Test Scores

Equating of test scores (briefly, *test equating*) is a statistical procedure used to present the scores across test forms on a common scale so that they can be used interchangeably. To be equated, the tests must measure the same latent variable (ability, trait) with the same precision. Thus, tests that differ in reliability cannot be equated. In the context of CTT, two popular approaches to test equating are the methods of linear equating and equipercentile equating (e.g., Kolen & Brennan, 2004). In the following, equating two tests refers to equating two test forms.

> **NOTE [1.4]** *Thurstone's method of absolute scaling*, mentioned earlier in regard to equal-interval scales, can also be used to equate two tests under the assumption that their scores are normally distributed for each of two equivalent samples of examinees. It should be noted, however, that the development of (even close to) equivalent samples involves carefully controlled and expensive sampling procedures.

Linear Equating

The method of *linear equating* can be used when the raw scores on the two tests to be equated are linearly related; that is, the raw-score distributions for the two tests have a similar shape. Under this condition, a score x on the scale of test X is equivalent to a score y on the scale of test Y if their standard scores are equal: $Z_x = Z_y$, that is:

$$\frac{x - \mu_X}{\sigma_X} = \frac{y - \mu_Y}{\sigma_Y}. \tag{1.12}$$

Thus, (a) $y = Z_x \sigma_Y + \mu_Y$, when a score x on test X is transformed to a score y on test Y, and conversely, $x = Z_y \sigma_X + \mu_X$, when a score y on test Y is transformed to a score x on test X. It should be noted that linear equating allows for the two tests to vary in difficulty across levels of the score scale. Under linear equating, the mean and standard deviation of the scores on test X equated to the scale of test Y are equal to the mean and standard deviation, respectively, of the scores on test Y (e.g., Kolen & Brennan, 2004).

Equipercentile Equating

If two tests, X and Y, are administered to two equivalent samples of examinees, scores at the same percentile in the distributions of scores for the two samples are treated as equivalent scores. For example, a score of 12 on test X is said to be equivalent to a score of 20 on test Y if 12 is, say, at the 45th percentile in the distribution of X scores and 20 is at the 45th percentile in the distribution of Y scores. The equipercentile equating is a nonlinear equating. If the distributions of X and Y scores differ only in their means and standard deviations, the equipercentile equating is equivalent to a linear equating of the scores (e.g., Kolen & Brennan, 2004).

CTT Strengths

The CTT is a simple yet powerful model of measurement and sets the foundation of reliability theory. Classical test models are often referred to as *weak models* because the assumptions of these models are fairly easily met by test data. CTT models do *not* require the strong assumption of unidimensionality; that is, the items that compose the test are not required to measure a single common trait or ability. As noted by Hambleton and Jones (1993), "it is only necessary to assume that the factor structure, whatever it is, is common across parallel forms" (p. 39). CTT can work efficiently with relatively small samples (e.g., 50–100 examinees). The true score theory can be used also in computer simulations as the basis for generating "observed" scores with desirable properties. The CTT provides simplicity and transparency in the computation and interpretation of test scores.

CTT Limitations

One of the main limitations of CTT is that (a) observed scores and true scores are test dependent and (b) item statistics (e.g., for *difficulty* and *discrimination*) depend on the sample of examinees (e.g., Lord, 1953). Thus, examinee characteristics and test characteristics are dependent on each other. A second limitation is that reliability coefficients depend on assumptions that are often not met with real data and, as a result, provide bias in the estimation of reliability. A third limitation is that the *SEM* is assumed to be the same for all examinees. As Hambleton, Swaminathan, and Rogers (1991) explained, "scores on any test are unequally precise measures for examinees of different ability, thus making the assumption of equal errors of measurement for all examinees implausible" (p. 4). A fourth limitation is that, given the test score of a person, one cannot predict the person's performance on individual test items. A fifth limitation is that observed scores and item difficulty, p_i, are not comparable as they are presented on different scales. This makes it difficult to evaluate the suitability of a test for a population of examinees.

CTT limitations have been addressed with understanding and caution in the profession of testing, and as Hambleton and Jones (1993) noted:

> "thousands of excellent tests have been constructed in this way (including all important tests up to the end of the 1960s), though special emphasis is placed on obtaining suitable examinee samples for obtaining item and test statistics and producing statistically parallel tests."
>
> (p. 38)

Furthermore, there are ongoing efforts on extending (or modifying) traditional CTT models and procedures. For example, issues related to error scores and reliability are addressed in the framework of generalizability theory by identifying components of error due to different sources, such as test scorer, item format, and conditions of test administration (e.g., Brennan, 2001; Shavelson & Webb, 1991). Numerous CTT issues are addressed via CTT extensions in the classical framework of the *D-scoring method of measurement* (DSM) presented in this book (see Chapter 4).

Summary Points

1. *Measurement* is a process that involves three components—an *object of measurement*, a *set of numbers*, and a *system of rules* that serve to assign numbers to the magnitudes of the variable being measured.
2. A *nominal scale* is used to classify persons (or objects) into mutually exclusive categories. The scale numbers serve only as "names" of such categories, so they cannot be ordered.
3. An *ordinal scale* is one in which the magnitudes of the variable being measured are ordered in the same way as the numbers assigned to these magnitudes.
4. An *interval scale* provides information about the *order* and *distances* between the actual magnitudes of the variable being measured.
5. A *ratio scale* provides information about the *order*, *distances*, and *ratios* of actual magnitudes of the variable being measured.
6. The *main CTT assumption* is that each observed score is a sum of a true score and an error score ($X = T + E$). The other four assumptions (analytically expressed) are $T = \varepsilon(X)$, $\rho_{TE} = 0$, $\rho_{E_1 E_2} = 0$, and $\rho_{T_1 E_2} = 0$.
7. *Parallel tests* satisfy the above five assumptions and have equal true scores and error variances.
8. *Essentially tau-equivalent tests* satisfy the above five assumptions, and the difference between their true scores is a constant.
9. Typical CTT scores are raw scores, percentiles, standard scores, standardized scores, and normalized scores.
10. CTT *item analysis* is based primarily on the concepts of *item difficulty* (proportion of correct responses), *item discrimination*, *item/total score correlation*, and ICC.
11. *Internal consistency reliability* is defined by the ratio of true score variance to observed score variance. The Cronbach's coefficient alpha is an accurate estimate of reliability under the assumptions that (a) the test measures are essentially tau-equivalent and (b) there are *no* correlated errors.
12. *Test-retest reliability* is estimated by the correlation between the observed scores of the same people taking the same test twice (or two parallel test forms). Test-retest reliability and internal consistency reliability are affected by different sources of error.
13. CTT assumes that the *SEM* is the same for all persons taking the test. The *SEM* is an overall estimate of differences between observed and true scores ($X - T$), whereas the *SEE* is an overall estimate of differences between actual and predicted true scores ($T - \hat{T}$).
14. *Linear equating* can be used when the raw scores on the two tests to be equated are linearly related; that is, the raw-score distributions for the two tests have a similar shape.
15. *Equipercentile equating* can be used when two tests are administered to two equivalent samples of examinees, so scores that are at the same percentile in the distributions of scores for the two samples are treated as equivalent scores.
16. CTT strengths: CTT is a simple yet powerful model of measurement and sets the foundation of reliability theory. CTT provides computational simplicity and transparency, and its assumptions are fairly easily met by test data.
17. CTT limitations: (a) Observed scores and true scores are test dependent, (b) item statistics are sample dependent, (c) *reliability* coefficients depend on assumptions that are often not met with real data, (d) *SEM* is (unrealistically) assumed to be the same for all examinees, (e) observed scores and item difficulties are not on the same scale, and (f) there are no models for predictions of examinees' performance (probability of correct response) on individual test items.

References

Allen, M. J., & Yen, W.M. (1979). *Introduction to measurement theory.* Monterey, CA: Brooks/Cole Publishing Company.

Brennan, R. L. (2001). *Generalizability theory.* New York: Springer-Verlag.

Crocker, L., & Algina, J. (1986). *Introduction to classical and modern test theory.* New York: Holt, Rinehart, & Winston.

Cronbach, L. J. (1951). Coefficient alpha and the internal structure of tests. *Psychometrika, 16,* 207–334.

Cronbach, L. J., & Furby, L. (1970). How we should measure "change"—Or should we? *Psychological Bulletin, 74,* 68–80.

Feldt, L. S., & Brennan, R. L. (1989). Reliability. In R. L. Linn (Ed.), *Educational measurement* (pp. 105–146). New York: Macmillan.

Gulliksen, H. (1950). *Theory of mental tests.* New York: Wiley.

Hambleton, R. K., & Jones, R. W. (1993). Comparison of classical test theory and item response theory and their applications to test development. *Educational Measurement: Issues and Practice, 12*(3), 38–47.

Hambleton, R. K, Swaminathan, H., & Rogers, H. J. (1991). *Fundamentals of item response theory.* Newbury Park, CA: Sage.

Kane, M. (1996). The precision of measurements. *Applied Measurement in Education, 9,* 355–379.

Kolen, M. J., & Brennan, R. L. (2004). *Test equating, scaling, and linking: Methods and practices* (2nd ed.). New York: Springer.

Lord, F. M. (1953). An application of confidence intervals and of maximum likelihood to the estimation of an examinee's ability. *Psychometrika, 18,* 57–76.

Lord, F. M. (1965). A strong true-score theory, with applications. *Psychometrika, 30,* 239–270.

Lord, F. M., & Novick, M. R. (1968). *Statistical theories of mental test scores.* The Addison Wesley series in behavioral science: Quantitative methods. Reading, MA: Addison-Wesley.

Nunnally, J. C., & Bernstein, I. H. (1994). *Psychometric theory* (3rd ed.). New York: McGraw-Hill.

Raykov, T. (2001). Bias of coefficient alpha for fixed congeneric measures with correlated errors. *Applied Psychological Measurement, 25,* 69–76.

Shavelson, R. J., & Webb, N. M. (1991). *Generalizability theory: A primer.* Newbury Park, CA: Sage.

Thorndike, E. L. (1904). *An introduction to the theory of mental and social measurements.* New York: Science Press.

Tisak, J., & Tisak, M. S. (1996). Longitudinal models of reliability and validity: A latent curve approach. *Applied Psychological Measurement, 20,* 275–288.

Wainer, H., & Thissen, D. (2001). True score theory: The traditional method. In D. Thissen & H. Wainer (Eds.), *Test scoring* (pp. 23–72). Lawrence Erlbaum Associates Publishers.

Zimmerman, D. W., & Williams, R. H. (1982). Gain scores in research can be highly reliable. *Journal of Educational Measurement, 19,* 149–154.

Zimmerman, D.W., Zumbo, B. D., & Lalonde, C. (1993). Coefficient alpha as an estimate of test reliability under violation of two assumptions. *Educational and Psychological Measurement, 53,* 33–49.

2 Item Response Theory

Basic Concepts and Features

Introduction

Item response theory (IRT) was developed to address the limitations of the classical test theory (CTT) and provide psychometric flexibility and rigor in a modern framework of measurement.

IRT is model-based measurement at item level. An IRT model is a mathematical model that specifies the relationship between a *dependent variable* ("observable" item responses) and *independent variables*—latent ability levels and item properties (*difficulty* and *discrimination*). In this context, the term "ability" is used to denote a latent trait measured by the test (e.g., cognitive ability, motivation, and anxiety). IRT models are referred to as *item response function* (IRF) models. An IRF describes the relationship between the ability level and the probability of correct item response. The IRF graphical depiction is referred to as *item characteristic curve* (ICC). The shape of the ICC is specified by the analytic form of the IRF. Sometimes IRF and ICC are used interchangeably.

Lord (1952) introduced a *two-parameter normal-ogive model* and developed the statistical framework of IRF-based psychometric analysis of test data. The two item parameters in this model are *item difficulty* and *item discrimination*. Birnbaum (1968) replaced the two-parameter normal-ogive model with the *two-parameter logistic* (2PL) model and introduced a *three-parameter logistic* (3PL) model to account for pseudo-guessing effects in examinees' responses on test items. A *one-parameter logistic* (1PL) model is obtained by fixing the item discrimination parameter to a constant in the 2PL model. The reader may refer to numerous excellent books on IRT (e.g., Bock & Gibbons, 2021; de Ayala, 2009; Embretson & Reise, 2000; Hambleton & Swaminathan, 1985; Raykov & Marcoulides, 2018; van der Linden, 2016).

Any IRF model is based on certain assumptions. For example, IRF models assuming that a single latent ability governs the examinee's responses on the test items are called *unidimensional* models. IRF models that assume two or more latent abilities, called *multidimensional* models, are treated in the framework of multidimensional IRT (MIRT; Reckase, 2009a). By the type of item scoring, there are IRT models for binary scored items and IRT models for polytomously scored items (e.g., Masters, 1982; Samejima, 1969, 1997, 2013; van der Linden, 2016). An IRT model must be tested for data fit to validate the results from the respective item analysis. Discussed in the following are only unidimensional IRT models for dichotomously scored test items.

IRT Assumptions

Unidimensionality

A key assumption in commonly used IRT models, referred to as *unidimensionality*, is that there is a single latent ability (trait) that governs the responses on test items for a target population of examinees. It should be noted that unidimensionality may hold for one population of examinees but not for another. For example, a math test can be unidimensional (measuring math ability) for a group of examinees who can understand properly the formulation of the test items, but not so for another group of examinees (say, of different culture) for whom reading comprehension would be a secondary dimension governing their item responses.

There are different approaches to testing for unidimensionality, mostly in the framework of IRT and factor analysis (e.g., for comprehensive reviews, see Hattie, 1985; Reise, Cook, & Moore, 2014), with some specific aspects in the context of Rasch measurement (e.g., Andrich, 1988; Rost, 2001; Smith, 2004). It should be noted that there is a (justified) skepticism in the ability of most approaches to properly detect unidimensionality (e.g., Hattie, 1985; Embretson & Reise, 2000; Ziegler & Hagemann, 2015). Furthermore, real data in testing are *not* strictly unidimensional as there are other factors (e.g., cognitive and personality) that influence the examinees' responses to test items. Effects of multidimensional data on the use of unidimensional IRT models have been

DOI: 10.4324/9781003343004-2

discussed in the extant literature (e.g., Kahraman, 2013). Reckase, Ackerman, and Carlson (1988) proposed an approach to building a unidimensional test using multidimensional items. They argued that "a test composed of items that measure the same weighted composite of multiple abilities will meet the requirements of unidimensional models even though multiple abilities are needed to derive the correct response" (Reckase et al., 1988, p. 193; see also Reckase, 2009b). In another study, Stucky and Edelen (2014) demonstrated how to use hierarchical IRT models to create unidimensional measures from multidimensional data.

Stout (1987, 1990) developed an approach to testing for *essential unidimensionality*, that is, testing for one dominant dimension and evaluating whether the effect of possible secondary dimensions is negligible. Specifically, after fitting a one-factor model, it is considered that the test data are essentially unidimensional if the average between-item covariance approaches zero when the number of test item increases. That is, when essential unidimensionality holds, minor secondary dimensions do not threaten the interpretation of item and person estimates under the IRT model of choice. This approach is implemented in the computer program DIMTEST (see Stout, Froelich, & Gao, 2001). Another efficient approach to testing for unidimensionality is based on *full-information factor analysis* (Bock, Gibbons, & Muraki, 1988; Muraki & Engelhard, 1985). This approach uses all the information encoded in the entire response matrix rather than only the covariance (or correlation) matrix. It is implemented in the computer program TESTFACT 4 (Wood et al., 2003). A particularly efficient in testing for unidimensionality of binary response data is the *full-information bifactor item-response model* (Gibbons & Hedeker, 1992) which is implemented, for example, in the R package "mirt" and Mplus (Muthén & Muthén, 1998–2017). A generalized version of this model, which handles an arbitrary mixing of dichotomous, ordinal, and nominal items, was proposed by Cai, Yang, and Hansen (2011).

Local Independence

The IRT *assumption of local independence* requires that a person's responses to the test items are statistically independent. This means that the person's probability of any response pattern (vector) of item scores is equal to the product of the probabilities of the scores (1 or 0) on all items regardless of the order of their presentation in the test. Under this assumption, if the response pattern of a person on a set of five items is (1 0 0 1 1), the person's probability of this response pattern to occur is P(1 0 0 1 1) = P(1).P(0).P(0).P(1).P(1), where P(1) is the probability of correct response and P(0) is the probability of incorrect response on the respective item. In other words, the assumption of local independence holds when the person's response (correct or incorrect) to an item does not depend on his/her responses to any other item; that is, at a fixed ability level, the responses to test items must be unrelated. A violation of the assumption of local independence is called *local dependence* (LD). For example, LD may occur (a) in a test on reading comprehension, where a group of items relate to the same word passage, or (b) in a math test, where a group of items relate to the same graph(s).

Let us denote (a) θ = person's ability level ("theta"); (b) U_i = person's response on item i, with two possible values: $u_i = 1$, if correct; $u_i = 0$, if incorrect; (c) $P(U_1 = u_1, ..., U_n = u_n | \theta)$ = the probability of a response pattern $(u_1, u_2, ..., u_n)$ at θ; and (d) $P(U_i = u_i | \theta)$ = the probability of getting a score u_i on the response U_i of item i; (i = 1, 2, ..., n) at θ. Under these notations, the analytic form of the assumption of local (statistical) independence is:

$$P(U_1 = u_1, U_2 = u_2, ..., U_n = u_n | \theta) = P(U_1 = u_1 | \theta).P(U_2 = u_2 | \theta)...P(U_n = u_n | \theta) \qquad (2.1)$$

or, in a product notation : $P(U_1 = u_1, U_2 = u_2, ..., U_n = u_n | \theta) = \prod_{i=1}^{n} P(U_i = u_i).$ \qquad (2.2)

If, for simplicity, we set $P_i = P(U_i = 1 | \theta)$ and $Q_i = P(U_i = 0 | \theta)$, that is, $Q_i = 1 - P_i$, then:

$$P(U_1 = u_1, U_2 = u_2, ..., U_n = u_n | \theta) = \prod_{i=1}^{n} P_i^{u_i} Q_i^{1-u_i} = \prod_{i=1}^{n} P_i^{u_i} (1 - P_i)^{1-u_i}. \qquad (2.3)$$

Equation 2.1 (or, equivalently, Equation 2.2 or 2.3) represents the *likelihood of a response pattern* of a person with ability θ. This equation, which is valid only under local independence, plays a key role in IRT estimations of person and item parameters (e.g., via maximum likelihood procedures). The presence of LD yields inaccuracy in such estimations and invalidates related results to a degree depending on the level of LD. For example, the presence of LD inflates the estimates of item discrimination parameters and test information, thus unduly reducing the conditional error of ability estimates (Yen, 1993). In a dissertation study, Fennessy (1995) found that high levels of LD cause underestimation of low ability scores and, conversely, overestimation of high ability scores. As Embretson and Reise (2000) noted, "all aspects of the IRT modeling process and application, such as computerized adaptive testing, are disturbed by the presence of local dependence" (p. 232).

There are different approaches to testing for LD, such as the Q_3 statistic (Yen, 1984), Pearson's χ^2 statistic (Chen & Thissen, 1997), score test statistic for pairs of items (Liu & Thissen, 2012), M_3 statistic for triplets of items (Maydeu-Olivares & Joe, 2006), and R_2 statistic (Liu & Maydeu-Olivares, 2012). It should be noted that the assumption of local independence cannot be isolated from the other assumptions of the IRT model. As Liu and Maydeu-Olivares (2012) noted,

> "all model assumptions (local independence, dimensionality, specification of the item characteristic curve, and specification of the latent trait density) are tested simultaneously when using an overall goodness-of-fit statistic for multivariate discrete data such as Pearson's χ^2, or the likelihood ratio test statistic."

(p. 255)

ICC Specification

An IRT model assumes that an ICC has a specified form that describes the relationship between the ability level and probability of a specified response (e.g., correct response to a binary item). The shape of the ICC is specified by the analytic expression of the respective IRF model which includes the person's ability level, θ, and item parameters (e.g., *difficulty* and *discrimination*). For binary items, it is assumed that the ICC is S-shaped and increases monotonically with the increase of θ. This is illustrated in Figure 2.1 with the ICCs of two hypothetical items

> **NOTE [2.1]** The assumptions of *local independence* and *unidimensionality* are equivalent if the IRT model contains parameters on only one dimension. Hambleton and Swaminathan (1985) noted that:
>
> "for fixed ability level, θ, if items were not statistically independent, it should imply that some examinees have higher expected test scores than other examinees of the same ability level. Consequently, more than one ability would be necessary to account for examinee test performance."
>
> (p. 24)

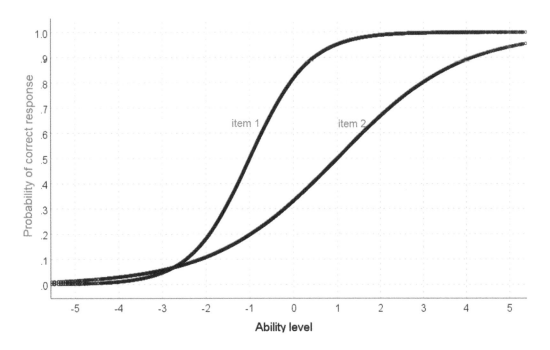

Figure 2.1. Item characteristic curves of two items under the 2PL model.

under the 2PL model (specified in the next section). In IRT, the ability scale is unlimited (i.e., θ can vary from $-\infty$ to $+\infty$) and its origin is zero ($\theta = 0$) but in practice the scale is usually restricted to an interval of choice (e.g., from -5 to $+5$). By definition, the *location* (*difficulty*) of an item is the location on the scale where the probability of correct response is 0.5 (i.e., 50% chance of success on the item). The steepness of the ICC indicates the discrimination power of the item; steeper ICCs are associated with more discriminating items.

In Figure 2.1, Item 1 is located at $\theta = -1.0$ (one unit below the mean), whereas Item 2 is located at $\theta = 1.0$ (one unit above the mean). For the most part (say, $\theta > -2.5$), the ICC of Item 2 is consistently below the ICC of Item 1, which indicates that Item 2 is more difficult than Item 1 for persons with ability in this range. On the other side, the ICC of Item 1 is steeper than that of Item 2 in the range, say, from -2.0 to 1.0, but the opposite holds in the range higher than 1.0. Thus, Item 1 is more discriminating than Item 2 among persons with ability levels between -2.0 and 1.0, but Item 2 is more discriminating than Item 1 among persons with ability levels higher than 1.0 on the scale. One can argue, for example, that if the purpose of the test is to select high-performing examinees, Item 2 might be preferable to Item 1.

Basic IRT Models

Presented in this section are widely used IRF models for unidimensional tests of binary items.

Two-Parameter Logistic Model

The analytic form of the two-parameter logistic (2PL) model (Birnbaum, 1968) is:

$$P_i(\theta) = \frac{\exp\left[D\alpha_i(\theta - \beta_i)\right]}{1 + \exp\left[D\alpha_i(\theta - \beta_i)\right]}, \quad (2.4)$$

where:

$P_i(\theta)$ = probability of correct response on item i for a person with ability θ,
β_i = item *difficulty* (i.e., the location on the ability scale where the probability of correct item response is 0.5),
α_i = item *discrimination* (α_i shows how well the item discriminates among persons with ability levels around the item location, β_i),
D = scaling constant (usually set to 1); when $D = 1.702$, the 2PL model in Equation 2.4 and the two-parameter normal-ogive model (Lord, 1952, 1953) produce almost identical ICCs (differ by less than 0.01 in absolute value), and
$\exp(.)$ = stands for the exponential function, $\exp(X) = e^X$.

The 2PL model of IRF is often presented in the following equivalent form:

$$P_i(\theta) = \frac{1}{1 + \exp\left[D\alpha_i(\beta_i - \theta)\right]}. \quad (2.5)$$

One-Parameter Logistic Model

The one-parameter logistic (1PL) model is obtained from the 2PL model by setting $D\alpha_i = 1$ in Equation 2.4 (or Equation 2.5):

$$P_i(\theta) = \frac{\exp(\theta - \beta_i)}{1 + \exp(\theta - \beta_i)}. \quad (2.6)$$

> **NOTE [2.2]** The item discrimination, α_i, indicates the steepness of the ICC at the item location, β_i, and shows how well the item discriminates among persons with ability levels close to β_i (*not* necessarily over other ranges on the ability scale). Mathematically, α_i equals the value of the first derivative of the 2PL function at the item location, β_i. That is, after differentiating $P_i(\theta)$ in Equation 2.4 (or Equation 2.5) and replacing θ with β_i in the derivative $P_i'(\theta)$, we obtain $\alpha_i = P_i'(\beta_i)$.

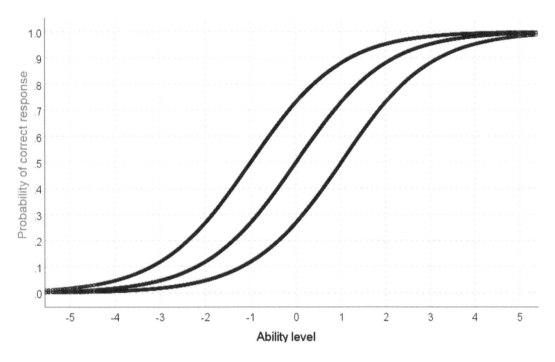

Figure 2.2. Item characteristic curves of three items (located at −1, 0, and 1 on the logit scale) under the 1PL model.

Under the 1PL model, the ICCs of the test items may differ in location but they have the same discrimination; that is, the ICCs have the same slope and look parallel. The ICCs of three items under the 1PL model are depicted in Figure 2.2, where the locations (difficulties) of the items (ICCs from left to right) are −1, 0, and 1, respectively. The 1PL model is usually referred to also as the Rasch model (Rasch, 1960). This is because, as shown in Appendix 2.1, the original Rasch model and the 1PL model in IRT are statistically equivalent. It should be noted, however, that there are some differences in their paradigms and estimation methods (e.g., Andrich, 1988; Engelhard, 2013; Smith & Smith, 2004; Wright & Stone, 1979).

Three-Parameter Logistic Model

In many test scenarios, especially with multiple-choice items, low-ability examinees tend to perform higher than expected on some items. In IRT, this issue is addressed by using the 3PL model for binary items (Birnbaum, 1968), which is obtained from the 2PL model by adding a third parameter, c_i, as follows:

$$P_i(\theta) = c_i + (1-c_i)\frac{\exp[D\alpha_i(\theta-\beta_i)]}{1+\exp[D\alpha_i(\theta-\beta_i)]}. \tag{2.7}$$

The parameter c_i is referred to as *pseudo-guessing parameter* as its purpose is to account for guessing or other causes of higher-than-expected performance of low-ability examinees. The c_i value of an item is usually smaller than the theoretical probability of selecting the correct answer under random guessing on the item. For example, the probability to select the correct answer via random guessing on a multiple-choice item with five response options (one correct option and four "distractors") is 1/5 = 0.20. Furthermore, c_i determines the lower asymptote of the ICC. This is illustrated in Figure 2.3, where $c_1 = 0.2$ and $c_2 = 0$ are the c_i values for Item 1 and Item 2, respectively. Note that the difficulty of Item 1 ($\beta_1 = 1$) is at the location on the ability scale that corresponds to the probability of correct response $(1 + c_1)/2 = (1 + 0.2)/2 = 0.6$. The difficulty of Item 2 ($\beta_2 = -1$), which does not involve pseudo-guessing, is the location that corresponds to the probability of correct response $(1 + c_2)/2 = (1 + 0)/2 = 0.5$.

The 3PL model typically provides a better fit to the data compared with the 2PL model but this comes with a "price" due to problems associated with the use of the third parameter, c_i, such as (a) lower estimation accuracy and (b) *item difficulty* is the location on the ability scale where the probability of correct item response is $(1 + c_i)/2$; that is, it would be 0.5 only when $c_i = 0$, and (c) the item difficulties are *not* comparable when the c_i parameter varies across items (e.g., for a detailed discussion of these problems, see Han, 2012).

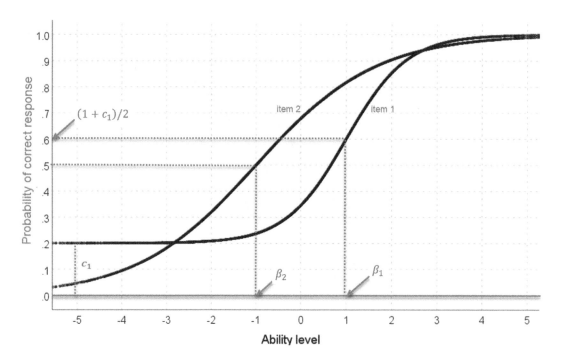

Figure 2.3. Item characteristic curves of two items under the 3PL model: Item 1 ($\alpha_1 = 1.2$, $\beta_1 = 1$, $c_1 = 0.2$) and Item 2 ($\alpha_2 = 0.75$, $\beta_2 = -1$, $c_2 = 0$).

Ability Scale

In IRT, the term "ability" connotes a latent trait (proficiency, affect) that underlies the responses of examinees on the items of an instrument (test, inventory, etc.). The ability scale commonly used in IRT is referred to as *logit scale*. The logit scale is an interval scale that theoretically ranges from $-\infty$ to $+\infty$. Both person ability and item difficulty, estimated under an IRT model (1PL, 2PL, or 3PL), are presented on the logit scale. The definition of logit scale is based on the concept "odds for correct item response" (or "odds for success"). Specifically, if $P_i(\theta)$ is the probability of correct response on item *i* by a person with ability θ, and $Q_i(\theta)$ is the probability of incorrect response on the item, the ratio $O_i = P_i(\theta)/Q_i(\theta)$ represents the "odds for success" on the item; note that $Q_i(\theta) = 1 - P_i(\theta)$. The analytic expressions of this odds ratio slightly differ across IRT models (1PL, 2PL, and 3PL) but the nature of the scale is generally the same.

IRT Logit Scale

Using Equation 2.6 for $P_i(\theta)$ under the 1PL model, $Q_i(\theta)$ can be represented as:

$$Q_i(\theta) = 1 - P_i(\theta) = \frac{1}{1 + \exp(\theta - \beta_i)}. \tag{2.8}$$

It can be easily verified that the odds ratio $O_i = P_i(\theta)/Q_i(\theta)$ can be represented as:

$$O_i = \exp(\theta - \beta_i). \tag{2.9}$$

Then, taking the natural logarithm of both sides of Equation 2.9, we obtain:

$$\ln(O_i) = \theta - \beta_i. \tag{2.10}$$

The $\ln(O_i)$ in Equation 2.10 produces "**log**-odds **units**" (abbreviated as "logits") that represent the difference between the ability level of a person, θ, and item difficulty, β_i (e.g., Wright, 1977). The resulting scale is the *logit scale*. For example, if the ability of a person is one unit above the difficulty of an item on the logit scale (i.e., $\theta - \beta_i = 1$), Equation 2.9 renders $O_i = \exp(1) = e^1 \approx 2.718$. Thus, the odds of this person for a correct response on the item are about 2.718; that is, the person's chances of correct response are 2.718 times higher than those of incorrect response on that item.

In addition to interpreting "person-item" differences, one can interpret "person-person" and "item-item" differences on the logit scale. Suppose that two persons with abilities θ and θ_2, respectively, are answering an item with difficulty β_i. Under Equation 2.10, their log-odds for item success are (a) $\ln(O_1) = \theta_1 - \beta_i$ and (b) $\ln(O_2) = \theta_2 - \beta_i$, respectively. By subtracting these two equations, we obtain:

$$\ln(O_1) - \ln(O_2) = \theta_1 - \theta_2$$

or, alternatively,

$$\ln(O_1/O_2) = \theta_1 - \theta_2. \tag{2.11}$$

For example, if $\theta_1 - \theta_2 = 1$, we have $\ln(O_1/O_2) = 1$ and, thus, $O_1/O_2 = \exp(1) = e^1 \approx 2.718$. The conclusion is that if two persons differ in ability by one unit on the logit scale, the odds for success on any item are about 2.718 times higher for the person with higher ability compared to the person with lower ability.

Now suppose that a person with ability θ is answering two items with difficulty β_1 and β_2. If O_1 and O_2 are the person's odds for success on the first and second items, respectively, it can be shown that the following equation holds:

$$\ln(O_1/O_2) = \beta_2 - \beta_1. \tag{2.12}$$

For example, suppose that the two items differ in difficulty by one unit, with the first item being more difficult; that is, $\beta_1 - \beta_2 = 1$ and, therefore, $\beta_2 - \beta_1 = -1$. Using Equation 2.12, we have: $\ln(O_1/O_2) = -1$ and, hence, $O_1/O_2 = \exp(-1) = e^{-1} = 1/e \approx 1/2.718 = 0.368$. Thus, $O_1 = 0.368 O_2$, which shows that the person's odds for success on the first (more difficult) item are smaller by a factor of 0.368 than the odds for success on the second (easier) item.

Under the 2PL model, the above transformations, based on $P_i(\theta)$ in Equation 2.4, result in the following equation of log-odds for success:

$$\ln(O_1/O_2) = D\alpha_i(\theta - \beta_i) \tag{2.13}$$

As the scaling factor is fixed ($D = 1$ or $D = 1.702$), interpretations of the log-odds for success are based on (a) $\ln(O_1/O_2) = \alpha_i(\theta - \beta_i)$ or (b) $\ln(O_1/O_2) = 1.702\alpha_i(\theta - \beta_i)$. In both cases, the discrimination parameter a_i is involved and, thus, should be accounted for in the interpretations.

Scale Indeterminacy

The estimation of person and item parameters under a specified IRT model (1PL, 2PL, or 3PL) can be performed via different estimation procedures (briefly discussed in the next section). In any case, the produced solution is *not* unique because an infinite number of other solutions can be obtained via linear transformations of the parameter estimates. Such "indeterminacy" of the logit scale (θ-scale) occurs because the probability of correct item response, $P_i(\theta)$, under the respective IRT model does not change upon the following linear transformations:

(a) 1PL model : $\theta^* = A\theta + B$; $\beta_i^* = A\beta_i + B$; (2.14)

NOTE [2.3] Under the 3PL model, the analytic form of the log-odds for success, $\ln(O_1/O_2)$, and related interpretations are more complicated because the "odds for success" is defined to account for the pseudo-guessing parameter, namely: $O_i = (P_i(\theta) - c_i)/Q_i(\theta)$. In this case, $\ln(O_1) = \ln\left(\frac{P_i(\theta) - c_i}{Q_i}\right) = D\alpha_i(\theta - \beta_i)$ (e.g., Hambleton & Swaminathan, 1985, p. 60).

(b)   2PL model : $\theta^\star = A\theta + B;\ \beta_i^\star = A\beta_i + B;\ \alpha_i^\star = \alpha_i/A$; and (2.15)

(c)   3PL model : $\theta^\star = A\theta + B;\ \beta_i^\star = A\beta_i + B;\ \alpha_i^\star = \alpha_i/A;\ \left(c_i^\star = c_i\right)$. (2.16)

The indeterminacy of the θ-scale is usually removed by fixing the *mean* and *standard deviation* of the distribution of θ estimates to 0 and 1, respectively ($\mu_\theta = 0$, $\sigma_\theta = 1$). Alternatively, one can fix the mean and standard deviation of the item difficulties to specific values. Theoretically, the θ-scale is unlimited ($-\infty$, $+\infty$), but in practice it is usually reported as a limited interval, say, [−5, 5], [−3, 3], or [−7,7], depending on the software for IRT analysis. To avoid issues with using and reporting negative values, the θ-scores on the logit scale are often transformed into positive scores on a scale with desired mean and standard deviation. For example, standard θ-scores ($\mu_\theta = 0$, $\sigma_\theta = 1$) can be presented on a scale with *mean* = 100 and *SD* = 15 using the transformation $\theta^\star = A\theta + B$, where $A = 15$ and $B = 100$.

True Domain Scores

As described earlier in this chapter, the ICC depicts the probability of correct response, $P_i(\theta)$, across ability levels on the θ-scale. The curve obtained by averaging the $P_i(\theta)$ values for all test items is referred to as *test characteristic curve* (TCC). That is, the TCC is a graphical depiction of the following *test characteristic function* (TCF):

$$\pi(\theta) = \frac{1}{n}\sum_{i=1}^{n} P_i(\theta). \qquad (2.17)$$

As shown in the literature on IRT (e.g., Lord & Novick, 1968), $P_i(\theta)$ is the classical *true score* on item *i* for a person with ability θ, and therefore, the sum of $P_i(\theta)$ values of all test items represents the person's classical *true score* on the test. The $\pi(\theta)$ score in Equation 2.17, referred to as *true domain score*, is simply the person's *true score* on the test divided by the number of test items. Thus, the TCF transforms the ability scores into true domain scores that are easy to interpret on a scale from 0 to 1. If the test items represent well a pool of items that ensure valid measurement of the targeted ability, the TCF in Equation 2.17 will produce unbiased domain scores (e.g., see Hambleton & Swaminathan, 1985, p. 67).

Ability Estimation

There are different approaches to estimating person ability, θ, and item parameters. The reader may refer, for example, to Baker and Kim (2004, 2017) for detailed descriptions of IRT-based estimation procedures and their implementation in a software package in R called "*birtr*" (Kim & Baker, 2018; https://cran.r-project.org). Brief descriptions of such procedures are provided in books on IRT methodology (e.g., De Ayala, 2009; Embretson & Reise, 2000; Hambleton & Swaminathan, 1985; van der Linden, 2016). Most approaches are based on the principle of *maximum-likelihood estimation* (MLE). In line with the scope and purpose of this book, presented in this section are only the logic and basic features of MLE (mathematical details, not presented here, differ across IRT models).

Let $\mathbf{u} = (u_1, u_2, \ldots, u_n \mid \theta)$ denote a response pattern of binary scores on *n* test items for a person with ability θ ($u_i = 1$, if correct; $u_i = 0$, if incorrect). Using Equation 2.3, the likelihood of this pattern to occur is:

$$L(\mathbf{u}\mid\theta) = \prod_{i=1}^{n} P_i^{u_i} Q_i^{1-u_i}, \qquad (2.18)$$

where P_i is the probability of correct response and Q_i is the probability of incorrect response ($Q = 1 - P_i$) on item *i* at ability level θ.

The value of θ that maximizes the *likelihood function*, $L(\mathbf{u}\mid\theta)$, is referred to as *maximum-likelihood estimator* (MLE) of the ability θ. As the product of probabilities on the right-hand side of Equation 2.18 produces very small numeric values, the natural logarithm of $L(\mathbf{u}\mid\theta)$ is used, $\ln L(u\mid\theta)$, to convert this product into the summation of probabilities as follows:

$$\ln L(\mathbf{u}\mid\theta) = \sum_{i=1}^{n}\left[u_i \ln(P_i) + (1-u_i)\ln(Q_i)\right] \qquad (2.19)$$

To maximize $L(\mathbf{u}|\theta)$ is equivalent to maximize $\ln L(\mathbf{u}|\theta)$ as these two functions are related monotonically. Thus, the MLE of θ is the location on the θ scale where the first derivative of $\ln L(\mathbf{u}|\theta)$ equals zero; that is, MLE of θ is a solution of the following equation:

$$\frac{d}{d\theta}\ln L(\mathbf{u}|\theta) = 0. \tag{2.20}$$

Graphically, the MLE of θ is depicted in Figure 2.4 for a response pattern of five items, (11010), with difficulties under the 1PL model as follows: $\beta_1 = -2$, $\beta_2 = -1$, $\beta_3 = 0$, $\beta_4 = 1$, and $\beta_5 = 2$ (in order from left to right in the response pattern). Using Equation 2.19, the $\ln L(u|\theta)$ function that is maximized is $\ln L(u|\theta) = \ln(P_1) + \ln(P_2) + \ln(1-P_3) + \ln(P_4) + \ln(1-P_5)$. As the item difficulties are known in this case, the probabilities P_1, P_2, P_3, P_4, and P_5 depend only on θ (see Equation 2.6). As shown in Figure 2.4, the $\ln L(\mathbf{u}|\theta)$ function reaches its maximum at $\theta = 0.5$ on the logit scale. Thus, $\hat{\theta} = 0.5$ is the ML-based estimate of θ in this illustration.

In real testing scenarios, both person and item parameters are unknown and estimated simultaneously using, for example, MLE-based methods such as the *joint maximum-likelihood* (JML) or *marginal maximumlikelihood* (MML) estimation. In general, MLE procedures are performed via an iterative process in two steps, (a) given some initial values of the item parameters, the person parameter, θ, is estimated, and then (b) using the resulting values of θ for all examinees, the item parameters are estimated. These two steps are repeated until a satisfactory solution is found (e.g., see Embretson & Reise, 2000; Hambleton & Swaminathan, 1985). As ML-based estimators may vary within the interval $(-\infty, +\infty)$, one cannot report θ scores corresponding to (a) perfect raw score—all test items were answered correctly, or (b) zero raw score—zero test items were answered correctly. This issue can be addressed by (a) using Bayesian estimators or (b) transforming the θ scores to domain true scores (see Equation 2.17).

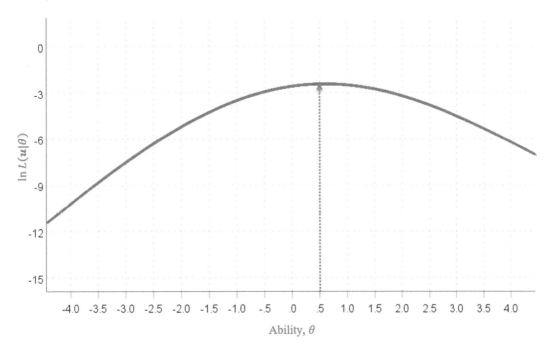

Figure 2.4. Log-likelihood function for a response pattern of five items, *ln*[L(1 1 0 1 0)], for a test of five hypothetical items under the 1PL model ($\beta_1 = -2$, $\beta_2 = -1$, $\beta_3 = 0$, $\beta_4 = 1$, and $\beta_5 = 2$).

NOTE [2.4] The IRT property of *invariance* ("sample free" estimation) holds theoretically *only* under the assumption that the respective (1PL, 2PL, or 3PL) model provides a perfect fit to the data for the population of examinees. In practical applications, the parameter estimates vary from sample to sample and, although they should be "in the same ballpark," rescaling procedures are needed to place them on a common scale (e.g., Kolen & Brennan, 2004).

Information Functions

In IRT context, the concept of "information" is associated with the precision of ability estimates, $\hat{\theta}$, in the sense that high precision provides more information about the examinee's ability level θ. That is, the amount of information, denoted I, is reciprocal to the variance of $\hat{\theta}$ at a given ability level $\theta: I = 1/\text{VAR}(\hat{\theta})$. As IRT operates at item level, precision-related information is defined for the entire test and individual items.

Test Information Function

One key property of ML estimators of θ is that their distribution is *asymptotically normal* (i.e., gets close to normal when the sample size increases) with *mean* = θ and the following variance:

$$\text{VAR}(\hat{\theta}) = 1 \Big/ \sum_{i=1}^{n} \left(P_i'^2 / P_i Q_i \right), \tag{2.21}$$

where P_i is the probability of correct item response, P_i' is its first derivative, and $Q_i = 1 - P_i$. Based on the conception that $I = 1/\text{VAR}(\hat{\theta})$, Lord (1980) provided the following analytic definition of *test information function* (TIF):

$$I(\theta) = \sum_{i=1}^{n} \left(P_i'^2 / P_i Q_i \right). \tag{2.22}$$

Thus, the standard deviation of $\hat{\theta}$ estimates at the ability level θ, referred to as *standard error of estimate*, $SE(\theta)$, is related to the TIF as follows:

$$SE(\theta) = \frac{1}{\sqrt{I(\theta)}}. \tag{2.23}$$

The $I(\theta)$ formulas for the 1PL, 2PL, and 3PL models, obtained from Equation 2.22, after developing the respective expression of the first derivative P_i', are as follows (e.g., Hambleton & Swaminathan, 1985, p. 91):

(a) $\quad$ 1PL : $I(\theta) = \sum_{i=1}^{n} (P_i Q_i);$ $\hfill (2.24)$

(b) $\quad$ 2PL : $I(\theta) = \sum_{i=1}^{n} \left(D^2 \alpha_i^2 P_i Q_i \right);$ $\hfill (2.25)$

(c) $\quad$ 3PL : $I(\theta) = \sum_{i=1}^{n} \left[D^2 \alpha_i^2 Q_i (P_i - c_i)^2 / (1 - c_i)^2 P_i \right].$ $\hfill (2.26)$

The behavior of the reciprocally related $I(\theta)$ and $SE(\theta)$ is illustrated in Figure 2.5 for a test of five hypothetical items with difficulties $\beta_1 = -2$, $\beta_2 = -1$, $\beta_3 = 0$, $\beta_4 = 1$, and $\beta_5 = 2$, using the 1PL model (same items were used for the illustration of log-likelihood function in Figure 2.4). As can be seen, (a) the $I(\theta)$ reaches its maximum, and conversely, $SE(\theta)$ reaches its minimum, at the middle of the scale, $\theta = 0$, and (b) the $I(\theta)$ and $SE(\theta)$ curves are symmetrical around $\theta = 0$. This is due to the special selection of five items with difficulties symmetrically located around the middle of the scale, $\theta = 0$, under the 1PL, but this is not the case in general. What is always the case, however, is that the $SE(\theta)$ increases toward the ends of the scale interval; that is, the precision of ability estimates, $\hat{\theta}$, is lower for low-performing and high-performing examinees.

Item Information Function

Equation 2.20 shows that the TIF, $I(\theta)$, is a sum of information "pieces" provided by individual test items. The additive contribution of an item to $I(\theta)$ is called *item information function*, denoted $I_i(\theta)$. That is:

$$I_i(\theta) = P_i'^2 / P_i Q_i. \tag{2.27}$$

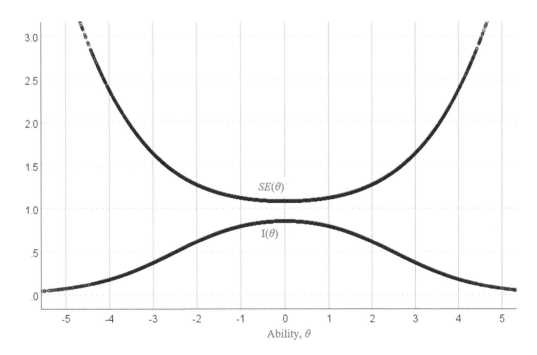

Figure 2.5. Reciprocally related test information function, $I(\theta)$, and standard error of estimate, $SE(\theta)$, for a test of five hypothetical items under the 1PL model ($\beta_1 = -2$, $\beta_2 = -1$, $\beta_3 = 0$, $\beta_4 = 1$, and $\beta_5 = 2$).

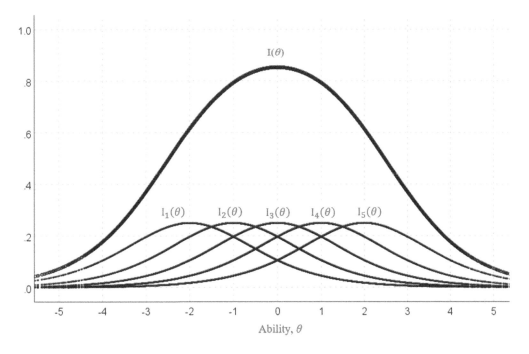

Figure 2.6. Test information function, $I(\theta)$, produced as a sum of the item information functions of five hypothetical items, $I_1(\theta)$, $I_2(\theta)$, $I_3(\theta)$, $I_4(\theta)$, and $I_5(\theta)$, under the 1PL model ($\beta_1 = -2$, $\beta_2 = -1$, $\beta_3 = 0$, $\beta_4 = 1$, and $\beta_5 = 2$).

Typically, the item information curve is bell shaped and reach its maximum (a) at the item difficulty location (i.e., $\theta_{\max} = \beta_i$) for the 1PL and 2PL models and (b) at a location slightly above β_i for the 3L model (e.g., Hambleton & Swaminathan, 1985, p. 105). For the 1PL model, this is illustrated in Figure 2.6 for the same five hypothetical items used in Figure 2.5 ($\beta_1 = -2$, $\beta_2 = -1$, $\beta_3 = 0$, $\beta_4 = 1$, and $\beta_5 = 2$).

Testing for Model–Data Fit

IRT models are based on strong assumptions which must be met to a degree that is considered sufficient for valid interpretations of results obtained under the model of choice. As it is not realistic to expect that an IRT model will provide an exact fit to the test data, it is reasonable to test for an approximate data fit instead. In a comprehensive review of goodness-of-fit assessment of IRT models, Maydeu-Olivares (2013) noted that:

> "the goodness of approximation of an IRT model should be regarded as the effect size of its misfit. As such, it is convenient that the goodness of approximation statistic can be interpreted qualitatively, for if a model is rejected, the researcher can judge whether the discrepancy is of substantive interest."
>
> (p. 72)

A *goodness-of-fit index* quantifies the discrepancy between the observed data and the data reproduced by a model. There is a variety of sources in the literature on statistical methods of testing for model-data fit in IRT (e.g., Andersen, 1973; Bock & Lieberman, 1970; Glas & Suárez-Falcón, 2003; Maydeu-Olivares, 2013, 2015; Maydeu-Olivares & Joe, 2006; Von Davier, 1997). This section provides only an overall description of likelihood ratio tests for data fit of IRT models. The assumptions of *unidimensionality* and *local independence*, described earlier, should be considered along with the testing for model-data fit.

Log-Likelihood Ratio Test

In general, the *likelihood ratio test* is a hypothesis test that compares the goodness of fit of two models based on the ratio of their likelihoods—an unconstrained model with all parameters free and a competing model which is constrained to fewer parameters. Let $L(\hat{\theta}_0)$ and $L(\hat{\theta}_1)$ denote the likelihood under the constrained and unconstrained model, respectively, where $\hat{\theta}_0$ and $\hat{\theta}_1$ are ML estimates of the parameter (or set of parameters) θ under the respective model. For convenience, the likelihood ratio $LR = L(\hat{\theta}_0)/L(\hat{\theta}_1)$ is replaced with its natural logarithm $\ln(LR) = \ln\left[L(\hat{\theta}_0)/L(\hat{\theta}_1)\right] = \ln\left[L(\hat{\theta}_0)\right] - \ln\left[L(\hat{\theta}_1)\right]$. It has been shown that the following statistic, referred to as *likelihood ratio test statistic* (*LRT*), follows asymptotically the chi-square (χ^2) distribution with *degrees of freedom* equal to the difference between the number of parameters of the two models (Wilks, 1938):

$$LRT = -2\left\{\ln\left[L(\hat{\theta}_0)\right] - \ln\left[L(\hat{\theta}_1)\right]\right\}. \tag{2.28}$$

The null hypothesis H_0, which favors the constrained model, is supported when $LRT\left(\approx \chi^2\right)$ is *not* statistically significant. The alternative hypothesis H_1, which favors the unconstrained model, is accepted when $LRT\left(\approx \chi^2\right)$ is statistically significant.

In IRT, testing for model fit against the data, called testing for *absolute* model fit, is performed by testing for the difference between the observed data and data that are reproduced (predicted) by the model. In this context, a widely used likelihood ratio test statistic, denoted G^2, is obtained as follows (McKinley & Mills, 1985):

$$G^2 = 2N\sum_{c=1}^{C} p_c \ln\left(p_c/\pi_c\right), \tag{2.29}$$

where:

N = number of examinees answering n test items with K response categories (0, 1, ..., $K-1$).
$C = K^n$ = number of cells in an n-dimensional contingency table of data (each cell contains one response pattern);
p_c = observed proportion of examinees with the response pattern in cell c ($c = 1, ..., C$);
π_c = probability of the response pattern in cell c, which is expected under the IRT model based on MLE of its parameters (e.g., θ, α_i, β_i, under the 2PL model).

The G^2 statistic is provided by commonly used IRT software programs such as BILOG-MG (Zimowski et al., 2003) and PARSCALE (Muraki & Bock, 1997).

Another widely used statistic for absolute model fit is the Pearson's chi-square statistic:

$$\chi^2 = N \sum_{c=1}^{C} \frac{(p_c - \pi_c)^2}{\pi_c}, \tag{2.30}$$

where N, C, p_c, and π_c have the same meaning as with Equation 2.29.

Testing for model-data fit using χ^2 involves assessing the discrepancy between the observed proportions p_c and the probabilities π_c across all cells of the contingency table. Under the null hypothesis that there is no such discrepancy, both statistics (G^2 and χ^2) are distributed asymptotically as a chi-square distribution with degrees of freedom: $df = C - q - 1$, where q is the number of item parameters estimated under the IRT model. For example, under the 2PL model for a test of 10 binary items, we have $n = 10$, $K = 2$, $C = 2^{10} = 1{,}024$ (number of different response patterns), and $q = 2$ (two model parameters, α_i, and β_i). In this case, $df = 1{,}024 - 2 - 1 = 1{,}021$.

$G^2(dif)$ Test

To avoid difficulties associated with the assessment of *absolute* model fit, researchers often times assess *relative* model fit by comparing a model of interest to a constrained version of that model. The constrained mode (M_0) is nested within the more general model (M_1) (e.g., M_0 = 1PL and M_1 = 2PL model). To test the relative fit of M_0 with respect to M_1, the principle of the *chi-square difference test* ($\Delta\chi^2 = \chi_0^2 - \chi_1^2$) is employed using the G^2 statistics of the two models. Specifically, $G^2(dif)$ statistic is computed as follows: $G^2(dif) = G_0^2 - G_1^2$, where G_0^2 and G_1^2 are the G^2 statistic (Equation 2.29) computed for the model M_0 and M_1, respectively.

Under the null hypothesis that the probabilities obtained under the M_0 and M_1 are equal, the $G^2(dif)$ statistic follows asymptotically a square distribution with degrees of freedom equal to the difference between the degrees of freedom for G_0^2 and G_1^2. That is, if the degrees of freedom for G_0^2 and G_1^2 are $df_0 = C - q_0 - 1$ and $df_1 = C - q_1 - 1$, respectively, the degrees of freedom for $G^2(dif)$ are $\Delta df = df_0 - df_1 = q_1 - q_0$, where q_1 and q_0 denote the number of parameters to be estimated (via MLE) in model M_1 and M_0, respectively. The null hypothesis is retained when the chi-square value of $G^2(dif)$ is not statistically significant, thus indicating that the two models do not differ in goodness-of-fit power for data fit. In such a case, the more parsimonious model M_0 should be preferred. Maydeu-Olivares and Cai (2006) provided a thorough discussion on using $G^2(dif)$ to assess relative model fit in categorical data analysis.

Item Fit

As IRT is item-level measurement, the evaluation of *item fit* (how well the IRT model predicts observed item responses) plays a key role in the assessment of model-data fit. The evaluation of item fit involves the use of statistical tests for item fit, visual inspection of the ICC behavior, and other elements of an overall judgment about item fit (e.g., Ames & Penfield, 2015; Embretson & Reise, 2000; Smith & Smith, 2004; Swaminathan, Hambleton, & Rogers, 2006).

Conceptually, the evaluation of *item fit* is based on information about how closely the observed item responses "fit" their predicted values under the IRT model. This is done by examining the residuals $R_{si} = X_{si} - P_{si}$ across all persons, with X_{si} being the (1/0) score and P_{si} being the probability of correct response of person s on item i under the IRT model. One limitation of examining such individual-level residuals is that (most of the time), they are not equal to zero even in the presence of a tenable model-data fit. This problem is avoided by using the so-called binned approach. Under this approach, the examinees are grouped into ranges of ability on the scale, called "bins," and residuals are computed by bins: $R_{hi} = O_{hi1} - P_{hi1}$, where O_{hi1} is the observed proportion of examinees

---

NOTE [2.5] When the number of response patterns increases, the π_c values become small (as their sum equals to 1), and as a result, the asymptotic *p*-values of the G^2 and χ^2 statistics are not trustworthy. To examine the validity of the *p*-values generated by these two statistics on the same data, one practical recommendation is to compare them: (a) if they are similar, it is likely that they are both correct; (b) if they slightly differ, χ^2 is to be preferred; and (c) if they are very different, then it is more likely that they are both incorrect (Koehler & Larntz, 1980).

in bin h who answered correctly item i, and P_{hi1} is the probability of correct item response in that bin ($h = 1, 2, \ldots, H$, where H is the total number of bins).

Most item-fit statistics are based on R_{hi} residuals and have an asymptotic chi-square distribution. The general form of a *chi-square test* for fit of binary items is (e.g., Ames & Penfield, 2015):

$$\chi_i^2 = \sum_{h=1}^{H} N_{hi} \frac{R_{hi}^2}{P_{hi1}(1 - P_{hi1})}, \quad (2.31)$$

where N_{hi} is the number of examinees in bin h, regardless of their score (1 or 0) on item i.

Two itemfit statistics, Yen's Q_1 (1981) and Bock's χ^2 (1960), are based on Equation 2.31 and follow asymptotically a chi-square distribution with degrees of freedom $df = H - q$, where H is the number of bins and q is the number of parameters estimated under the IRT model. For example, if 10 bins are used ($H = 10$) and the probabilities are estimated under the 2PL ($q = 2$), the degrees of freedom will be $df = 10 - 2 = 8$. It should be noted that these two statistics use a different number of bins and different ways of computing the bin probability, P_{hi1}. Specifically, Yen's Q_1 is based on 10 bins ($H = 10$), and P_{hi1} is the average of the model-based probabilities of correct item response for the examinees in the bin. In contrast, Bock's χ^2 allows for any number of bins, and P_{hi1} is the median of the model-based probabilities of correct item response for the examinees in the bin.

The general form of a likelihood-ratio statistic for item fit, denoted LR_i, is:

$$LR_i = 2 \sum_{h=1}^{H} \left[N_{hi1} \ln\left(\frac{N_{hi1}}{N_{hi} P_{hi1}}\right) + N_{hi0} \ln\left(\frac{N_{hi0}}{N_{hi}(1 - P_{hi1})}\right) \right], \quad (2.32)$$

where N_{hi1} and N_{hi0} represent the number of examinees in bin h with correct and incorrect responses to item i, respectively, and $N_{hi} = N_{hi1} + N_{hi0}$.

McKinley and Mills (1985) used G_i^2 statistic for item fit based on Equation 2.32, allowing for any number of bins and P_{hi1} defined as the model-based probability computed at the average value of ability estimates, $\hat{\theta}$, for the examinees in the bin. G_i^2 follows an asymptotic chi-square distribution with degrees of freedom equal to the number of bins ($df = H$).

One common limitation of the itemfit statistics, Yen's Q_1, Bock's χ^2, and G_i^2, is that they depend on (a) the arbitrary choice of the number of bins and (b) model-based ability estimates, $\hat{\theta}$. To address this issue, Orlando and Thissen (2000) created bins based on the raw scores (number of correct responses, NCR) with the number of bins computed as $H = n - 1$, where n is the total number of test items. Also, they computed the bin probabilities, P_{hi1}, using a recursive algorithm (Lord & Wingersky, 1984). For zero and perfect scores, $P_{hi1} = 0$ at $NCR = 0$, and $P_{hi1} = 1$ at $NCR = n$. Under this approach, (a) the χ_i^2 statistic in Equation 2.31 becomes a statistic denoted $S - X^2$, and (b) the LR_i statistic in Equation 2.32 becomes a statistic denoted $S - G^2$. Both $S - X^2$ and $S - G^2$ follow an asymptotic chi-square distribution with degrees of freedom: $df = n - 1 - q$, where n is the total number of test items and q is the number of model parameters. For example, in case of the 2PL model for a test with 30 binary items, $df = 30 - 1 - 2 = 27$. These two itemfit statistics are provided, for example, by the IRT software program IRTPRO (Cai, Thissen, & du Toit, 2011).

In the context of Rasch measurement, the χ_i^2 statistic in Equation 2.31 is used with one examinee per bin; that is, for a sample of N examinees, $H = N$. The residual for an examinee h is computed as $R_{hi} = X_{hi} - P_{hi}$, where X_{hi} is the examinee's score (1 or 0) on item i and P_{hi} is the probability of correct item response under the 1PL model. Given that $\mathrm{VAR}(X_{hi}) = P_{hi}(1 - P_{hi})$ and $N_{hi} = 1$ (one person per bin), the term under summation in Equation 2.31 is a squared standard score, Z_{hi}^2. Hence, $\chi_i^2 = \sum_{h=1}^{N} Z_{hi}^2$. Using these notations, the *OUTFIT* statistic for item i, based on a sample of N examinees, is defined as follows:

$$OUTFIT_i = \frac{1}{N} \sum_{h=1}^{N} Z_{hi}^2 \quad (2.33)$$

It should be noted that $OUTFIT_i$ does not follow a chi-square distribution but rather indicates the magnitude of "lack of fit." Hence, a tenable item fit is accepted when the $OUTFIT_i$ value is close to 1 (from 0.5 to 1.5, according to a widely used rule of thumb).

The *INFIT* statistic for item i, based on a sample of N examinees, is computed as follows:

$$INFIT_i = \frac{\sum_{h=1}^{N} Z_{hi}^2 \cdot w_{hi}}{\sum_{h=1}^{N} w_{hi}}, \tag{2.34}$$

where the "weight" for person h on item i is the variance of the person's score on the item, that is, $w_{hi} = \text{VAR}(X_{hi}) = P_{hi}(1 - P_{hi})$. (Note that this is also the item information function under the 1PL model.) Clearly, the $INFIT_i$ statistics gives more weight to examinees with ability level, θ, closer to the item difficulty, β_i. The underlying idea is that an examinee with ability level close to the item's difficulty will provide more information about the item's fit to the data than an examinee whose ability level is more distant from the item's difficulty. The rule of thumb for item fit indicated by $INFIT_i$ is the same as that used for $OUTFIT_i$; that is, a tenable item fit is flagged when $0.5 \leq INFIT_i \leq 1.5$. Conversely, item misfit is signaled when $INFIT_i$ is out of the interval [0.5, 1.5]. The $OUTFIT_i$ and $INFIT_i$, as well as their transformations to a t-statistic, are produced by the computer program Winsteps (Linacre, 2014). The reader may consult the literature on Rasch measurement for extended presentations of item fit procedures and their advantages, drawbacks, etc. (e.g., Andrich, 1988; Bond & Fox, 2007; de Ayala, 2009; Smith, 1991; Smith & Smith, 2004; Wu & Adams, 2013).

Person Fit

The assessment of IRT model-data fit at the level of individual examinees is called *person-fit* assessment. More specifically, person fit refers to statistical procedures used to evaluate the fit of a person's response pattern to the model being used. As noted by Embretson and Reise (2000), "person-fit indices attempt to assess the validity of the IRT measurement model at the individual level and the meaningfulness of a test score derived from the IRT model" (p. 238). Person measurement disturbances (aberrant response patterns) can be (a) *random* disturbances, associated with factors such as guessing or carelessness in responding to items, or (b) *systematic* disturbances, which may occur, say, with a deficiency in the content area, test bias, or instructional differences. The person-fit indices can be classified as (a) norm-based indices, such as the caution index (Sato, 1975) and the consistency index (Cliff, 1979), (b) IRT-based indices, such as the standardized index Z_3 (or l_z; e.g., Drasgow, Levine, & Williams, 1985; Levine & Drasgow, 1988), (c) Rasch model indices, such as the cube root transformation of the mean square statistic (e.g., Smith, Schumacker, & Bush, 1998), or its adjustment through the use of symmetric functions (Dimitrov & Smith, 2006), and (d) covariance-based indices, such as $ECI2_z$ and $ECI4_z$ (Tatsuoka, 1984) and H^T (Sijtsma, 1986; Sijtsma & Meijer, 1992). Described briefly in the following are the widely used IRT-based Z_3 statistic and the nonparametric H^T statistic.

The IRT-based Z_3 statistic is a *standardized likelihood-based personfit statistic* computed as:

$$Z_3 = \frac{l_0 - E(l_0 \mid \hat{\theta}_s)}{\left[\text{VAR}(l_0 \mid \hat{\theta}_s)\right]^{1/2}}, \tag{2.35}$$

where $\hat{\theta}$ is the maximum likelihood estimate of the ability of person s on the logit scale, l_0 is the natural logarithm of the likelihood for the response pattern at $\hat{\theta}_s$, and $VAR(l_0 \mid \hat{\theta}_s)$ is the conditional variance of l_0 at $\hat{\theta}_s$. For a test of n binary items, l_0 is estimated as follows (see Equation 2.19):

$$l_0 = \sum_{i=1}^{n} \left\{ X_{si} \ln P_i(\hat{\theta}_s) + (1 - X_{si}) \ln \left[1 - P_i(\hat{\theta}_s)\right] \right\} \tag{2.36}$$

> **NOTE [2.6]** According to Linacre (2002), "outfit" means "outlier-sensitive fit" as the outfit statistic is more sensitive to responses to items with difficulty far from a person's location on the ability scale. On the other side, "infit" means "inlier-sensitive" as the infit statistic is more sensitive to the pattern of responses to items targeted on the person (e.g., overfit for Guttman patterns or underfit for alternative curricula or idiosyncratic clinical groups).

where X_{si} is the binary (1/0) score of person s on item i. The expected value of l_0 is:

$$E(l_0 \mid \hat{\theta}_s) = \sum_{i=1}^{n} \left\{ P_i(\hat{\theta}_s) \ln P_i(\hat{\theta}_s) + \left[1 - P_i(\hat{\theta}_s)\right] \ln\left[1 - P_i(\hat{\theta}_s)\right] \right\}, \tag{2.37}$$

and the conditional variance of l_0 is:

$$\mathrm{VAR}(l_0 \mid \hat{\theta}_s) = \sum_{i=1}^{n} P_i(\hat{\theta}_s)\left[1 - P_i(\hat{\theta}_s)\right] \left[\ln \frac{P_i(\hat{\theta}_s)}{1 - P_i(\hat{\theta}_s)} \right]^2. \tag{2.38}$$

The H^T *statistic* is a nonparametric statistic for person fit (Sijtsma, 1986; Sijtsma & Meijer, 1992). To describe this statistic, let β_i and β_j denote the expected proportions of correctly answered items for two examinees, i and j, and β_{ij} is the expected proportion of items to which both examinees responded correctly. Then, the covariance between the item scores of these two examinees is $\sigma_{ij} = \beta_{ij} - \beta_i \beta_j$, with a maximum value $\sigma_{ij}^{max} = \beta_i(1 - \beta_j)$. The person-fit statistic H^T is computed as follows:

$$H^T = \left(\sum_{i \neq j} \sigma_{ij} \right) \bigg/ \left(\sum_{i \neq j} \sigma_{ij}^{\max} \right). \tag{2.39}$$

The H^T statistic reaches a maximum value of 1 when for all pairs of examinees $\sigma_{ij} = \sigma_{ij}^{\max}$, a value of 0 when $\sum_{i \neq j} \sigma_{ij} = 0$, and a negative value ($H^T < 0$) when $\sum_{i \neq j} \sigma_{ij} < 0$. In essence, H^T measures the lack of fit between a given response vector and the response vector summarized over the remaining response vectors.

Research on person-fit statistics indicates that, overall, H^T tends to do better than Z_3. For example, in the context of Rasch measurement, Dimitrov and Smith (2006) found that H^T outperforms Z_3 on tests of 20 and 30 items, but not on very short tests of 10 items. In a simulation study on person-fit statistics under the Rasch model, Karabatsos (2003) also reported that H^T outperformed Z_3 (and many other parametric and nonparametric person-fit statistics) for tests of 17, 33, and 65 items. It should be noted, however, that the power of Z_3 and H^T (and other person-fit statistics) depends largely on factors such as test difficulty, ranges of ability levels, θ, and the specific IRT model (e.g., Meijer & Sijtsma, 1995). For comprehensive studies on this issue, one can refer, for example, to Armstrong et al. (2007), regarding Z_3, and Karabatsos (2003), regarding H^T.

Differential Item Functioning

Issues of validity and fairness in testing involve the examination of *differential item functioning* (DIF). Specifically, DIF occurs when respondents from different groups, but with the same level of ability measured by the test, differ in chances to endorse the respective response categories of the item. The presence of DIF threatens the validity of comparing groups on the ability measured by the test (e.g., Holland & Wainer, 1993; Osterlind & Everson, 2009; Penfield & Camilli, 2007). Procedures for DIF testing are under ongoing development, mostly in the frameworks of IRT (e.g., Andrich & Hagquist, 2015; Lord, 1980; Oshima & Morris, 2008; Oshima, Raju, & Nanda, 2006; Raju, 1988, 1990; Raju, van der Linden, & Fleer, 1995; Thissen, Steinberg, & Wainer, 1993) and *confirmatory factor analysis* (CFA; e.g., Cheung & Rensvold, 1999; Dimitrov, 2010; Raykov et al., 2015). There are studies on DIF that deal with comparisons and integration of IRT and CFA frameworks (e.g., Dimitrov, 2017; Stark, Chernyshenko, & Drasgow, 2006). For the case of binary test items, the integration of CFA and IRT frameworks is based on an equivalence between a one-factor CFA model and the two-parameter normal-ogive IRT model (Takane & de Leeuw, 1987; see also Dimitrov, 2017). Out of the IRT and CFA frameworks are DIF testing procedures such as the Mantel–Haenszel method and its refinement (e.g., Holland & Thayer, 1988; Zwick, 2012), logistic regression modeling (e.g., Swaminathan & Rogers, 1990; Zumbo, 1999), log-linear analysis (e.g., Green, Crone, & Folk, 1989), and descriptive standardizations (e.g., Dorans, 1989; Dorans, Schmitt, & Bleistein, 1992).

In IRT, most approaches to testing for DIF are based on the discrepancy between the ICCs of two groups—a majority group called *reference group* and a minority group, against which DIF is suspected, called *focal group* (e.g., Dimitrov, 2017; Oshima et al., 2006; Raju, 1988, 1990; Raju et al., 1995). Two types of DIF may occur, (a) *uniform* DIF—the ICCs of the two groups do *not* cross (see Figure 2.7), and (b) *nonuniform* DIF—the ICCs cross (see Figure 2.8). In this context, a key role in testing for DIF plays the difference:

$$d_{is} = P_{iF}(\theta_s) - P_{iR}(\theta_s), \tag{2.40}$$

where $P_{iF}(\theta_s)$ and $P_{iR}(\theta_s)$ are the probabilities of correct item response for examinees with the same ability, θ_s, that belong to the focal and reference group, respectively.

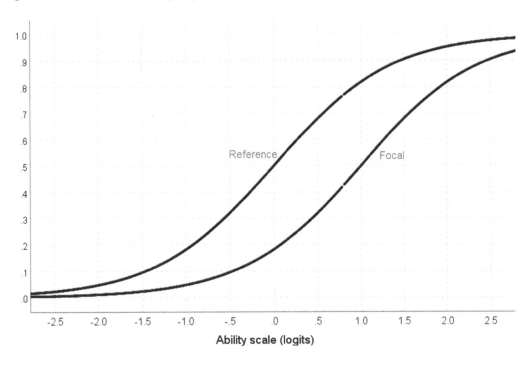

Figure 2.7. Uniform DIF—the item characteristic curves of the reference and focal groups do not cross. The item parameters for the two groups, presented on a common scale, are as follows: Reference ($\alpha_i = 1$, $\beta_i = 0$) and Focal ($\alpha_i = 1$, $\beta_i = 1$).

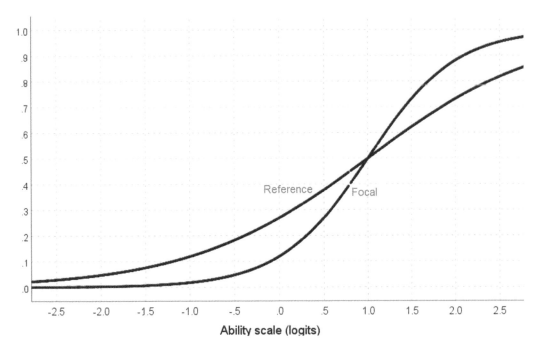

Figure 2.8. Nonuniform DIF—the item characteristic curves of the reference and focal groups cross. The item parameters for the two groups, presented on a common scale, are as follows: Reference ($\alpha_i = 2$, $\beta_i = 1$) and Focal ($\alpha_i = 1$, $\beta_i = 1$).

Differential Test Functioning

At the test level, DTF refers to the discrepancy between the TCCs of the reference and focal groups. Testing for DTF is based on examining the overall difference across the item-level differences d_{is} in Equation 2.40, that is, $D_s = \sum_{i=1}^{n} d_{is}$, where n is the number of test items. Raju et al. (1995) proposed an overall measure of DTF based on the expected value (theoretical mean) of the squared D_s values over the ability distribution of one of the two groups (reference or focal):

$$\text{DTF} = E(D_s^2) = \sigma_D^2 + \mu_D^2 = \sum_{i=1}^{n} \left[\text{Cov}(d_i, D) + \mu_{d_i} \mu_D \right], \quad (2.41)$$

where d_i and D are estimated from d_{is} and D_s, respectively, over all ability levels, θ_s, and μ_{d_i} and μ_D are their theoretical means. (For specificity, θ_s are taken for the focal group, but they can be taken for the reference group as well.)

A Compensatory DIF Index

Raju et al. (1995) used the term under summation in Equation 2.41 to define an additive DIF index that allows to evaluate the contribution of individual items to the differential functioning of the entire test. Specifically:

$$CDIF_i = \text{Cov}(d_i, D) + \mu_{d_i} \mu_D. \quad (2.42)$$

Thus, $\text{DTF} = \sum_{i=1}^{n} CDIF_i$, which shows how much each item's $CDIF_i$ contributes to DTF. Raju et al. (1995) noted that "unlike other DIF indices, the $CDIF_i$ includes information about bias from other items in the test" ... which "will influence differential functioning at the test level" (p.355). The $CDIF_i$ is a "compensatory" index in the sense that it may have positive or negative values, which allows DIF effects across items to "cancel out" to a certain degree. As Raju et al. (1995) stated, "the proposed DTF index takes into account compensating bias across items at the examinee level" (p. 355).

A Noncompensatory DIF Index

Equation 2.42 produces a *noncompensatory* DIF index under the assumption that, excluding item i, all other items in the test are unbiased and, thus, $d_j = 0$ for all $j \neq i$. The resulting DIF index is:

$$NCDIF_i = \sigma_{d_i}^2 + \mu_i^2. \quad (2.43)$$

> **NOTE [2.7]** Dimitrov and Atanasov (2022) proposed an approach to testing for differential functioning of items and tests, referred to as P-Z method, under which the comparison of ICCs for the reference and focal groups, $P_{iF}(\theta_s)$ and $P_{iR}(\theta_s)$, is reduced to comparing their Z-scale normal deviates, Z_{iF} and Z_{iR}, which are linearly related. This approach, described in Chapter 8, is designed for DIF and DTF testing in the context of the D-scoring method of measurement. (Research on its efficiency in the IRT context is underway.)

Test Equating

Test equating is a psychometric procedure of presenting test scores on a common scale using an appropriate equating design, such as (a) *single-group design*: the same group of examinees take two different test forms, (b) *equivalent-group design*: two groups of examinees, equivalent in ability measured by the test, take two different test forms, and (c) *anchor-test design*: two groups of examinees that differ in ability measured by the test take two different test forms containing a set of common (anchor) items. In large-scale assessments, for example, multiple test forms are administered to different groups of examinees for security reasons, so test equating is necessary to validate the comparison of test scores obtained by examinees who took different test forms. In general, the equating of two tests requires that they are unidimensional and measure the same ability (trait) with equal precision. In addition, the validity of score comparison across test forms must *not* depend on whether test X is equated to the scale of test Y or vice-versa ("symmetry"). An elaboration of these requirements, known together as "equity" in test equating, is provided by Lord (1980, p. 195) (e.g., see also Lord, 1982; Hambleton & Swaminathan, 1985, p.199).

There is a variety of classical and IRT-based methods of test equating (e.g., Dorans, Moses, & Eignor, 2010; Kolen & Brennan, 2004; Lee & Fitzpatrick, 2008; Von Davier & Von Davier, 2007). In line with the purpose of this book, provided here is only a brief description of IRT-based equating under the anchor-test design, referred to also as the *nonequivalent groups with anchor test* (NEAT) design. This approach is based on the IRT property of *invariance* under which the ability estimates of examinees remain invariant across sets of items, and the item parameter estimates remain invariant across samples of examinees; that is, the IRF remains invariant across different sets of items. Theoretically, the invariance holds only under the assumption of a perfect model-data fit in the population of examinees. In practice, when the person and item parameters are unknown, the IRFs remain invariant up to a linear transformation of the ability and item parameters. The analytic form of this linear transformation was provided earlier (see Equations 2.14–2.16).

Under the NEAT design, the equating of two test forms, X and Y, is based on the following linear relationship between the parameters of the common items of X and Y:

$$\beta_{ic}^\star = A.\beta_{ic} + B \tag{2.44}$$

and

$$\alpha_{ic}^\star = \alpha_{ic}/A, \tag{2.45}$$

where α_{ic} and β_{ic} are the item *discrimination* and *difficulty*, respectively, for the common items in test X, and $\alpha_{ic}^\star$ and $\beta_{ic}^\star$ are their rescaled counterparts on the scale of test Y. (A and B are rescaling constants.) Under the "mean and sigma method" (Loyd & Hoover, 1980; Marco, 1977) (e.g., see also Hambleton & Swaminathan, 1985, p. 207), the rescaling constants are obtained from Equation 2.39 by taking the standard deviation and the mean of the terms on both sides:

$$A = \sigma_{\beta_{ic}^\star}/\sigma_{\beta_{ic}} \tag{2.46}$$

and

$$B = \mu_{\beta_i^\star} = A.\mu_{\beta_i}. \tag{2.47}$$

After the rescaling constants A and B are obtained, the parameters of all items in test X are rescaled to the scale of test Y using the linear transformations in Equations 2.44 and 2.45 for all items in X. Then, the ability scores θ of examinees who took test X are rescaled to $\theta^\star$ scores on the scale of test Y as follows: $\theta^\star = A.\theta + B$. When the 3PL model is used, the pseudo-guessing parameter is kept the same upon rescaling (i.e., $c_i^\star = c_i$). Lee and Fitzpatrick (2008) proposed an approach to equating test scores using the 3PL model with fixed c_i parameter (i.e., c_i = const.).

A modification of the mean and sigma method, called "robust mean and sigma method," is based on "weights" taking into account the accuracy of person and item parameter estimates (Linn et al., 1981). Stocking and Lord (1983) proposed a *robust iterative weighted mean and sigma* method that assigns low weights to estimates with low accuracy and to outliers. They proposed also the *characteristic curve* method which produces better results by minimizing the difference between the two ICCs, but at the "price" of more complicated and time-consuming numerical procedures. As IRT test equating is based on the rescaling of parameters, it is also referred to as *scale linking* (e.g., for a unified approach to scale linking, see von Davier & von Davier, 2007).

True-Score Equating

True-score equating refers to the equating of *number-correct true scores* on test form X to the scale of number-correct true scores on a test form Y. IRT true-score equating (Lord, 1982) is based on the known relationship between the number-correct true score, τ, on a test of n items and the IRT score, θ, of an examinee: $\tau(\theta) = \sum_{i=1}^{n} P_i(\theta)$. The *true domain score*, $\pi(\theta)$, relates to the *number-correct true score* as follows: $\pi(\theta) = \tau(\theta)/n$ (see Equation 2.17). Here, the term "true score" will be used to indicate the number-correct true score, denoted $\tau(\theta)$ (or just τ).

Described next are the main steps in a widely used IRT approach to true-score equating (e.g., Kolen & Brennan, 2004, pp. 175–180).

Step 1. The item parameters of test X, obtained, say, under the 2PL model $(\alpha_{iX}, \beta_{iX})$, are rescaled to their counterparts $(\alpha_{iY}, \beta_{iY})$ on the scale of test Y.

Step 2. If τ_X is a given true score on test form X, the corresponding ability score, θ_X, can be found as a numerical solution of the equation $\sum_{i=1}^{n} P_i(\theta_X, \alpha_{iX}, \beta_{iX}) - \tau_X = 0$.

Step 3. The true score τ_Y, that corresponds to τ_X on the true-score scale of test Y, is obtained as follows: $\tau_Y = \sum_{i=1}^{n} P_i(\theta_X, \alpha_{iY}, \beta_{iY})$, where θ_X is a solution of the equation in Step 2.

The above three-step approach to true-score equating is illustrated in Figure 2.9. In this case, we have (a) $\theta_X = 0.5$ corresponding to $\tau_X = 10$ and (b) $\tau_Y = 14$ corresponding to $\theta_X = 0.5$. Thus, the true score of 10 on the scale of test X is equated to a true score of 14 on the scale of test Y. In general, the most difficult part is to find a solution, θ_X, of the equation in Step 2. The widely used Newton-Raphson method of solving this equation involves tedious iterative procedures that can run into convergence problems.

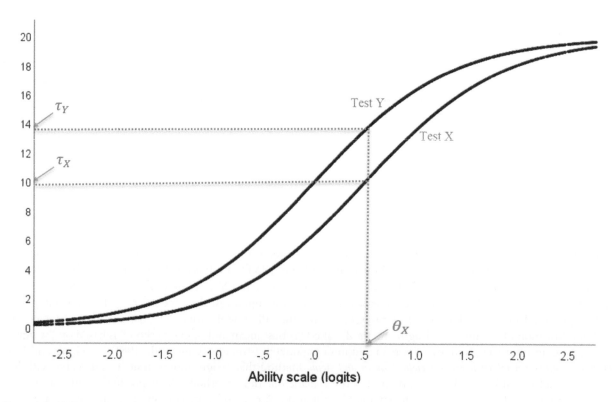

Figure 2.9. IRT equating of a true score τ_X on test X to a true score τ_Y on the scale of test Y.

NOTE [2.8] When the goal is to equate *observed number-correct scores* on two test forms, an IRT-based procedure is used to produce an estimated distribution of such scores for each test form. The observed scores of these distributions are then equated using the equipercentile method (e.g., Kolen & Brennan, 2004, pp. 181–190). A drawback of this approach is that the results are sample dependent. Some studies suggest that very similar results are obtained by using the IRT equating of number-correct true scores and then treating the true scores as observed scores, but there is no theoretical justification for that (Lord & Wingersky, 1984).

In any case, IRT equating (of true or observed scores) was found to perform better than the traditional equipercentile equating (e.g., Han, Kolen, & Pohlman, 1997; Holland & Sinharay, 2010).

Summary Points

1. IRT is model-based measurement at item level. An IRF model specifies the relationship between a *dependent variable* (observable item responses) and *independent variables*—unobservable (latent) ability level and item properties (e.g., *difficulty* and *discrimination*).
2. The assumption of *unidimensionality* implies that there is a single latent ability (trait) that governs the responses on test items for a target population of examinees.
3. The assumption of *local independence* implies that the person's responses to the test items are statistically independent; that is, the person's probability of any response pattern of item scores equals the product of probabilities of the scores on all test items regardless of the order of their presentation in the test.
4. The assumptions of *local independence* and *unidimensionality* are equivalent if the IRT model contains parameters on only one dimension.
5. An IRT model assumes that an ICC has a specified form that describes the relationship between the ability level and probability of a specified response.
6. The ability scale commonly used in IRT is referred to as *logit scale*. The logit scale is an interval scale that theoretically ranges from $-\infty$ to $+\infty$. The definition of the logit scale is based on the concept "odds for correct item response" (O_i). The $\ln(O_i)$ produces "**log**-odds un**its**" (abbreviated as "logits") that represent the difference between the person ability and item difficulty, $\ln(O_i) = \theta - \beta_i$.
7. *Indeterminacy* of the logit scale occurs because the probability of correct item response does not change upon the linear transformation of the person and item parameters (see Equations 2.14–2.16).
8. The IRT property of *invariance* ("sample free" estimation) holds theoretically *only* under the assumption that the IRF model provides a perfect fit to the data for the examinee population.

    At sample level, the invariance of person and item parameters holds up to linear transformations.
9. The TCC is obtained by averaging the ICCs over the logit scale. The TCC value at a given ability level is referred to as *true domain score* at that ability level (see Equation 2.17). The true domain score of a person is simply the person's *true score* on the test divided by the number of test items.
10. A *maximum-likelihood estimator* (MLE) of a person's ability level is the scale value that maximizes the likelihood of the person's response pattern of the test items (Equation 2.19).
11. In the IRT context, the concept of "information" is associated with the precision of ability estimates—high precision provides more information about the examinee's ability level. The TIF is a sum of the *item information functions* (see Equation 2.22). The *SEE* at a given ability level is reciprocal to the square root of the TIF (see Equation 2.23).
12. In the testing for model-data fit, a *goodness-of-fit index* quantifies the discrepancy between the observed data and the data reproduced by a model. The *likelihood-ratio test* compares the goodness of fit of two models based on the ratio of their likelihoods—an unconstrained model with all parameters free and a competing model constrained to fewer parameters.
13. The evaluation of *item fit* is based on information about how closely the observed item responses "fit" their predicted values under the IRT mode. It involves the use of statistical tests for item fit, visual inspection of the ICC behavior, and other elements of an overall judgment about item fit.
14. *Person fit* refers to statistical procedures used to evaluate the fit of a person's response pattern to the IRT model being used. Person-fit indices attempt to assess the validity of the IRT measurement model at the individual level and the meaningfulness of a test score derived from the IRT model.

15 DIF occurs when respondents from different groups (e.g., *reference* and *focal*), but with the same level of ability measured by the test, differ in chances to endorse the respective response categories of the item. The presence of DIF threatens the validity of comparing groups on the ability measured by the test.
16 DTF refers to the discrepancy between the TCCs of the reference and focal groups.
17 *Test equating* is a psychometric procedure of presenting test scores on a common scale using an appropriate equating design. Under the *anchor-test design*, also called the NEAT design, two groups of examinees that can differ in ability measured by the test take two different test forms that contain a set of common (anchor) items. Under the NEAT design, equating of two tests is based on a linear relationship between the parameters of the common items of the tests (see Equations 2.44 and 2.45).
18 *True-score equating* refers to the equating of *number-correct true scores* on test form X to the scale of number-correct true scores on a test form Y. IRT true score equating is based on the relationship between the number-correct true score and the IRT score of an examinee (see Equation 2.17).

Appendix 2.1: Rasch Model

The Danish mathematician George Rasch (1960) proposed a probabilistic model referred to as the *Rasch model*. The original form of the Rasch model for the probability of item success (e.g., see also, Hambleton, Swaminathan, & Rogers, 1991, p. 81) is:

$$P_i = \frac{\theta^\star}{\theta^\star + b_i^\star}, \tag{A2.1}$$

where P_i is the probability of correct response on item i, with difficulty $b_i^\star$ for a person with ability level $\theta^\star$ on the latent ability (trait) measured by the test.

The 1PL model (Equation 2.6) is obtained from the Rasch model in Equation A2.1 using the following non-linear exponential transformations:

$$\theta^\star = e^\theta \text{ and } b_i^\star = e^{b_i} \tag{A2.2}$$

Indeed, using the transformations in Equations (A2.2), the probability of correct response under the model in Equation A2.1 becomes:

$$P_i = \frac{e^\theta}{e^\theta + e^{b_i}} = \frac{1}{1 + e^{b_i - \theta}} = \frac{e^{\theta - b_i}}{1 + e^{\theta - b_i}}. \tag{A2.3}$$

Rasch Ratio Scale Property

Under the Rasch model, a simple algebra shows that the *odds for success* on an item are:

$$O_i = \frac{P_i}{1 - P_i} = \frac{\theta^\star}{b_i^\star}. \tag{A2.4}$$

Thus, for two examinees with ability $\theta_1^\star$ and ability $\theta_2^\star$, responding to an item i, the *odds ratio for success* on the item is:

$$\frac{O_{1i}}{O_{2i}} = \frac{\theta_1^\star / b_i^\star}{\theta_2^\star / b_i^\star} = \frac{\theta_1^\star}{\theta_2^\star}. \tag{A2.5}$$

Equation A2.5 shows that the odds ratio for the item success of two examinees equals the ratio of their ability levels on the $\theta^\star$ scale. For example, if $\theta_1^\star = 2\theta_2^\star$, then $O_{1i} = 2O_{2i}$. Thus, the ratio scale property holds for the $\theta^\star$ scale.

Now assume that an examinee with ability $\theta^\star$ has responded to two items with difficulty $b_1^\star$ and $b_2^\star$. Using Equation A2.4, the examinee's odds for success on the two items is:

$$\frac{O_1}{O_2} = \frac{\theta^\star / b_1^\star}{\theta^\star / b_2^\star} = \frac{b_2^\star}{b_1^\star}. \tag{A2.6}$$

Equation A2.6 shows that the ratio scale property holds for the $b^\star$ scale. For example, if the first item is twice as difficult as the second item ($b_1^\star = 2b_2^\star$), then the examinee's odds for success on the more difficult item are two times smaller than those for success on the easier item ($O_1 = O_2/2$).

References

Ames, A., & Penfield, R. D. (2015). An NCME instructional module on item fit statistics for item response theory models. *Educational Measurement: Issues and Practice, 34*(3), 39–48.

Andersen, E. B. (1973). A goodness of fit test for the Rasch model. *Psychometrika, 38*, 123–140.

Andrich, D. (1988). *Rasch models of measurement*, Beverly Hills, CA: Sage Publications.

Andrich, D., & Hagquist, C. (2015). Real and artificial differential item functioning in polytomous items. *Educational and Psychological Measurement, 75*(2), 185–207.

Armstrong, R. D., Stoumbos, Z. G., Kung, M. T., & Shi, M. (2007). On the performance of the l_z person-fit statistic. *Practical Assessment, Research & Evaluation, 12*(16), 1–15.

Baker, F. B., & Kim, S.-H. (2004). *Item response theory: Parameter estimation techniques* (2nd ed.). Boca Raton, FL: CRC Press.

Baker F. B., & Kim S.-H. (2017). *The basics of item response theory using R*. New York: Springer.

Birnbaum, A. (1968). Some latent trait models and their use in inferring an examinee's ability. Part 5. In F.M. Lord & M.R. Novick (Eds.), *Statistical Theories of mental test scores* (pp. 395–4790). Reading, MA: Addison-Wesley.

Bock, R. D. (1960). *Methods and applications of optimal scaling*. Chapel Hill, NC: L.L. Thurstone Psychometric Laboratory.

Bock, R. D., & Gibbons, R. D. (2021). *Item response theory*. New York: Wiley.

Bock, R. D., Gibbons, R. D., & Muraki, E. (1988). Full-information item factor analysis. *Applied Psychological Measurement, 12*, 261–280.

Bock, R. D., & Lieberman, M. (1970). Fitting a response model for n dichotomously scored items. *Psychometrika, 35*, 179–197.

Bond, T. G., & Fox, C. M. (2007). *Applying the Rasch model: Fundamental measurement in the human sciences* (2nd ed.). New York: Routledge.

Cai, L., Thissen, D., & du Toit, S. H. C. (2011). *IRTPRO for Windows* [Computer software]. Lincolnwood, IL: Scientific Software International.

Cai, L., Yang, J. S., & Hansen, M. (2011). Generalized full-information item bifactor analysis. *Psychological Methods, 16*(3), 221–248.

Chen, W.-H., & Thissen, D. (1997). Local dependence indexes for item pairs using item response theory. *Journal of Educational and Behavioral Statistics, 22*, 265–289.

Cheung, G. W., & Rensvold, R. B. (1999). Testing factorial invariance across groups: A reconceptualization and proposed new method. *Journal of Management, 25*, 1–27.

Cliff, N. (1979). Test theory without true scores? *Psychometrika, 44*, 373–393.

De Ayala, R. J. (2009). *The theory and practice of item response theory* (2nd ed.). New York: The Guilford Press.

Dimitrov, D. M. (2010). Testing for factorial invariance in the context of construct validation. *Measurement and Evaluation in Counseling and Development, 43*(2), 121–149.

Dimitrov, D. M. (2017). Examining differential item functioning: IRT-based detection in the framework of confirmatory factor analysis. *Measurement and Evaluation in Counseling and Development, 50*(3), 183–200.

Dimitrov, D. M., & Atanasov, D. V. (2022). Testing for differential item functioning under the D-scoring method. *Educational and Psychological Measurement, 82*(1), 107–121.

Dimitrov, D. M., & Smith, R. M. (2006). Adjusted Rasch person-fit statistics. *Journal of Applied Measurement, 7*(2), 170–183.

Dorans, N. J. (1989). Two new approaches to assessing differential item functioning: Standardization and the Mantel-Haenszel method. *Applied Measurement in Education, 2*(3), 217–233.

Dorans, N. J., Moses, T., & Eignor, D. (2010). *Principles and practices of test score equating*. ETS Research Report No. RR-10-29. Princeton, NJ: Educational Testing Service.

Dorans, N. J., Schmitt, A. P., & Bleistein, C. A. (1992). The standardization approach to assessing comprehensive differential item functioning. *Journal of Educational Measurement, 29*(4), 309–319.

Drasgow, F., Levine, M. V., & Williams, E. A. (1985). Appropriateness measurement with polychotomous item response models and standardized indices. *British Journal of Mathematical and Statistical Psychology, 38*, 67–86.

Embretson, S. E., & Reise, S. P. (2000). *Item response theory*. Mahwah, NJ: Erlbaum Publishers.

Engelhard, G. (2013). *Invariant measurement: Using Rasch models in the social, behavioral, and health sciences*. New York: Routledge.

Fennessy, L. M. (1995). *The impact of local dependencies on various IRT outcomes*. (Publication No. AAI9524701) [Doctoral dissertation, University of Massachusetts Amherst]. Proquest. https://scholarworks.umass.edu/dissertations/AAI9524701.

Gibbons, R. D., & Hedeker, D. R. (1992). Full-information item bi-factor analysis. *Psychometrika, 57*(3), 423–436.

Glas, C. A. W., & Suárez-Falcón, J. C. (2003). A comparison of item-fit statistics for the three-parameter logistic model. *Applied Psychological Measurement, 27*(2), 87–106.

Green, B. F., Crone, C. R., & Folk, V. G. (1989). A method for studying differential distractor functioning. *Journal of Educational Measurement, 26*(2), 147–160.

Hambleton, R. K., & Swaminathan, H. (1985). *Item response theory: Principles and applications*. Hingham, MA: Kluwer, Nijhoff.

Hambleton, R. K, Swaminathan, H., & Rogers, H. J. (1991). *Fundamentals of item response theory*. Newbury Park, CA: Sage.

Han, K. T. (2012). Fixing the c parameter in the three-parameter logistic model. *Practical Assessment, Research & Evaluation, 17*(1), 1–24.

Han, T., Kolen, M., & Pohlman, J. (1997). A comparison among IRT true- and observed-score equatings and traditional equipercentile equating. *Applied Measurement in Education, 10*(2), 105–121.

Hattie, J. (1985). Methodology review: Assessing unidimensionality of tests and items. *Applied Psychological Measurement, 9*, 139–164.

Holland, P. W., & Sinharay, S. (2010). A new approach to comparing several methods in the context of the NEAT design. *Journal of Educational Measurement, 47*(3), 261–285.

Holland, P. W., & Thayer, D. T. (1988). Differential item performance and the Mantel-Haenszel procedure. In H. Wainer & H. I. Braun (Eds.), *Test validity* (pp. 129–145). Mahwah, NJ: Lawrence Erlbaum.

Holland, P. W., & Wainer, H. (1993). *Differential item functioning*. Mahwah, NJ: Lawrence Erlbaum.

Kahraman, N. (2013). Unidimensional interpretations for multidimensional test items. *Journal of Educational Measurement, 50*(2), 227–246.

Karabatsos, G. (2003). Comparing the aberrant response detection performance of thirty-six person-fit statistics. *Applied Measurement in Education, 16*(4), 277–298.

Kim, S. H., & Baker, F. B. (2018). birtr: A package for "The basics of item response theory using R." *Applied Psychological Measurement, 42*(5), 403–404.

Koehler, K., & Larntz, K. (1980). An empirical investigation of goodness of fit statistics for sparse multinomials. *Journal of the American Statistical Association, 75*, 336–344.

Kolen, M. J., & Brennan, R. L. (2004). *Test equating, scaling, and linking: Methods and practice* (2nd ed.). New-York: Springer-Verlag.

Lee G., & Fitzpatrick, A. R. (2008). A new approach to test score equating using item response theory with fixed c-parameters. *Asia Pacific Education Review, 9*(3), 248–261.

Levine, M. V. & Drasgow, F. (1988). Optimal appropriateness measurement. *Psychometrika, 53*, 161–176.

Linacre, M. (2002). What do infit and infit, mean-square and standardized mean? *Rasch Measurement Transactions, 16*(2), 878.

Linacre, J. M. (2014). *Winsteps, Rasch measurement computer program*. Beaverton, OR: Winsteps.com

Linn, R. L., Levine, M. V., Hastings, C. N., & Wardrop, J. L. (1981). An investigation of item bias in a test of reading comprehension. *Applied Psychological Measurement, 5*, 159–173.

Liu, Y., & Maydeu-Olivares, A. (2012). Local dependence diagnostics in IRT modeling of binary data. *Educational and Psychological Measurement, 73*(2), 254–274.

Liu, Y., & Thissen, D. (2012). Identifying local dependence with a score test statistic based on the bifactor logistic model. *Applied Psychological Measurement, 36*(8), 670–688.

Lord, F. M. (1952). *A theory of test scores (Psychometric* Monograph, 7). Richmond: VA: Psychometric Corporation. 7, 1–84.

Lord, F. M. (1953). The relation of test score to the trait underlying the test. *Educational and Psychological Measurement, 13*, 517–548.

Lord, F. M. (1980). *Applications of item response theory to practical testing problems*. Hillsdale, NJ: Erlbaum Publishers.

Lord, F. M. (1982). Item response theory and equating-A technical summary. In P.W. Holland & D.B. Rubin (Eds.), *Testing equating* (pp. 141–161). New York: Academic.

Lord, F. M., & Novick, M. R. (1968). *Statistical theories of mental test scores*. The Addison Wesley series in behavioral science: Quantitative methods. Reading, MA: Addison- Wesley.

Lord, F. M., & Wingersky, M. S. (1984). Comparison of IRT true-score and equipercentile observed-score "equatings." *Applied Psychological Measurement, 9*, 49–57.

Loyd, B. H., & Hoover, H. D. (1980). Vertical equating using the Rasch model. *Journal of Educational Measurement, 17*, 179–193.

Marco, G. L. (1977). Item characteristic solution to three intractable testing problems. *Journal of Educational Measurement, 14*, 139–160.

Masters, G. (1982). Rasch model for partial credit scoring. *Psychometrika, 47*, 149–174.

Maydeu-Olivares, A. (2013). Goodness-of-fit assessment of item response theory models. *Measurement, 11*, 71–101.

Maydeu-Olivares, A. (2015). Evaluating fit in IRT models. In S.P. Reise & D. A. Revicki (Eds.), *Handbook of item response theory modeling: Applications to typical performance assessment* (pp. 111–127). New York: Routledge.

Maydeu-Olivares, A., & Cai, L. (2006). A cautionary note on using G^2(dif) to assess relative model fit in categorical data analysis. *Multivariate Behavioral Research, 41*(1), 55–64.

Maydeu-Olivares, A., & Joe, H. (2006). Limited information goodness-of-fit testing in multidimensional contingency tables. *Psychometrika, 71*, 713–732.

McKinley, R. L., & Mills, C. N. (1985). A comparison of several goodness-of-fit statistics. *Applied Psychological Measurement, 9*, 49–57.

Meijer, R. R., & Sijtsma, K. (1995). Detection of aberrant item score patterns: A review of recent developments. *Applied Measurement in Education, 8*, 261–272.

Muraki, E., & Bock, R. D. (1997). *PARSCALE: IRT item analysis and test scoring for rating scale data* [Computer software]. Chicago, IL: Scientific Software.

Muraki, E., & Engelhard, G. (1985). Full information factor analysis: Applications of EAP scores. *Applied Psychological Measurement, 9*, 417–430.

Muthén, L. K. and Muthén, B. O. (1998–2017). *Mplus user's guide (8th ed.)*. Los Angeles, CA: Muthén & Muthén.

Orlando, M., & Thissen, D. (2000). Likelihood-based item-fit indices for dichotomous item response theory models. *Applied Psychological Measurement, 24*(1), 50–64.

Oshima, T. C., & Morris, S. B. (2008). Raju's differential functioning of items and tests (DFIT). *Educational Measurement: Issues and Practice, 27*(3), 43–50.

Oshima, T. C., Raju, N. S., & Nanda, A. O. (2006). A new method for assessing the statistical significance in the differential functioning of items and tests (DFIT) framework. *Journal of Educational Measurement, 43*(1), 1–17.

Osterlind, S., & Everson, H. (2009). *Differential item functioning*. Newbury Park, CA: Sage.

Penfield, R. D., & Camilli, G. (2007). Differential item functioning and item bias. In C. R. Rao & S. Sinharay (Eds.), *Handbook of statistics* (Vol. 26, pp. 125–167). Amsterdam, North Holland: Elsevier.

Raju, N. S. (1988). The area between two item characteristic curves. *Psychometrika, 53*(4), 495–502.

Raju, N. S. (1990). Determining the significance of estimated signed and unsigned areas between two item response functions. *Applied Psychological Measurement, 14*(2), 197–207.

Raju, N. S., van der Linden, W. J., & Fleer, P. F. (1995). IRT-based internal measures of differential functioning of items and tests. *Applied Psychological Measurement, 19*(4), 353–368.

Rasch, G. (1960). *Probabilistic models for some intelligence and attainment tests*. Copenhagen: Danish Institute for Educational Research.

Raykov, T., & Marcoulides, G. (2018). *A course in item response theory and modeling with Stata*. College Station, TX: Stata Press.

Raykov, T., Marcoulides, G. A., Lee, C. L., & Chan, C. (2015). Studying differential item functioning via latent variable modeling: A note on a multiple-testing procedure. *Educational and Psychological Measurement, 73*(5), 898–908.

Reckase, M. (2009a). *Multidimensional item response theory*. New York: Springer.

Reckase, M. (2009b). Unifactor latent trait models applied to multifactor tests: Results and implications. *Journal of Educational Statistics, 4*, 207–230.

Reckase, M. D., Ackerman, & Carlson, J. E. (1988). Building a unidimensional test using multidimensional items. *Journal of Educational Measurement, 25*(3), 193–203.

Reise, S. P., Cook, K. F., & Moore, T. M. (2014). Evaluating the impact of multidimensionality on unidimensional item response theory model parameters. In S.P. Reise & D.A. Revicki (Eds.), *Handbook of item response theory modeling: Applications to typical performance assessment* (pp. 13–41). New York: Routledge.

Rost, J. (2001). The growing family of Rasch models. In A. Boomsma, M. J. van Duijn, & T. B. Snijders (Eds.), *Essays on item response theory* (Vol. 157, pp. 25–42). New York: Springer

Samejima, F. (1969). *Estimation of latent ability using a response pattern of graded scores* (Psychometric Monograph No. 17). Richmond, VA: Psychometric Society.

Samejima, F. (1997). Graded response model. In W.J. van der Linden & R. Hambleton (Eds.), *Handbook of modern item response theory* (pp. 85–100). New York: Springer.

Samejima, F. (2013). "Graded response models," in W.J. van der Linden (Ed.), *Handbook of item response theory*, Vol. 1 (pp. 95–108). Raton, FL: Taylor and Francis.

Sato, T. (1975). *The construction and interpretation of S-P tables*. Tokyo: Meiji Tokyo.

Sijtsma, K. (1986). A coefficient of deviant response patterns. *Kwantitative Methoden, 7*, 131–145.

Sijtsma, K., & Meijer, R. R. (1992). A method for investigating the intersection of item response functions in Mokken's nonparametric IRT model. *Applied Psychological Measurement, 16*, 149–157.

Smith, Jr., E. V. (2004). Detecting and evaluating the impact of multidimensionality using item fit statistics and principal component analysis of residuals. In E.V. Smith Jr. & R. M. Smith (Eds.), *Introduction to Rasch measurement* (pp. 460–517). Maple Grove, MN: JAM Press Publisher.

Smith, Jr., E. V., & Smith, R. M. (2004). *Introduction to Rasch measurement*. Maple Grove, MN: JAM Press Publisher.

Smith, R. M. (1991). The distributional properties of Rasch item fit statistics. *Educational and Psychological Measurement, 51*, 541–565.

Smith, R. M., Schumacker, R. E., & Bush, M. J. (1998). Using item mean squares to evaluate fit to the Rasch model. *Journal of Outcome Measurement, 2*, 66–78.

Stark, S., Chernyshenko, O. S., & Drasgow, F. (2006). Detecting differential item functioning with CFA and IRT: Toward a unified strategy. *Journal of Applied Psychology, 91*(6), 1292–1306.

Stocking, M. L., & Lord, F. M. (1983). Developing a common metric in item response theory. *Applied Psychological Measurement, 7*(2), 201–210.

Stout, W. (1987). A nonparametric approach for assessing latent trait unidimensionality. *Psychometrika, 52*, 589–617.

Stout, W. (1990). A new item response theory modeling approach with applications to unidimensional assessment and ability estimation. *Psychometrika, 55*, 293–326.

Stout, W., Froelich, A. G., & Gao, F. (2001). Using resampling methods to produce an improved DIMTEST procedure. In A. Boomsma (Ed.), *Essays on item response theory* (pp. 357–375). New York: Springer.

Stucky, B., & Edelen, M. O. (2014). Using hierarchical IRT models to create unidimensional measures from multidimensional data. In S.P. Reise & D.A. Reiki (Eds.), *Handbook of item response theory modeling: Application to typical performance assessments* (pp. 183–206). New York: Routledge.

Swaminathan, H., Hambleton, R. K., & Rogers, H. J. (2006). Assessing the item fit of item response theory models. In C.R. Rao & S. Sinharay (Eds.), *Handbook of statistics*, vol. 26 (pp. 683–718). Amsterdam, North Holland: Elsevier.

Swaminathan, H., & Rogers, H. J. (1990). Detecting differential item functioning using the logistic regression procedure. *Journal of Educational Measurement, 27*(4), 361–370.

Takane, Y., & de Leeuw, J. (1987). On the relationship between item response theory and factor analysis of discretized variables. *Psychometrika, 52*, 393–408.

Tatsuoka, K. K. (1984). Caution indices based on item response theory. *Psychometrika, 49*, 95–110.

Thissen, D., Steinberg, L., & Wainer, H. (1993). Detection of differential item functioning using the parameters of item response theory. In P.W. Holland & H. Wainer (Eds.), *Differential item functioning* (pp. 67–113). Mahwah, NJ: Lawrence Erlbaum.

van der Linden, W. J. (Ed.). (2016). *Handbook of item response theory, Volume two: Statistical tolls*. Boca Raton, FL: Taylor and Francis Group.

Von Davier, M. (1997). Bootstrapping goodness-of-fit statistics for sparse categorical data: Results of a Monte Carlo study. *Methods of Psychological Research Online, 2*(2), 29–48.

Von Davier, M., & Von Davier, A. A. (2007). A unified approach to IRT scale linking and scale transformation. *Methodology: European Journal of Research Methods for the Behavioral and Social Sciences, 3*(3), 115–124.

Wilks, S. S. (1938). The large-sample distribution of the likelihood ratio for testing composite hypotheses. *Annals of Mathematical Statistics. 9*, 60–62.

Wood, R., Wilson, D. T., Gibbons, R., Scilling, S., Muraki, E., & Bock, R. D. (2003). *TESTFACT 4: Classical item and item factor analysis [Computer software]*. Chicago, IL: Scientific Software.

Wright, B. D. (1977). Solving measurement problems with the Rasch model. *Journal of Educational Measurement, 14*, 97–166.

Wright, B. D., & Stone, M. A. (1979). *Best test design*. Chicago, IL: MESA Press.

Wu, M., & Adams, R. J. (2013). Properties of Rasch residual fit statistics. *Journal of Applied Measurement, 14*, 400–413.

Yen, W. M. (1981). Using simulation results to choose a latent trait model. *Applied Psychological Measurement, 5*, 245–262.

Yen, W. M. (1984). Effects of local item dependence on the fit and equating performance of the three-parameter logistic model. *Applied Psychological Measurement, 8*, 125–145.

Yen, W. M. (1993). Scaling performance assessments: Strategies for managing local item dependence. *Journal of Educational Measurement, 30*, 187–213.

Ziegler, M., & Hagemann, D. (2015). Testing the unidimensionality of items: Pitfalls and loopholes. *European Journal of Psychological Assessment, 31*(4), 231–237.

Zimowski, M. F., Muraki, E., Mislevy, R. J., & Bock, R. D. (2003). *BILOGMG for Windows: Multiple-group IRT analysis and test maintenance for binary items (Version 3.0)* [Computer software]. Chicago, IL: Scientific Software International.

Zumbo, B. D. (1999). A handbook on the theory and methods of differential item functioning (DIF): Logistic regression modeling as a unitary framework for binary and Likert-type (ordinal) item scores. Ottawa, ON: Directorate of Human Resources Research and Evaluation, Department of National Defense.

Zwick, R. (2012). A review of ETS differential item functioning assessment procedures: Flagging rules, minimum sample size requirements, and criterion refinement (RR-12-08). Educational Testing Service. https://doi.org/10.1002/j.2333-8504.2012.tb02290.

3 CTT-IRT

Comparison and Connections

Introduction

Basic concepts and features of the traditional *classical test theory* (CTT) and *item response theory* (IRT) are presented in Chapters 1 and 2, respectively. Efforts to benefit from the advantages of both frameworks in practical applications have resulted in numerous studies on comparing, connecting, and integrating CTT and IRT (e.g., Bechger et al., 2003; Brennan, 1998; Hambleton & Jones, 1993; Hu et al., 2021; Dimitrov, 2003a, 2003b; Fan, 1998; Jabrayilov, Emons, & Sijtsma, 2016; Lin, 2008; Lord, 1980; Oswald, Shaw, & Farmer, 2015; Raykov et al., 2019a, 2019b; Raykov & Marcoulides, 2016). A brief overview of the findings and methodological points provided in such studies is presented next.

CTT-IRT Comparison

CTT and IRT Models and Assumptions

The main aspect of CTT-IRT comparison relates to their models and underlying assumptions. The CTT is based on a simple linear model presenting an *observable* test score as a sum of two unobservable (latent) scores, referred to as *true* score and *error* score ($X = T + E$). The CTT assumptions, referred to as *weak assumptions*, state that (a) T and E scores are uncorrelated, (b) the expected error score for the population is zero, $\mu_E = 0$, and (c) error scores on parallel tests are uncorrelated. (*Parallel tests* are equal on true scores and error variances.)

An IRT model is based on an *item response function* (IRF) that describes the relationship between the examinee's ability level and the probability of a specified response (e.g., correct response to a binary item). The IRT assumptions are referred to as "strong" assumptions as they are more difficult to meet with real-data assessments. Key assumptions in commonly used IRT models (e.g., 1PL, 2PL, and 3PL) are those of *unidimensionality* and *local independence*. These two assumptions are equivalent when the IRT model contains parameters on only one dimension. Also, an IRT model assumes that the item characteristic curve (ICC) has a specified form—e.g., for binary test items, it is assumed that the ICC is S-shaped and increases monotonically with the increase in the ability level, θ. Furthermore, the validity of results obtained under an IRT model depends on the degree of model-data fit at test level and individual levels for items and persons.

Hambleton and Jones (1993) made an important methodological comment regarding the use of (CTT or IRT) models, stating that:

> "the meaningful question is not whether a model is correct or incorrect: All models are incorrect in the sense that they provide incomplete representations of the data to which they are applied. The question instead is whether a model fits the data well enough to be useful in guiding the measurement process. Statistical evidence and judgment play important roles in answering the question."
>
> (p. 39)

In this line of reasoning, Brennan (1998) stated that "the crux of the matter, then, is not that we pick models with correct assumptions but rather that we recognize and acknowledge the fallibility of our models and assumptions, qualify results accordingly, and not mislead test users" (p. 5).

CTT Advantages

The main *advantages* of the traditional CTT are as follows:

1. CTT assumptions are easy to meet in real test data. For example, the assumption of unidimensionality is not required. It is only necessary to assume that the factor structure of the test data is the same across parallel forms.
2. CTT produces meaningful results even with relatively small samples.
3. CTT provides computational simplicity, transparency, and clarity of interpretations.
4. CTT does not involve testing for model-data fit. Regarding the CTT model ($X = T + E$), Brennan (1998) noted that "this is a tautology, and, as such, it is not capable of being proved or disproved" (p. 6).

CTT Disadvantages

The main *disadvantages* of the traditional CTT are as follows:

1. CTT is test-dependent measurement; that is, person scores depend on the set of test items, and, on the other hand, estimates of item parameters depend on the sample of examinees.
2. In CTT, person scores (number correct responses) do not account for (a) the person's response pattern and (b) item features such as difficulty and discrimination. As a result, persons at different ability levels may have the same test score.
3. In CTT, persons scores (number correct responses) do not produce an interval scale, so additional efforts are needed to present such scores on a (close to interval) scale.
4. In CTT, person scores (number correct responses) and item difficulties are *not* on the same scale, which makes it difficult to evaluate the match of person abilities and item difficulties.
5. The CTT does not provide modeling of the relationship between test scores of examinees and their chances of success on individual items.
6. In CTT, the standard error of measurement is (unrealistically) assumed to be the same for all examinees.

IRT Advantages

IRT is a more comprehensive, rigorous, and flexible framework of measurement, with key advantages over CTT as follows:

1. IRT provides IRF models of the relationship between person ability levels and chances of success on individual test items.
2. IRT estimates of person and item parameters are "sample free"; that is, estimates of person ability do not depend on the set of test items, and, on the other hand, estimates of item parameters do not depend on the sample of examinees. However, such "invariance" holds under the assumption of perfect model-data fit for the population of examinees. In practice, person and item parameters obtained under an IRT model are *not* necessarily the same across different samples, but they are linearly related, which allows for their presentation on a common scale.
3. The IRT standard error of ability estimates, $SE(\hat{\theta})$, is *not* the same for all examinees but, instead, varies across ability levels.
4. The IRT test information function is a sum of item information functions, which allows to assess the contribution of individual test items to the precision of ability score estimates.
5. IRT estimates of person ability and item difficulty are on the same scale (in logits). This allows, for example, to evaluate the match between person ability levels and item difficulties.
6. IRT-based procedures of test equating are more accurate and stable compared to CTT-based equating (e.g., IRT observed score equating compared to CTT equipercentile equating).

IRT Disadvantages

1. IRT assumptions, such as unidimensionality, local independence, and model-data fit, are often difficult to meet in real test data.
2. IRT estimations require relatively large samples of examinees.

3   IRT models are mathematically complex and involve iterative computations that may not always produce a desirable solution (or any solution at all in lack of convergence).
4   Commonly used maximum-likelihood estimations on the logit scale (−∞, +∞) do not produce θ-scores corresponding to the perfect raw score or zero raw score.
5   The estimation error of ability scores increases toward the ends of the scale, thus reducing their accuracy for low- and high-performing examinees.
6   Person ability scores on the logit scale, θ, are difficult to understand and interpret by large audiences of practitioners, educators, and other stakeholders. Transformations of θ scores, often used to avoid negative scores in reports of test results, do not help to clarify (in fact, may further obscure) the interpretation of person scores on the test.

Problems with IRT estimations over the whole real numeric line (−∞, +∞) were signaled by researchers calling for "optimal" scoring on a bounded metric (e.g., Ramsay & Wilberg, 2017) or reporting true domain scores ranging from 0 to 1 (e.g., Hambleton & Swaminathan, 1985).

Comparing CTT-IRT Performance

Numerous studies compare the performance of CTT and IRT from different perspectives. For example, Jabrayilov et al. (2016) compared CTT and IRT in the assessment of individual change. They concluded that:

> "IRT is superior to CTT, provided that tests contain, say, at least 20 items, but in general the differences between the two methods are small. For shorter tests, results are ambiguous and using CTT seems to be a good choice assessment."
>
> (p. 568)

As another example, some researchers examined CTT and IRT methods of scoring multiple-choice items comparing the classical number-correct and classical optimal scoring (COS) versus binary 3PL and nominal response methods in IRT (e.g., DeMars, 2008; Haladyna & Kramer, 2005; Warrens, de Gruijter, & Heiser, 2007). Among other things, they reported that (a) for scales composed of dichotomous items, COS scores were quite similar to the IRT scores (Haladyna & Kramer, 2005; Warrens et al., 2007); (b) for scales composed of ordered-category items, COS scores were similar to graded response scores (Warrens et al., 2007); and (c) the COS scores were as reliable, sometimes more reliable, than the IRT polytomous scores (DeMars, 2008).

Findings that CTT and IRT perform quite similarly under certain conditions were reported in many other studies as well (e.g., Davey & Hendrickson, 2010; Fan, 1998; Ferrando & Chico, 2007; MacDonald & Paunonen, 2002; Ourania, Elmore, & Headrick, 2001; Polat, 2022; Sćbille et al., 2010). In a study on the prediction of true scores from a possibly nonparallel test, Holland and Machteld (2002) used an approach that treats the "CTT as a very general version of IRT, and the commonly used IRT models as detailed elaborations of CTT for special purposes" (p. 1). From a methodological perspective, Brennan (1998) stated that:

> "classical theory is an incredibly simple, but not simplistic, model. It postulates that an observed score can be split into two latent parts (a true score and an error score), … yet, this simple notion is fundamental to all of measurement. I believe, therefore, that it is misleading to view new models as replacements for classical theory—extensions or liberalizations, yes, but not replacements."
>
> (p. 6)

Under both CTT and IRT, the assembly of alternate test forms involves statistical specifications which require that the performance characteristics of items are known in advance. Under CTT, such specifications are stated in terms of the mean, variance, marginal, or joint distributions of item difficulty and discrimination indices. Under IRT, statistical specifications are stated in terms of target information functions. Davey and Hendrickson (2010) conducted a simulation study to evaluate the stability of test forms assembled to meet either classical and IRT or IRT statistical specifications. They stated that "the most notable result of the study was the relatively small difference evident between the performance of the classical and IRT assembly methods. Both methods were capable of producing a series of test forms whose characteristics resembled the target form" and concluded that "the similarity in performance across methods may mean that the practitioner's choice depends largely on preference or operational convenience" (Davey & Hendrickson, 2010, p.2).

CTT-IRT Connections

Although the CTT and IRT differ in key psychometric features, there are important connections between them that can be useful in integrated applications of the two methodologies in research and practices. One key connection is the relationship between the CTT true domain score and IRT ability score (see Chapter 2, Equation 2.15). There are also analytic relationships between CTT and IRT item parameters. For example, Lord (1980) derived approximate relationships between two CTT item parameters (item-test biserial correlation, r_{ib}, and item difficulty, p_i) and their IRT counterparts—item discrimination α_i, and difficulty, β_i, under the two-parameter model. Specifically:

$$\alpha_i \approx \frac{r_{ib}}{\sqrt{1-r_{ib}^2}} \tag{3.1}$$

and

$$\beta_i \approx \frac{\gamma_i}{r_{ib}}, \tag{3.2}$$

where γ_i is the normal deviate that corresponds to the ability score beyond which the p_i proportion of examinees fall.

In Equation 3.1, α_i and r_{ib} are in a monotonic positive relationship; that is, as r_{ib} increases so does α_i. A practical extension of the Lord's (1980) formula in Equation 3.1 is provided by Kulas, Smith, and Xu (2017). In Equation 3.2, β_i and p_i are implicitly related because γ_i depends on p_i. Given that (a) γ_i decreases when p_i increases, and (b) β_i increases when γ_i increases, it follows that β_i and p_i are in a monotonic negative relationship; that is, as p_i increases, β_i decreases. This makes sense, given that p_i represents item "easiness," whereas β_i is model-based item difficulty.

Dimitrov (2003a, 2003b) derived numerous analytic relationships between CTT true-score measures and reliability of binary items as a function of their IRT item parameters. Presented here is only the relationship between the expected item score and IRT item parameters, which relates to concepts of the D-scoring method introduced in Chapter 4. Let π_i denote the *expected item score* (population proportion of correct responses on item i), and IRT parameters (α_i and β_i) are estimated under the 2PL model, with a scaling factor $D = 1.702$ to approximate the two-parameter normal-ogive model (see Chapter 2, Equation 2.4). Dimitrov (2003a) showed that:

$$\pi_i = \frac{1 - erf(X_i)}{2}, \tag{3.3}$$

where $X_i = \alpha_i \beta_i / \sqrt{2(1+\alpha_i^2)}$, *erf* is the known mathematics function called *error function*, a_i is the *item discrimination*, and b_i is the *item difficulty*. With a relatively simple approximation provided by Hastings (1955, p. 185), the error function (for $X > 0$) can be evaluated with an absolute error smaller than 0.0005 as follows:

$$erf(X) = 1 - \left(1 + m_1 X + m_2 X^2 + m_3 X^3 + m_4 X^4\right)^{-4}, \tag{3.4}$$

where $m_1 = 0.278393$, $m_2 = 0.230389$, $m_3 = 0.000972$, and $m_4 = 0.078108$. When $X < 0$, one can use that $erf(-X) = -erf(X)$. Also, $erf(X_i)$ is directly executable in software packages such as R and MATLAB (MathWorks, Inc., 2010).

In the case of IRT calibrations under the 1PL model, Equation 3.3 is used with $a_i = 1$. In the case of 3PL model, the expected item score is given by $c_i + (1 - c_i)\pi_i$, where c_i is the pseudo-guessing parameter in the 3PL model and π_i is obtained for the 2PL model (via Equation 3.3).

> **NOTE [3.1]** Equation 3.3 is derived under the assumption that the latent ability, θ, which is measured by the test, is normally distributed. A simulation study showed that the estimates of π_i remain stable under deviations from normality, except for cases where the distribution of θ is very skewed (Atanasov & Dimitrov, 2014).

It is important to note that π_i represents the expected item "easiness" because higher π_i values indicate easier items. The *expected item difficulty*, denoted hereafter δ_i ("delta"), is $\delta_i = 1 - \pi_i$. Using Equation 3.3, a simple algebra yields the following presentation of δ_i as a function of the 2PL item parameters α_i and β_i:

$$\delta_i = \frac{1 + \mathit{erf}(X_i)}{2}, \tag{3.5}$$

with the notations for X_i and $\mathit{erf}(X_i)$ used in Equation 3.3.

Analytic connections between CTT and IRT concepts are very useful from both theoretical and practical perspectives. In this regard, Bechger et al. (2003) noted that "when an appropriate IRT model is found, one is able to calculate and use classical indices for properties of items and tests in situations when CTT could normally not be applied" (p. 319). For example, some researchers used IRT information to derive estimates of measurement precision in CTT context and provided useful practical applications (e.g., Bechger et al., 2003; Dimitrov, 2003a, 2003b, Kolen, Zeng, & Hanson, 1996; Mellenbergh, 1996). As another example in this regard, useful perspectives on true score evaluation for binary and polytomous test items, using IRT, were provided by Raykov et al. (2019a, 2019b).

Summary Points

1. The traditional CTT is based on a simple linear model ($X = T + E$) and "weak" assumptions that (a) $r_{TE} = 0$, (b) $\mu_E = 0$, and (c) $r_{E_1 E_2} = 0$, for the error scores on parallel tests. (*Parallel tests* are equal on true scores and error variances.)
2. An IRT model is based on (a) IRF that describes the relationship between the examinee's ability level and the probability of a specified response, and (b) "strong" assumptions such as unidimensionality, local independence, and model fit.
3. Regarding the use of (CTT or IRT) models, the question is not whether a model is correct or incorrect but, rather, whether a model fits the data well enough to be useful in guiding the measurement process. CTT and IRT perform quite similarly under certain conditions.
4. Main advantages of CTT are that (a) it provides simplicity, transparency, and clear interpretations of person scores and item statistics, (b) does not require testing for strong assumptions and model-data fit, and (c) produces meaningful results even with relatively small samples.
5. Main disadvantages of CTT are that (a) it is test-dependent measurement, (b) assumes the same error of measurement for all examinees, (c) does not provide modeling of the chances of correct response on individual test items, and (d) person ability and item difficulty are not on the same scale.
6. Main advantages of the IRT are that (a) it provides IRF *models*, (b) the estimates of person and item parameters are sample free, assuming a perfect model-data fit for the population (and invariant up to linear transformations for samples), (c) the standard error of estimate varies across ability levels, and (d) person ability and item difficulty are on the same scale.
7. Main disadvantages of IRT are that (a) it is based on strong assumptions, (b) it requires large samples, (c) the estimation error of ability scores increases towards the ends of the scale thus reducing their accuracy for low- and high-performing examinees, and (d) person ability scores on the logit scale are not transparent and difficult to interpret by practitioners, educators, and other stakeholders.
8. Although CTT and IRT differ in key psychometric features, there are connections between them that can be useful in integrated applications of the two methodologies. For example, the expected item difficulty, δ_i, can be presented as a function of IRT-based item parameters.

References

Atanasov, D. V., & Dimitrov, D. M. (2014). *Robustness of the expected item score as a function of IRT item parameters.* (RR 04-2014) Riyadh, Saudi Arabia: National Center for Assessment at ETEC.

Bechger, T. M., Maris, G., Verstralen, H. H. F. M., & Beguin, A. A. (2003). Using classical test theory in combination with item response theory. *Applied Psychological Measurement, 27*(5), 319–334.

Brennan, R. L. (1998). Misconceptions at the intersection of measurement theory and practice. *Educational Measurement: Issues and Practice, 17*(1), 5–30.

Davey, T., & Hendrickson, A. (2010, May). *Classical versus IRT statistical test specifications for building test forms.* Paper presented at the Annual Conference of the National Council for Measurement in Education Denver, Colorado.

DeMars, C. E. (2008, March). Scoring multiple choice items: *A comparison of IRT and classical polytomous and dichotomous methods.* Paper presented at the annual meeting of the National Council on Measurement in Education, New York.

Dimitrov, D. M. (2003a). Marginal true-score measures and reliability of binary items as a function of their IRT parameters. *Applied Psychological Measurement, 27*(6), 440–458.

Dimitrov, D. M. (2003b). Reliability and true-score measures of binary items as a function of their Rasch difficulty parameter. *Journal of Applied Measurement, 4*(3), 222–233.

Fan, X. (1998). Item response theory and classical test theory: An empirical comparison of their item/person statistics. *Educational and Psychological Measurement, 58*(3), 357–381.

Ferrando, P. J., & Chico, E. (2007). The external validity of scores based on the two-parameter logistic model: Some comparisons between IRT and CTT. *Psicológica, 28*, 237–257.

Haladyna, T. M., & Kramer, G. (2005, April). *An empirical investigation of poly-scoring of multiple-choice item responses.* Paper presented at the annual meeting of the National Council on Measurement in Education, Montreal, Canada.

Hambleton, R. K., & Jones, R. W. (1993). Comparison of classical test theory and item response theory and their applications to test development. *Educational Measurement: Issues and Practice, 12*(3), 38–47.

Hambleton, R. K., & Swaminathan, H. (1985). *Item response theory: Principles and applications.* Hingham, MA: Kluwer, Nijhoff.

Hastings, C., Jr. (1955). *Approximations for digital computers.* Princeton, NJ: Princeton University Press.

Holland, P. W., & Machteld, H. (2002). *Classical test theory as a first-order item response theory: Application to true-score prediction form a possibly nonparallel test.* ETS Research Report (RR-02-20) (pp. 1–40).

Hu, Z., Lin, L., Wang, Y., & Li, J. (2021). The integration of classical testing theory and item response theory. *Psychology, 12*, 1397–1409.

Jabrayilov, R., Emons, W. H. M., & Sijtsma, K. (2016). Comparison of classical test theory and item response theory in individual change assessment. *Applied Psychological Measurement, 40*(8), 559–572.

Kolen, M. J., Zeng, L., & Hanson, B. A. (1996). Conditional standard errors of measurement for scale scores using IRT. *Journal of Educational Measurement, 33*, 129–140.

Kulas, J. T., Smith, J. A., & Xu, H. (2017). Approximate functional relationship between IRT and CTT item discrimination indices: A simulation, validation, and practical extension of Lord's (1980) formula. *Journal of Applied Measurement, 18*(4), 393–407.

Lin, C.-J. (2008). Comparison between classical test theory and item response theory in automated assembly of parallel test forms. *Journal of Technology, Learning, and Assessment, 6*(8). Retrieved 07/09/2022 from https://files.eric.ed.gov/fulltext/EJ838620.pdf.

Lord, F. M. (1980). *Applications of item response theory to practical testing problems.* Hillsdale, NJ: Erlbaum.

MacDonald, P., & Paunonen, S. V. (2002). A Monte Carlo comparison of item and person statistics based on item response theory versus classical test theory. *Educational and Psychological Measurement, 62*, 921–943.

MathWorks, Inc. (2010). *MATLAB. The language of technical computing* (Version 7.10.0). Natick, MA: Author.

Mellenbergh, G. J. (1996). Measurement precision in test score and item response models. *Psychological Methods, 1*(3), 293–299.

Oswald, F. L., Shaw, A., & Farmer, W. L. (2015). Comparing simple scoring with IRT scoring of personality measures: The Navy Computer Adaptive Personality Scales. *Applied Psychological Measurement, 39*, 144–154.

Ourania, R., Elmore, P. B., & Headrick, T. C. (2001, April). *Number correct scoring: Comparison between classical true score theory and multidimensional item response theory.* Paper presented at the Annual Meeting of the American Educational Research Association, Seattle.

Polat, M. (2022). Comparison of performance measures obtained from foreign language tests according to item response theory vs classical test theory. *International Online Journal of Education and Teaching (IOJET), 9*(1), 471–485.

Ramsay, J. O., & Wilberg, M. (2017). A strategy for replacing sum scoring. *Journal of Educational and Behavioral Statistics, 42*(3), 282–307.

Raykov, T., Dimitrov, D. M., Marcoulides, G. A., & Harrison, M. (2019a). On true score evaluation using item response modeling. *Educational and Psychological Measurement, 79*(4), 796–807.

Raykov, T., Dimitrov, D. M., Marcoulides, G. A., & Harrison, M. (2019b). On the connections between item response theory and classical test theory: A note on true score evaluation for polytomous items via item response modeling. *Educational and Psychological Measurement. 79*(6), 1198–1202.

Raykov, T., & Marcoulides, G. A. (2016). On the relationship between classical test theory and item response theory: From one to the other and back. *Educational and Psychological Measurement, 76*, 325–338.

Sébille, V., Hardouin, J. B., Le Néel, T., Kubis, G., Boyer, F., Guillemin, F., & Falissard, B. (2010). Methodological issues regarding power of classical test theory (CTT) and item response theory (IRT) for the comparison of patient-reported outcomes in two groups of patients – a simulation study. *BMC Medical Research Methodology, 10*(24), 1–10.

Warrens, M. J., de Gruijter, D. N. M., & Heiser, W. J. (2007). A systematic comparison between classical optimal scaling and the two-parameter IRT model. *Applied Psychological Measurement, 31*, 106–120.

4 Classical *D*-scoring Method

Introduction

There are ongoing efforts in the field of measurement to address drawbacks of the traditional classical test theory (CTT) and item response theory (IRT) and enhance their connection from methodological and practical perspectives. For example, some researchers emphasized problems with using unweighted sum scores in CTT, as well as problems with IRT score estimations over the whole real numeric line ($-\infty$, $+\infty$), calling for "optimal" scoring via weighted scores on a bounded metric, such as from 0 to 100 (e.g., Ramsay & Wilberg, 2017; Ramsay, Wilberg, & Li, 2020). The methods used in these studies, although psychometrically sound, are technically complicated (e.g., involving spline smoothing techniques in multi-step procedures) and address mainly the scoring aspect of CTT-IRT issues. Other researchers have also emphasized the advantages of using bounded scales, such as the *true domain scale* (e.g., Brennan, 1998; Hambleton & Swaminathan, 1985).

The D-*scoring method of measurement* (DSM) is designed to combine merits of the traditional CTT and IRT, *not* to replace them, in a unified framework of classical and latent scoring of tests and their psychometric analysis (e.g., Dimitrov, 2016, 2018, 2020; Dimitrov & Atanasov, 2021). The DSM is developed in classical and latent versions denoted DSM-C and DSM-L, respectively. In essence, DSM-L is a latent analog to DSM-C, both sharing the same scale on a bounded metric for person scores and item difficulties, same analytic models for item response functions, and other psychometric features, but they differ in approaches (latent vs. classical) used for the estimation of person ability and item parameters. The DSM is developed for dichotomously scored items, but it is readily applicable to polytomous items upon a simple recoding of their ordered categories (see Chapter 9). Presented in the following are concepts, models, and features of the classical *D*-scoring version, DSM-C.

DSM-C provides key extensions of the traditional CTT such as (a) scoring based on the examinee's response pattern and expected item difficulties, (b) intervalness of the scoring scale, (c) same scale for person scores and item difficulties, (d) classical modeling of item response functions (IRFs), and (e) conditional standard error of test scores. Under DSM-C, the person's score on a test is a weighted sum of the binary (1/0) scores on the test items, where the item "weight" depends on the expected item difficulty, δ ("*delta*"), hence the name "*Delta*-scoring" ("*D*-scoring," for short). The *D*-scores range from 0 to 1, but they are usually multiplied by 100 to place them on a scale from 0 to 100 in reports of test results.

Expected Item Difficulty

The expected item difficulty, δ ("*delta*"), represents the true difficulty of an item for a target population of examinees. That is, $\delta_i = 1 - \pi_i$, where π_i is the expected "easiness" of the item (i.e., the population proportion of correct item responses). In CTT, "item difficulty" is a (misfortunate) term which actually indicates *easiness* of the item as it represents the sample proportion of correct item responses, p_i. Under DSM-C, (a) higher values of δ_i indicate higher level of item difficulty, and (b) δ_i is sample independent as it represents the expected item difficulty for a target population (*not* a sample) of examinees. Some approaches to estimating δ_i are described next.

Bootstrap Estimation of δ_i

Given a sample of (1/0) scores on a test item, the method of bootstrap resampling (Efron, 1979) provides dependable estimates of the expected item difficulty, δ_i, along with the distribution of its sample values across numerous bootstrap replications (e.g., > 1,000) and their standard error, $SE(\hat{\delta}_i)$. It should be noted that (a) $SE(\hat{\delta}_i)$ decreases with the increase of the sample size, and (b) regardless of the sample size, $SE(\hat{\delta}_i)$ reaches its highest value when

DOI: 10.4324/9781003343004-4

δ_i is located at the middle of the D-scale ($\delta_i = 0.5$) and decreases when δ_i approaches the ends of the scale (0 or 1). For example, the bootstrapping of a sample of 10,000 examinees produces $SE(\hat{\delta}_i) = 0.009$, when $\delta_i = 0.10$ or $\delta_i = 0.90$ (i.e., close to the ends of the D-scale), and $SE(\hat{\delta}_i) = 0.016$ (its highest value), when $\delta_i = 0.5$ (e.g., Dimitrov, 2018, p. 808). The computation of δ_i values is facilitated by the availability of bootstrapping in SPSS, R, and other popular statistical packages.

Estimation of δ_i via IRT Item Parameters

As shown in Chapter 3, Equation 3.3, the population proportion of correct item responses, π_i, can be represented as a function of IRT-based item parameters (Dimitrov, 2003, p. 443). Then, given that $\delta_i = 1 - \pi_i$, the following equation holds for δ_i as a function of the item parameters under the 2PL model in IRT:

$$\delta_i = \frac{1 + erf(X_i)}{2}, \tag{4.1}$$

where $X_i = \alpha_i \beta_i / \sqrt{2(1+\alpha_i^2)}$, erf is the known mathematical function called *error function*, α_i is *item discrimination*, and β_i is *item difficulty* (under the 2PL). The $erf(X)$ is directly executable in R, MATLAB, and other software packages. An approximation of the $erf(X)$, provided by Hastings (1955, p. 185), is given in Chapter 3, Equation 3.4. When the 1PL model is used, Equation 4.1 holds with $a_i = 1$. When the 3PL model in IRT is used, with a pseudo-guessing parameter c_i, the expected item difficulty is $\delta_i^* = c_i + (1-c_i)\delta_i$, where δ_i is computed via Equation 4.1 under the 2PL model (Dimitrov, 2003, p. 446).

> **NOTE [4.1]** An application of Equation 4.1 in the context of confirmatory factor analysis is presented in Chapter 12 (Appendix 12.1). Also, for quick practical applications, when the sample of item responses is very large (e.g., > 10,000), the sample-based δ_i can be used as a close estimate of the population δ_i.

Computation of Classical D-scores

Under DSM-C, the person's D-score on a test of n binary items is computed as a weighted sum of the (1/0) item scores, with weights $w_i = \delta_i / \sum \delta_i$. Note that $\sum w_i = 1$; ($i = 1, \ldots, n$). Thus, w_i is a ratio of the expected item difficulty to the total expected difficulty of the test ($\sum \delta_i$). The weighted score is $D_w = \sum w_i X_i$, where X_i is the person score (1/0) on item i. An equivalent form of this formula is:

$$D_w = \frac{\sum_{i=1}^{n} \delta_i X_i}{\sum_{i=1}^{n} \delta_i}. \tag{4.2}$$

D_w scores range from 0 to 1 ($0 \le D_w \le 1$), with $D_w = 0$ if all item responses are incorrect ($X_1 = 0, \ldots, X_n = 0$), and $D_w = 1$ if all item responses are correct ($X_1 = 1, \ldots, X_n = 1$). In reports of test results, the D_w scores are usually multiplied by 100 to place them on a scale from 0 to 100. One can interpret the D_w score of a person as indicating what proportion (or %) of the ability required for "total success on the test" is demonstrated by that person.

Example 4.1

The computation of D_w scores is illustrated in Table 4.1 for hypothetical response patterns of four persons on a test of five items. For example, the second and third persons have the same unweighted sum score ($\sum X_i = 3$), but they have different D_w scores (0.48 and 0.60, respectively) because of their different response patterns. The score of the

Table 4.1 Computation of D_w scores for hypothetical responses of four persons on five items

	$\delta_1 = 0.20$	$\delta_2 = 0.35$	$\delta_3 = 0.50$	$\delta_4 = 0.65$	$\delta_5 = 0.80$			
Person	X_1	X_2	X_3	X_4	X_5	$\sum \delta_i X_i$	$\sum \delta_i$	D_w score
1	0	0	0	0	0	0	2.50	0
2	1	1	0	1	0	1.20	2.50	0.48
3	1	0	1	0	1	1.50	2.50	0.60
4	1	1	1	1	1	2.50	2.50	1

first person is $D_w = 0$ as all item responses are incorrect. The fourth person has a perfect score ($D_w = 1$) as all item responses are correct; that is, this person demonstrated 100% of the ability required for total success on the test.

Intervalness of the *D*-Scale

An important question about the *D*-scale is whether it is an *interval scale*. Theoretically, an interval scale exists when the axioms of additive conjoint measurement (ACM) hold within a given dataset (Luce & Tukey, 1964). Referring to a scale, the term "intervalness" is used to indicate the degree to which the scale data are consistent with the axioms of ACM (e.g., Domingue, 2014). From this perspective, a study comparing the intervalness of D_w scores and IRT scores, θ, on the logit scale demonstrated that the D_w scores produce a *D*-scale with high level of intervalness—in fact, slightly higher than that of the IRT logit scale by criteria of the additive conjoint measurement, with the difference decreasing with the increase of the number of items (Domingue & Dimitrov, 2021).

Item Response Function Models

A key extension of the traditional CTT, provided by the classical DSM-C, is the modeling of *item response functions* (IRFs) on the *D*-scale. Specifically, DSM offers IRF models, referred to as *rational function models* (RFMs), with *one parameter* (RFM1), *two parameters* (RFM2), and *three parameters* (RFM3). The analytic derivation of the RFMs is described in Chapter 12.

Two-Parameter RFM (RFM2)

Under the RFM2, the probability of correct item response for a person with a given D_w score, $P_i(D_w)$, is estimated as a predicted value of the person's item score ($X_i = 1 / 0$) using a two-parameter nonlinear regression model, where the independent variable (predictor) is the D_w score, obtained *a priori* via Equation 4.2, that is, $P_i(D_w) = \hat{X}_i(D_w)$. The RFM2 analytic form is:

$$P_i(D_w) = \frac{1}{1 + \left[\dfrac{b_i(1 - D_w)}{D_w(1 - b_i)}\right]^{s_i}}, \qquad (4.3)$$

where b_i and s_i are referred to as item parameters for *difficulty* and *shape*, respectively.

In Equation 4.3, the *item difficulty*, b_i, is the location on the *D*-scale where the probability $P_i(D_w) = 0.5$ (50% chance for success on the item). The *shape* parameter, s_i, is an indicator of item *discrimination*—higher s_i values produce steeper IRFs (e.g., see Figure 4.1 and NOTE [4.2]). The IRFs of four items in Figure 4.1, produced by using the RFM2 in Equation 4.3, are denoted as follows: (a) P1 = IRF of item 1, with $b_1 = 0.8$, $s_1 = 2.0$; (b) P2 = IRF of item 2, with $b_2 = 0.5$, $s_2 = 2.0$; (c) P3 = IRF of item 3, with $b_3 = 0.4$, $s_3 = 3.0$; and (d) P4 = IRF of item 4, with $b_4 = 0.3$, $s_4 = 1.5$.

One-Parameter RFM (RFM1)

The RFM1 is obtained from the RFM2 by fixing the shape parameter, s_i, to a prespecified value in Equation 4.3. The resulting IRFs over the *D*-scale do not cross. For example, Figures 4.2 and 4.3 show the IRFs of four items

48 *Classical D-scoring Method*

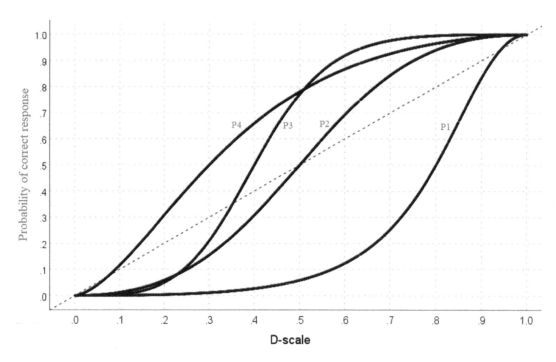

Figure 4.1 Item characteristic curves of four items under the RFM2 model on the *D*-scale: P1 ($b_1 = 0.8$, $s_1 = 2$), P2 ($b_2 = 0.5$, $s_2 = 2$), P3 ($b_3 = 0.4$, $s_3 = 3$), and P4 ($b_4 = 0.3$, $s_4 = 1.5$).

NOTE [4.2] In IRT, *item discrimination*, α_i (see Chapter 2, Equation 2.4) is defined as the value of the first derivative of the IRF at the location of item difficulty, β_i, i.e., $\alpha_i = P_i'(\beta_i)$. In the context of DSM, the first derivative of the IRF under the RFM2 has the following analytic form (Dimitrov, 2020, p. 130):

$$P_i'(D) = \frac{s_i P_i(D)[1 - P_i(D)]}{D(1-D)}. \tag{4.4}$$

Thus, using that $P_i(b_i) = 1/2$, the RFM2-based *item discrimination* at the location $D = b_i$ is:

$$a_i = P_i'(b_i) = \frac{s_i}{4b_i(1-b_i)}. \tag{4.5}$$

with different locations on the *D*-scale (0.8, 0.6, 0.4, and 0.2) obtained via the RFM1 with fixed values of the shape parameter $s_i = 1$ and $s_i = 2$, respectively.

Three-Parameter RFM (RFM3)

In some test scenarios (e.g., with multiple-choice items), low-ability examinees tend to perform higher than expected on some items. In IRT, this issue is addressed by extending the 2PL model to 3PL model where, in addition to the item parameters β_i and α_i, a *pseudo-guessing parameter*, c_i, is added to account for guessing or other causes of higher-than-expected performance of low-ability examinees (Chapter 2, Equation 2.7). Likewise, the RFM2 in Equation 4.3 is extended to a *rational function model with three parameters* (RFM3) as follows:

$$P_i(D_w) = c_i + \frac{1 - c_i}{1 + \left[\dfrac{b_i(1 - D_w)}{D_w(1 - b_i)}\right]^{s_i}}. \tag{4.6}$$

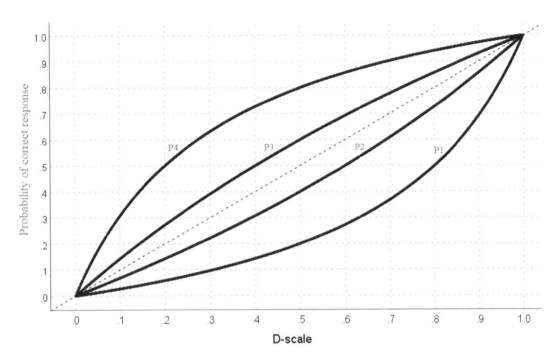

Figure 4.2 Item characteristic curves of four items under the RFM1 model (with $s = 1$) on the *D*-scale: P1 ($b_1 = 0.8$), P2 ($b_2 = 0.6$), P3 ($b_3 = 0.4$), and P4 ($b_4 = 0.2$).

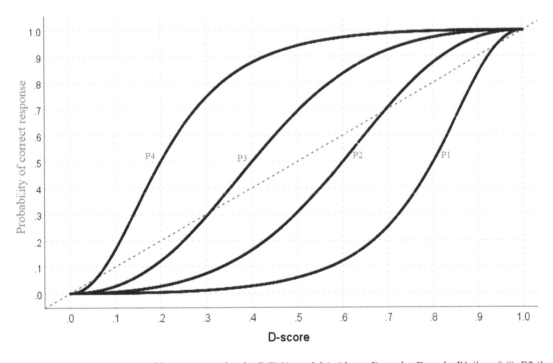

Figure 4.3 Item characteristic curves of four items under the RFM1 model (with $s = 2$) on the *D*-scale: P1 ($b_1 = 0.8$), P2 ($b_2 = 0.6$), P3 ($b_3 = 0.4$), and P4 ($b_4 = 0.2$).

NOTE [4.3] Under the RFM1, the discrimination index a_i in Equation 4.5 depends only on the item location, b_i. For example, if $s_i = 1$, we have $a_i = 1/4b_i(1-b_i)$. Furthermore, a_i has the same value for any two items located symmetrically around the *mean* of the *D*-scale (0.5) because the product $b_i(1-b_i)$ has the same value for such items. In Figures 4.2 and 4.3, for example, a_i has the same value for the two items in each pair of items with (a) $b_1 = 0.8$ and $b_4 = 0.2$, and (b) $b_2 = 0.6$ and $b_3 = 0.4$.

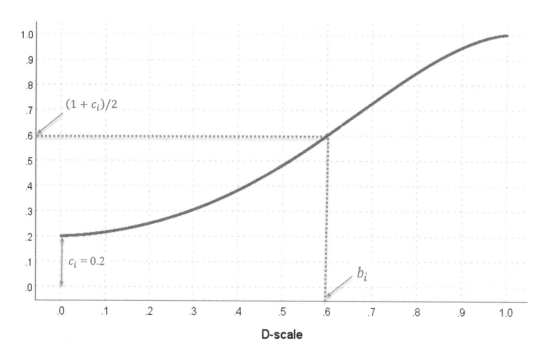

Figure 4.4 An item characteristic curve under the 3PL model for an item with a pseudo-guessing parameter $c_i = 0.2$.

Under the RFM3, the item difficulty, b_i, is the location on the D-scale where the probability of correct item response is $P_i = (1 + c_i)/2$ (e.g., see Figure 4.4). As noted in Chapter 2, the same holds for the difficulty parameter β_i under the 3PL model in IRT. Thus, it is inappropriate to compare item difficulties, b_i, when the third parameter, c_i, varies across items. It might be useful in some situations to fix the pseudo-guessing parameter c_i to validate the comparison of b_i values (e.g., $c_i = 0.20$ for multiple-choice items with five response options). For the case of 3PL in IRT, this issue is discussed by Han (2012).

NOTE [4.4] Under the RFM3, the discrimination index at the item location, b_i, on the D-scale, $a_i = P'_i(b_i)$, has the following analytic form (Dimitrov, 2020, p. 135):

$$a_i = \frac{s_i(1-c_i)}{4b_i(1-b_i)}.$$

True Values and Standard Errors of D_w Scores

The *true* (expected) value of an observed D_w score, $E(D_w)$, is obtained via Equation 4.2 by replacing the observed item scores, X_i, with their expected values, $P_i(D_w)$, obtained under the selected IRF model (e.g., RFM2). The resulting equation for the true value of D_w on a test of n items is (Dimitrov, 2018, p. 811):

$$E(D_w) = \frac{\sum \delta_i P_i}{\sum \delta_i}, \qquad (4.7)$$

where $P_i = P_i(D_w)$; ($i = 1, ..., n$).

The error associated with the observed score D_w, denoted $\varepsilon(D_w)$, is the difference between D_w and its expected value, $\varepsilon(D_w) = D_w - E(D_w)$. The standard deviation of this error, referred to as *standard error* of D_w, is denoted $SE(D_w)$. The formula for $SE(D_w)$ is (Dimitrov, 2018, p. 811):

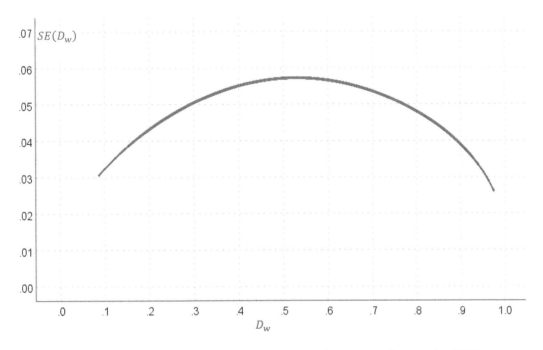

Figure 4.5 Standard error of D_w scores, $SE(D_w)$, for real data on a test of 75 binary items for a sample of 7,754 examinees.

$$SE(D_w) = \left(\frac{1}{\sum \delta_i}\right)\sqrt{\sum_{i=1}^{n}\left[\delta_i^2 P_i(1-P_i)\right]}, \qquad (4.8)$$

where $P_i = P_i(D_w)$; $(i = 1, \ldots, n)$.

The $SE(D_w)$ decreases toward the ends of the D-scale. This can be seen by examining the values of the product $P_i(1-P_i)$ in the right-hand side of Equation 4.8. Specifically, when D_w tends to 0, $P_i(D_w)$ approaches 0, and thus, the product $P_i(1-P_i)$ approaches $0.(1-0) = 0$. When D_w tends to 1, $P_i(D_w)$ also approaches 1, so the product $P_i(1-P_i)$ approaches $1.(1-1) = 0$. One can also note that the product $P_i(1-P_i)$ reaches its highest value at $D_w = 0.5$. Figure 4.5 shows the $SE(D_w)$ of D_w scores obtained for real data on a teacher certification test of 75 binary items administered to 7,754 examinees.

NOTE [4.5] The $SE(D_w)$ is a *conditional standard error*, whereas the standard error in the traditional CTT is assumed to be the same for all examinees, regardless of their test score. Also, the $SE(D_w)$ decreases toward the ends of the D-scale, whereas the standard error in IRT, $SE(\theta)$, increases when θ tends to $+\infty$ or $-\infty$ on the logit scale $(-\infty, +\infty)$.

Item-Person Map on the D-scale

The *item-person map* (IPM) represents the distributions of person ability scores and item difficulties on the same scale. The match of such distributions is an important condition for the accuracy of test measures. In the context of IRT, IPMs are routinely used in examining the psychometric properties of test data. IPMs cannot be produced in the traditional CTT context because the person scores on a test (number correct responses) are *not* on the same scale with the item difficulty (i.e., item "easiness"—proportion of correct item responses).

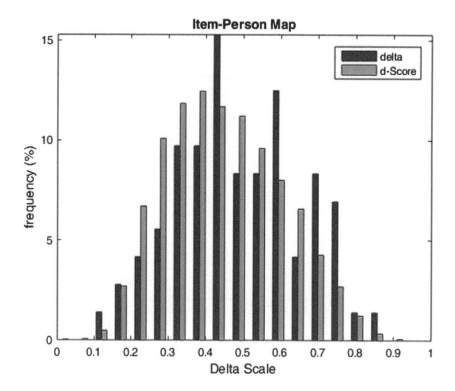

Figure 4.6 Item-person map (IPM) for the distributions of expected item difficulties (δ_i, "*delta*") and person D_w scores on the D-scale for real data on a test of 72 binary items for a sample of 3,460 examinees. The IPM is produced by the computer program DELTA (Atanasov & Dimitrov, 2018).

Under DSM-C, the person D_w scores and the expected item difficulties, δ_i, are on the same scale [0, 1] which allows for the development of IPMs by graphing the frequency distributions of D_w scores and δ_i values on the D-scale. This is illustrated with the IPM in Figure 4.6, which is obtained via DSM-C analysis of real data from a general aptitude test of 72 binary items and a sample of 3,460 examinees, using the computer program DELTA (Atanasov & Dimitrov, 2018). As can be seen, the IPM in this example shows a good overlap between the distributions of the person D_w scores and δ_i values on the D-scale.

NOTE [4.6] In the DSM-C framework, the IPM is usually developed for the distributions of D_w scores and expected item difficulties, δ_i, both used in Equation 4.2. However, depending on the purpose, IPMs can be developed also for the match between the D_w scores and item difficulties, b_i, obtained via the respective regression model (e.g., RFM2 in Equation 4.3).

"Odds for Success" Properties

Provided here are some properties related to *odds for success* on test items, where $P_i = P_i(D_w)$ is the probability of correct item response estimated under RFM2 (Equation 4.3). These properties, derived with a simple algebra over the ratio $P_i/(1-P_i)$ (Dimitrov, 2020, p. 141), are as follows:

1   The *odds for correct response* (OCR) on an item with parameters b_i and s_i for a person with a score D_w are:

$$\mathrm{OCR}_i = P_i/(1-P_i) = \left[\frac{D_w(1-b_i)}{b_i(1-D_w)}\right]^{s_i} \tag{4.9}$$

2   The *odds ratio for correct response* (ORCR) on one item (b_i, s_i) by two persons with scores D_{w1} and D_{w2} are:

$$\text{ORCR}_i = \left[\frac{D_{w1}(1-D_{w2})}{D_{w2}(1-D_{w1})}\right]^{s_i} \tag{4.10}$$

3   The ORCR on two items with parameters (b_1, s_1) and (b_2, s_2) by a person with a score D_w are:

$$\text{ORCR}_{(1,2)} = \frac{\text{OCR}_1}{\text{OCR}_2} = D_w^{s_1-s_2}(1-D_w)^{s_2-s_1}\left[\frac{1-b_1}{b_1}\right]^{s_1}\left[\frac{b_2}{1-b_2}\right]^{s_2}. \tag{4.11}$$

4   Under RFM1, Equations 4.9 and 4.10 can be used directly with the selected fixed value of the shape parameter (e.g., $s_1 = 1$).
5   Under RFM1, Equation 4.11, when $s_1 = s_2 = s$, takes the following simpler form:

$$\text{ORCR}_{(1,2)} = \left[\frac{b_2(1-b_1)}{b_1(1-b_2)}\right]^s \tag{4.12}$$

NOTE [4.7] Under RFM3, the respective equations for "odds of success" are more complex and not very useful because the item locations, b_i, are not comparable when the values of the pseudo-guessing parameter, c_i, vary across test items.

Features and Practical Applications of D_w Scores

Questions related to psychometric properties of the classical D_w scores need to be addressed from different perspectives. First, the D_w scores are based on information about the person response patterns and expected item difficulties, δ_i (see Equation 4.2). It is worth noting that δ_i incorporates information related to the IRT (model-based) item parameters for difficulty, β_i, and discrimination, α_i, because δ_i can be presented as a function of α_i and β_i (see Equation 4.1). Thus, D_w scores provide more refined information about the persons' performance compared to CTT scores (number correct responses). Persons with the same CTT score, but different response patterns, have different (more differentiating and more accurate) D_w scores.

Second, as noted earlier in this chapter, the D_w scores produce a scale with high level of intervalness by the criteria of additive conjoint measurement (Domingue & Dimitrov, 2021). Third, the D_w scores highly correlate ($r \approx 0.99$) with latent scores obtained for the same data using different estimation methods, such as latent D-scoring (Chapter 5) or IRT-based D-scoring (Chapter 12). Fourth, the standard errors of D_w scores are conditional and decrease toward the ends of the scale; that is, D_w scores are more accurate for low-performing and high-performing examinees. More details on the relationship between classical D_w scores and latent estimates of D-scores are provided in Chapter 5.

The derivation of the analytic forms of the RFM models and their mathematical equivalence to the IRT models is described in Chapter 12. In DSM-C, the RFM models (RFM1, RFM2, and RFM3) are treated as classical nonlinear regression models, where the D_w score, computed *a priori* via Equation 4.2, is used as an independent variable (predictor) and the resulting regression coefficients are item parameters. In the latent framework (DSM-L), presented in Chapter 5, the same RFMs are treated as latent models for simultaneous estimations of person and item parameters via latent estimation methods used in IRT (e.g., maximum-likelihood estimations). Furthermore, the classical D_w scores are (a) always highly correlated with latent D-scores, regardless of the estimation method, and (b) close in values to latent D-scores, obtained via a specific estimation approach, on a *base D-scale* (see JML-NCO method in Chapter 5).

In some testing scenarios, classical D_w scores can be preferred for their computational simplicity, transparency, clarity of interpretation, and comprehensive psychometric features. The R code in Appendix 4.1 can be used to compute D_w scores and estimates of item parameters under a selected IRF model (RFM1, RFM2, or RFM3). More comprehensive analysis can be performed using, for example, the computer program DELTA (Atanasov & Dimitrov, 2018) (see also the DSM software section in Chapter 13). Furthermore, equating of D_w scores across different test forms is pretty straightforward as it is based on a simple rescaling of δ_i values. (Equating procedures for classical and latent *D*-scores are provided in Chapter 6.) As discussed in Chapter 11, for example, the simple procedure of presenting D_w scores on a common scale is efficiently used in multistage testing (MST) where D_w scores are computed across MST tracks using δ_i values of precalibrated items (see also, Han, Dimitrov, & Al-Mashari, 2019). As another example, D_w scores are used in an approach to standard setting (see Chapter 10; Dimitrov, 2022). Also, DSM-C provides a dependable framework for comprehensive psychometric evaluation of test data (e.g., Dimitrov & Alsadaawi, 2018).

Summary Points

1. There are ongoing research efforts to address CTT-IRT drawbacks in attempts to improve test scoring, scaling, and item analysis in the field of measurement. In response to such calls, the DSM is designed to combine the merits of the traditional CTT and IRT, *not* to replace them, in a unified framework of classical and latent scoring of test data and their psychometric analysis.
2. The DSM is developed in classical and latent versions (DSM-C and DSM-L) sharing the same scale on a bounded metric [0,1] for person scores and item difficulties, same analytic models for item response functions (IRFs), and other psychometric features, but differ in approaches (classical vs. latent) used for the estimation of person ability and item parameters.
3. Under DSM-C, the test score of a person is a weighted sum of the person's binary (1/0) scores on the test items, where the item "weight" depends on the *expected item difficulty*, δ_i ("delta"), hence the name "Delta-scoring" (or "*D*-scoring," for short) (see Equation 4.2).
4. The expected item difficulty, δ_i, can be estimated (a) via bootstrapping, (b) as a function of IRT-based item parameters for *difficulty* and *discrimination*, if available, or (c) as $\hat{\delta}_i = 1 - p_i$, where p_i is the proportion of correct item responses for a very large sample of examinees (e.g., $N > 10{,}000$), if other options are not available. For example, bootstrapping is used for the estimation of δ_i values in the computer program DELTA (Atanasov & Dimitrov, 2018).
5. Main properties of DSM-C are:
   a. the D_w scores form a bounded interval scale [0,1];
   b. person scores and item difficulties are placed on the same scale;
   c. item response functions (IRFs) are estimated via rational function models (RFMs) used as classical regressions, where the D_w score (computed *a priori*) is a predictor;
   d. the *standard error* of D_w scores, $SE(D_w)$, is conditional, whereas the standard error of test scores in the traditional CTT is assumed to be the same for all examinees.
   e. the standard error of D_w scores, $SE(D_w)$, decreases toward the ends of the *D*-scale [0, 1], whereas its IRT counterpart, $SE(\theta)$, increases when θ tends to $+\infty$ or $-\infty$ on the logit scale.

Appendix 4.1: R Code for Classical *D*-scores and Item Parameters

Step 1. Install the following R packages:

```
install.packages("devtools")
library(devtools)
install_github("amitko/DScoring")
library(DScoring)
```

Step 2. Run the following R code:

```
library("DScoring")


# Load item response data
itemData = read.csv('item_scores.csv', header = FALSE)


# Estimate the expected item difficulty ('delta')
db<-DS.deltaBootstrap(itemData)
db$delta
```

```
# Compute classical D-scores
PS<-DS.personDscore(itemData,db$delta)
PS


# Select RFM model (1=RFM1, 2=RFM2, 3=RFM3)
o = DS.options()
o$model = 2


# Estimate item parameters (nonlinear RFM regression)
Fit<-DS.logitDeltaFit(itemData,Dscore = PS,o)
Fit$parameters


# Export results
write.csv(db$delta, "cls-delta.csv")
D<-list("Dw" = PS)
write.csv(D, "cls-Dscore.csv")
write.csv(data.frame(Fit$parameters,Fit$MAD), "cls-parameters.csv")
```

Notes:
1. The input data file, which contains the person scores (1/0) on the test items, must be in a "comma separated values" (.csv) format. Missing values must be replaced by zero prior to using the data file. In the R code here above, the name of the input data file is "item_scores.csv" but it could be a different name.
2. The command "**o$model = 2**" will result in the selection of the two-parameter model (RFM2). The user must type 1, 2, or 3 for the selection options: 1 = RFM1, 2 = RFM2, 3 = RFM3.
3. The results are exported in three (.csv) files named as follows:
    cls-DScore.csv: contains classical D_w scores.
    cls-delta.csv: contains expected item difficulty, δ_i ("delta"), and
    cls-parameters.csv: contains item parameters (under the selected model, RFM) and an item fit statistic "MAD" (mean absolute difference) indicating (a) good item fit, if MAD ≤ 0.07; (b) tolerable item fit, if 0.07 < MAD ≤ 0.10; and (c) poor item fit, if MAD > 0.10 (see Chapter 7).
4. The R code is provided also at https://github.com/amitko/Dscoring (folder: "samples/DSM-C").

References

Atanasov, D. V., & Dimitrov, D. M. (2018). *DELTA: A computer program for test scoring, equating, and item analysis under the D-scoring method.* Riyadh, Saudi Arabia: National Center for Assessment at ETEC.

Brennan, R. L. (1998). Misconceptions at the intersection of measurement theory and practice. *Educational Measurement: Issues and Practice, 17*(1), 5–30.

Dimitrov, D. M. (2003). Marginal true-score measures and reliability of binary items as a function of their IRT parameters. *Applied Psychological Measurement, 27*(6), 440–458.

Dimitrov, D. M. (2016). An approach to scoring and equating tests with binary items: Piloting with large-scale assessments. *Educational and Psychological Measurement, 76*, 954–975.

Dimitrov, D. M. (2018). The delta scoring method of tests with binary items: A note on true score estimation and equating. *Educational and Psychological Measurement, 78*, 805–825.

Dimitrov, D. M. (2020). Modeling of item response functions under the *D*-scoring method. *Educational and Psychological Measurement, 80*(1), 126–144.

Dimitrov, D. M., & Atanasov, D. V. (2021). Latent *D*-scoring modeling: Estimation of item and person parameters. *Educational and Psychological Measurement, 81*(2), 388–404.

Dimitrov, D. M. (2022). The response vector for mastery (RVM) method of standard setting. *Educational and Psychological Measurement, 82*(4), 719–746.

Dimitrov, D. M., & Alsadaawi, A. (2018). Psychometric features of the *General Teacher Test* under the *D*-scoring model: The case of teacher certification assessment in Saudi Arabia. *World Journal of Social Science Research, 5*(2), 107–126.

Domingue, B. (2014). Evaluating the equal-interval hypothesis with test score scales. *Psychometrika, 79*, 1–19.

Domingue, B. W., & Dimitrov, D. M. (2021). *A comparison of IRT theta estimates and delta scores from the perspective of additive conjoint measurement*. EdArXiv Preprints (https://edarxiv.org/amh56/).

Efron, B. (1979). Bootstrap methods: Another look at the jackknife. *Annals of Statistics, 7*, 1–26.

Hambleton, R. K., & Swaminathan, H. (1985). *Item response theory: Principles and applications*. Hingham, MA: Kluwer, Nijhoff.

Han, K. T. (2012). Fixing the c parameter in the three-parameter logistic model. *Practical Assessment, Research & Evaluation, 17*(1), 1–24.

Han, K. T., Dimitrov, D. M., & Al-Mashari, F. (2019). Developing multistage tests using D-scoring method. *Educational and Psychological Measurement, 79*(5), 988–1008.

Hastings, C., Jr. (1955). *Approximations for digital computers*. Princeton, NJ: Princeton University Press.

Luce, R. D., & Tukey, J. W. (1964). Simultaneous conjoint measurement: A new type of fundamental measurement. *Journal of Mathematical Psychology, 1*, 1–27.

Ramsay, J. O., & Wilberg, M. (2017). A strategy for replacing sum scoring. *Journal of Educational and Behavioral Statistics, 42*(3), 282–307.

Ramsay, J. O., Wilberg, M., & Li, J. (2020). Full information optimal scoring. *Journal of Educational and Behavioral Statistics, 45*(3), 297–315.

5 Latent *D*-scoring Method

Introduction

As described in Chapter 4, the classical *D*-scoring method of measurement, DSM-C, extends the traditional classical test theory (CTT) by providing new features, such as (a) weighted *D*-scores, D_w, are computed on a bounded *D*-scale [0,1], taking into account the person's response pattern and expected item difficulties; (b) classical modeling of item response functions (IRFs) using nonlinear regression models, where the observed D_w scores (computed *a priori*) serve as a predictor variable; and (c) conditional standard error of estimates on the *D*-scale. The latent DSM, denoted DSM-L, is also developed on the bounded scale [0,1] and uses the same analytic models of IRFs, but the DSM-C and DSM-L differ in approaches (classical vs. latent) to the estimation of person and item parameters.

Latent Rational Function Models of IRFs

Two-Parameter Rational Function Model (RFM2)

In DSM-L, the RFM2 for item response functions (IRFs) has the following analytic form (same as in DSM-C):

$$P_i = \frac{1}{1 + \left[\frac{b_i(1-D)}{D(1-b_i)}\right]^{s_i}} \quad (5.1)$$

where P_i is the probability of correct response for a person with a latent ability score D on item i with *difficulty* b_i and *shape* parameter s_i.

In DSM-L, the RFM2 in Equation 5.1 is treated as a latent model for simultaneous estimation of person ability scores, D, and item parameters b_i and s_i. (An estimation method is described later in this chapter.) The item difficulty, b_i, is the location on the *D*-scale where $P_i(D) = 0.5$ (i.e., 50% chance for success on the item), and the *shape* parameter, s_i, is an indicator of item discrimination (higher s_i values produce steeper IRFs). Furthermore, the comment in NOTE [4.2] (Chapter 4) applies here for the role of s_i in the discrimination power of the item at the location of item difficulty, b_i, namely: $a_i = s_i/4b_i(1-b_i)$.

One-Parameter Rational Function Model (RFM1)

The *one-parameter rational function model* (RFM1) is obtained from the RFM2 by fixing the shape parameter, s_i, to a prespecified value (constant, s) (i.e., $s_i = s$). For example, $s_i = 1$ produces the following RFM1 analytic form:

$$P_i = \frac{1}{1 + \frac{b_i(1-D)}{D(1-b_i)}}. \quad (5.2)$$

Under the RFM1, the item characteristic curves (ICCs) do not cross. As the shape parameter is fixed ($s_i = s$), the item discrimination at the location for item difficulty, b_i, on the *D*-scale is $a_i = s/4b_i(1-b_i)$. Thus, if $s = 1$, $a_i = 1/4b_i(1-b_i)$ (see also NOTE [4.3] in Chapter 4).

Three-Parameter Rational Function Model (RFM3)

The *three-parameter rational function model* (RFM3) involves a pseudo-guessing parameter, c_i:

$$P_i = c_i + \frac{1 - c_i}{1 + \left[\dfrac{b_i(1-D)}{D(1-b_i)}\right]^{s_i}}. \tag{5.3}$$

Under the RFM3, the item discrimination at the location for item difficulty, b_i, on the D-scale is: $a_i = \left[s_i(1-c_i)\right]/\left[4b_i(1-b_i)\right]$ (see also NOTE [4.4] in Chapter 4).

> **NOTE [5.1]** Under the RFM3, the item difficulty, b_i, is the location on the D-scale where the probability of correct item response is $P_i = (1+c_i)/2$ (e.g., see Figure 4.4. in Chapter 4). Thus, it is inappropriate to compare item difficulties, b_i, when the parameter c_i varies across items. In some scenarios, it might be useful to fix c_i to a prespecified value (e.g., $c_i = 0.25$ for multiple-choice items with four response options of which only one is correct).

The derivation of the *item response function models* RFM1, RFM2, and RFM3 is described in Chapter 12. These models have the same analytic form under the DSM-C and DSM-L, but under the DSM-C they are treated as classical nonlinear regression models, where the observed score D_w (computed *a priori*) is a predictor, whereas under the DSM-L they are used as latent models for simultaneous estimation of person and item parameters. For example, the item characteristic curves (ICCs) in Figures 4.1–4.4 (Chapter 4) can be used to illustrate ICCs under the DSM-L, assuming that they were produced using latent estimations of person ability and item parameters via the RFMs in Equations 5.1–5.3.

Item and Test Information Functions

The IRT concepts of *item information function* (IIF), denoted $I_i(\theta)$, and *test information function* (TIF), denoted $I(\theta)$, are presented in Chapter 2 (see Equations 2.22 and 2.27). These concepts remain applicable in the framework of latent estimations under DSM-L.

Item Information Function (IIF)

Using the IRT analytic expressions for $I_i(\theta)$ (Birnbaum, 1968; see also Lord, 1980; Hambleton et al., 1991) in the context of DSM-L, we have the following analytic expressions for IIF, $I_i(D)$, on the D-scale:

$$I_i(D) = \frac{\left[P_i'(D)\right]^2}{P_i(D)\left[1 - P_i(D)\right]}, \tag{5.4}$$

where $P_i(D)$ is the item response function under the selected IRF model (RFM1, RFM2, or RFM3), and $P_i'(D)$ is its first derivative. Provided next are formulas for $I_i(D)$ obtained via simple algebra from Equation 5.4 for each IRF model.

1. Under the RFM2, the derivative $P_i'(D)$ has the following analytic form (see Chapter 4, Equation 4.4):

$$P_i'(D) = \frac{s_i P_i(1-P_i)}{D(1-D)}, \tag{5.5}$$

   where $P_i = P_i(D)$ is obtained via the RFM2 in Equation 5.1.
2. By replacing $P_i'(D)$ in Equation 5.4 with its analytic expression in Equation 5.5, we obtain the following analytic expression for IIF under the RFM2:

$$I_i(D) = \frac{s_i^2 P_i[1-P_i]}{\left[D(1-D)\right]^2}. \tag{5.6}$$

3. Under the RFM1, the $I_i(D)$ formula is obtained from Equation 5.6 by setting s_i to a prespecified value s. For example, if $s = 1$, the IIF is:

$$I_i(D) = \frac{P_i[1 - P_i]}{[D(1 - D)]^2}, \tag{5.7}$$

where $P_i = P_i(D)$ is obtained via the RFM1 in Equation 5.2.

4. Under the RFM3, the derivative $P_i'(D)$ has the following analytic form:

$$P_i'(D) = \frac{s_i(P_i - c_i)(1 - P_i)}{D(1 - D)(1 - c_i)}, \tag{5.8}$$

where $P_i = P_i(D)$ is obtained via the RFM3 in Equation 5.3.

5. By replacing $P_i'(D)$ in Equation 5.4 with its analytic expression in Equation 5.8, we obtain the following equation for IIF under the RFM3:

$$I_i(D) = \frac{s_i^2 (P_i - c_i)^2 (1 - P_i)}{[D(1 - D)]^2 (1 - c_i)^2 P_i}, \tag{5.9}$$

where $P_i = P_i(D)$ is obtained via the RFM3 in Equation 5.3.

NOTE [5.2] The analytic formulas for $I_i(D)$ under the RFM1, RFM2, and RFM3 have the same structure as those for $I_i(\theta)$ under the 1PL, 2PL, and 3PL models in IRT, respectively (see Chapter 2, Equations 2.24–2.26), except that the RFM-based Equations 5.7, 5.6, and 5.9 contain the "rescaling" term $[D(1 - D)]^2$ in the denominator of the respective analytic expressions in the right-hand side of these equations.

Test Information Function (TIF)

As shown in Chapter 2, the TIF in IRT is a sum of the IFFs, that is, $I(\theta) = \sum_{i=1}^{n} I_i(\theta)$ (see Equation 2.22). Likewise, the TIF in DSM-L, denoted $I(D)$, is a sum of the IIFs, that is:

$$I(D) = \sum_{i=1}^{n} I_i(D), \tag{5.10}$$

where $I_i(D)$ is obtained via Equation 5.6, 5.7, or 5.9 for RFM2, RFM1, or RFM3, respectively.

Standard Error of Estimation

As shown in Chapter 2, the conditional standard error of IRT scores, $SE(\theta)$, is reciprocal to the TIF: $SE(\theta) = 1/\sqrt{I(\theta)}$ (see Equation 2.23). Likewise, the *conditional standard error* of latent D-scores in DSM-L is:

$$SE(D) = \frac{1}{\sqrt{I(D)}}, \tag{5.11}$$

where the TIF, $I(D)$, is obtained via Equation 5.10.

The analytic formulas for $SE(D)$ are provided next for a test of n binary items, when the TIF, $I(D)$, is obtained under the RFM2, RFM1, and RFM3, respectively.

1. Under the RFM2, the $I(D)$ term in Equation 5.11 is replaced with its analytic expression in Equation 5.10, where the IIFs, $I_i(D)$, are obtained via Equation 5.6,

$$SE(D) = \frac{1}{\sqrt{I(D)}} = \frac{D(1 - D)}{\sqrt{\sum_{i=1}^{n} s_i^2 P_i(D)[1 - P_i(D)]}}. \tag{5.12}$$

2 Under the RFM1, the $I(D)$ term in Equation 5.11 is replaced with its analytic expression in Equation 5.10, where the IIFs, $I_i(D)$, are obtained via Equation 5.7 for a fixed value of s_i. Specifically, when $s_i = 1$, the analytic form of $SE(\hat{D})$ is:

$$SE(D) = \frac{1}{\sqrt{I(D)}} = \frac{D(1-D)}{\sqrt{\sum_{i=1}^{n} P_i(D)[1 - P_i(D)]}}. \tag{5.13}$$

3 Under the RFM3, the $I(D)$ term in Equation 5.11 is replaced with its analytic expression in Equation 5.10, where $I_i(D)$ are obtained via Equation 5.9:

$$SE(D) = \frac{1}{\sqrt{I(D)}} = \frac{D(1-D)}{\sqrt{\sum_{i=1}^{n} \left\{ \frac{s_i^2 [1 - P_i(D)][P_i(D) - c_i]^2}{(1 - c_i)^2 P_i(D)} \right\}}}. \tag{5.14}$$

NOTE [5.3] In DSM-L, the TIF is a direct summation of the IIFs, which allows test developers and researchers to control the additive contribution of individual items to the TIF. This is not the case under the DSM-C, where the person score, D_w, is a weighted sum of the item scores, with weights $w_i = \delta_i / \sum \delta_i$ (see Chapter 4, Equation 4.2). Specifically, as shown by Lord, 1980, p.73), the TIF for weighted scores has the following analytic form:

$$I(D_w) = \frac{\left(\sum_{i=1}^{n} w_i P_i' \right)^2}{\sum_{i=1}^{n} w_i^2 P_i (1 - P_i)}, \tag{5.15}$$

where w_i is the "weight" for the score on item i, P_i is the probability of correct response, and P_i' is the first derivative of P_i under the respective IRF model.

RFM-Based Estimations

The simultaneous estimation of person and item parameters under the respective IRF model in DSM-L is performed using IRT estimation approaches (e.g., MLE-based or Bayesian methods). The difference is that IRT estimations are conducted over the unlimited interval $(-\infty, +\infty)$, whereas DSM-L estimations are conducted on a bounded D-scale ranging from 0 to 1. Thus, DSM-L estimations address IRT issues with estimations over the unlimited interval $(-\infty, +\infty)$ and calls for using bounded scales raised by some researchers (e.g., Brennan, 1998; Hambleton & Swaminathan, 1985; Ramsay & Wilberg, 2017; Ramsay, Wilberg, & Li, 2020).

NOTE [5.4] As shown in Chapter 12, the two-parameter model RFM2 is mathematically equivalent to the 2PL model in IRT. Specifically, the RFM2 can be obtained from the 2PL model using the transformations: $\theta = \ln[D/(1 - D)]$, $\beta_i = \ln[b_i/(1 - b_i)]$, and $\alpha_i = s_i$ (Robitzsch, 2021). Conversely, the 2PL model can be obtained from the RFM2 via the transformations: $D = 1/[1 + \exp(-\theta)]$, $b_i = 1/[1 + \exp(-\beta)]$, and $s_i = \alpha_i$. Under these transformations, the IRT scale $(-\infty, +\infty)$ maps onto the D-scale, namely: (a) $D = 0$, when θ tends to $-\infty$, and (b) $D = 1$, when θ tends to $+\infty$. In essence, RFM-based estimations in the framework of DSM-L can be treated as IRT estimations on a bounded scale (0,1).

JML-CNO Estimation

Under DSM-L models (RFM1, RFM2, or RFM3), the simultaneous estimation of person and item parameters is efficiently performed via a variant of the *joint maximum-likelihood* (JML) method with iterations under *constraint nonlinear optimization* (CNO). This method, referred to as JML-CNO method, is used under the constraints (a) $0 \leq D \leq 1$, (b) $0 \leq b_i \leq 1$, and (c) $0 < s_i < C$, where C is an upper-limit constant (say, $C = 5$), and maximizes the likelihood of the examinees' response vectors. The JML-CNO method does *not* impose restrictions typically used with MLE or Bayesian methods, such as fixing the mean and standard deviation of the ability distribution (e.g., $\mu = 0$, $\sigma = 1$). The JML-CNO method (see Appendix 5.1) is implemented in the computer program DELTA which is written in MATLAB (MathWorks, Inc., 2018) and performs DSM-based test scoring, equating, and item analysis (Atanasov & Dimitrov, 2018).

Base D-scale

The scale of D-scores obtained via *JML-CNO* estimations is referred to as *base D-scale* and its D-scores are denoted D_B. An important feature of the *base D-scale*, verified in numerous simulations and real-data analyses, is that the latent D_B scores are closely related to the classical D_W scores (see Chapter 4, Equation 4.2). Specifically, D_W and D_B scores, computed for the same data, are highly correlated ($R_{D_W D_B} \approx 0.99$) and their difference varies in a small range, typically $|D_W - D_B| < 0.10$.

Example 5.1

Figure 5.1 displays the relationship between D_W and D_B scores, obtained for real data on a teacher certification test of 71 items administered to 2,662 examinees. The correlation between these D_W and D_B scores was very high ($R_{D_W D_B} = 0.989$) and their differences ranged from 0 to 0.07 in absolute value (*Mean* = 0.018, *SD* = 0.013). The standard errors of the D_W and D_B scores are depicted in Figure 5.2. As expected, the estimated latent D_B scores are more accurate than their classical counterparts, D_W, but in both cases the standard errors do not exceed 0.06 and their difference is very small, ranging from 0.00 to 0.01. Also, as shown in Table 5.1, there are very high correlations between (a) the D_W, D_B, and IRT scores, θ, and (b) the expected item difficulty, δ, and the model-based item difficulty in DSM-L and IRT (b_i and β_i, respectively) for the data in this example. Similar results hold in general, with small variations depending on factors such as sample size, test length, and reliability (e.g., Dimitrov & Atanasov, 2021).

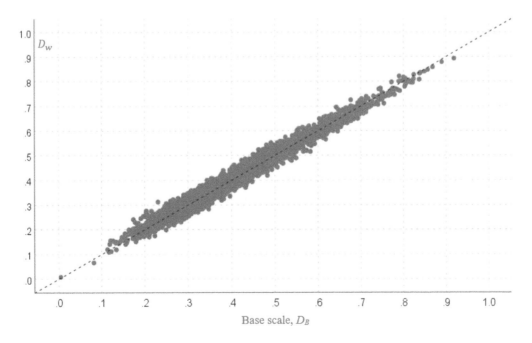

Figure 5.1 Relationship between classical D_W scores and latent D_B scores (on the base D-scale) for data on a teacher certification test of 71 items administered to 2,662 examinees. The correlation between the D_W and D_B scores is 0.989 and their differences range from 0 to 0.07 in absolute value (*Mean* = 0.018, *SD* = 0.013).

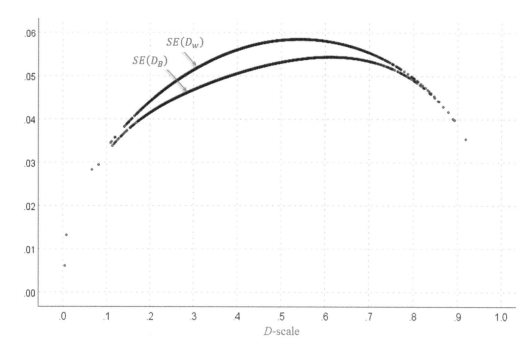

Figure 5.2 Standard errors of the D_w and D_B scores for data on a teacher certification test of 71 items administered to 2,662 examinees.

Table 5.1 Real-data correlations between DSM- and IRT-based estimates of person and item parameters

	Ability scores		Item parameters	
Parameter	D_B	θ	b	β
D_w	0.987	0.980		
D_B		0.998		
δ			0.971	0.970
b				0.998

Note. D_w = classical D-scores; D_B = latent D-scores (*base D-scale*); θ = IRT scores (on the logit scale); δ = expected item difficulty; b = item difficulty (via the latent RFM2 of DSM); β = item difficulty (via the 2PL model in IRT).

Rescaling D-scores to the Base D-scale

Consider the case where latent D-scores are estimated using an approach different from the JML-CNO method (say, Bayesian method), and the goal is to present such scores on the *base D-scale*. This case may occur, for example, when a software implementing the JML-CNO method is not available or in research scenarios involving D-scoring. In this situation, D_B scores (*base D-scale*) are not available. One practical solution is to use the scale of classical D_w scores as a "proxy" of the *base D-scale*, given that the D_w scores are easy to compute and closely related to the latent D_B scores. An algorithm for the general case of rescaling D-scores on a scale X (e.g., Bayesian estimates) to scale Y (e.g., D_w scores) is provided in Appendix 5.2. This algorithm can be easily implemented via simple programming (e.g., syntax codes in SPSS and R are provided in Appendix 5.2). An application with real data is provided next in Example 5.2.

Example 5.2

For the real data used in Example 5.1, latent D-scores were estimated via the Hamiltonian Monte Carlo (HMC) algorithm applied under the RFM2 model in DSM-L using the Bayesian statistical software program STAN in R. The goal was to rescale these latent D-scores, denoted here D_{hmc}, to the scale of classical D_w scores, computed for the same data; that is, the D_w scale is used as a "proxy" of the *base D-scale* of latent D_B scores. For verification purposes only, the latent D_B scores were also computed for the same data, using the *JML-CNO* algorithm implemented in the computer program DELTA (Atanasov & Dimitrov, 2018).

The D_{hmc} scores were rescaled to $D_{hmc}^\star$ scores on the D_w scale using the rescaling procedure in Appendix 5.2, with $X = D_{hmc}$ and $Y = D_w$. Figure 5.3 shows the relationship between the D_{hmc} scores (*prior* to rescaling) and the latent D_B scores for the same data. The D_{hmc} and D_B scores are highly correlated ($r = 0.998$), yet nonlinearly related. The relationship between the rescaled D_{hmc} scores, $D_{hmc}^\star$, and the latent D_B scores is depicted in Figure 5.4. The $D_{hmc}^\star$ and D_B scores are linearly related ($r = 0.999$), and their differences over the D-scale are practically negligible, ranging from 0 to 0.020 in absolute value (*Mean* = 0.005, *SD* = 0.003).

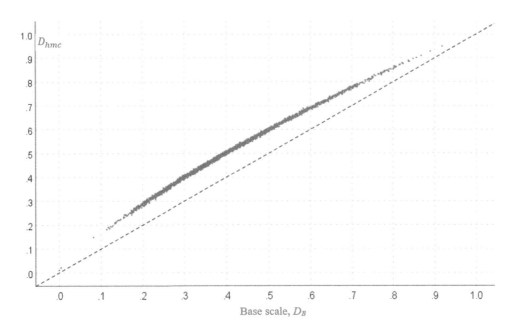

Figure 5.3 Relationship between latent scores obtained via two different estimation methods applied for the RFM2 model, (a) D_{hmc}, via the Hamiltonian Monte Carlo (HMC) algorithm using the Bayesian statistical software program STAN in R, and (b) D_B scores on the base D-scale, using the *JML-CNO* algorithm in the computer program DELTA (Atanasov & Dimitrov, 2018).

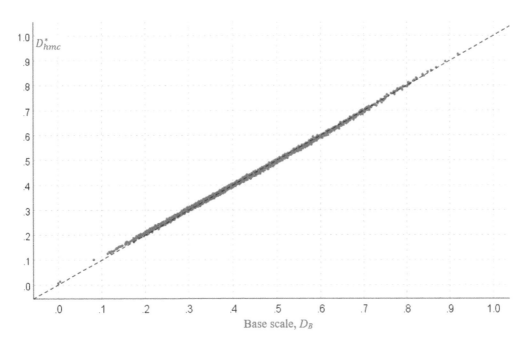

Figure 5.4 Relationship between the rescaled scores, $D_{hmc}^\star$, obtained via rescaling the D_{hmc} scores on the scale of classical D_w scores, and the latent D_B scores (on the base D-scale). The correlation between the $D_{hmc}^\star$ and D_B scores is 0.999 and their differences range from 0 to 0.020 in absolute value (*Mean* = 0.005, *SD* = 0.003).

Summary Points

1. The latent version of the D-scoring method, DSM-L, can be seen as a latent analog of the classical DSM-C version in the sense that they share the same scale, same analytic forms of item response function models (RFM1, RFM2, and RFM3), and same psychometric concepts and interpretations.
2. The DSM-L and DSM-C differ in the approaches used for the estimation (latent vs. classical) of person ability and item parameters under the respective IRF model (RFM1, RFM2, or RFM3) and related features—e.g., the additive property of the TIF in DSM-L does not hold under the classical weighted scoring in DSM-C (see NOTE [5.3]).
3. In DSM-L, the *standard error of estimate*, $SE(\theta) = 1/\sqrt{I(\theta)}$, decreases toward the ends of the D-scale [0, 1].
4. The JML-CNO method (*joint maximum-likelihood* estimation with iterations under *constraint nonlinear optimization*) is used under the following restrictions of person ability scores and items parameters: (a) $0 \leq D \leq 1$, (b) $0 \leq b_i \leq 1$, and (c) $0 < s_i < C$, where C is an upper-limit constant (say, $C = 5$). The JML-CNO maximizes the log-likelihood function of the examinees' response vectors, $\ln L([\mathbf{X}]|\mathbf{D}, v)$ (see Appendix 5.1, Equation A5.4).
5. The scale produced by the JML-CNO method is referred to as *base D-scale*. When the JML-CNO procedure is not available, a practically efficient solution is to rescale latent D-scores, obtained via different (e.g., Bayesian-based) estimation approach, to the scale of classical D_w scores computed for the same data. The rescaled D-scores are very close (practically equal) to D-scores on the *base D-scale*, that is, if they were obtained via the JML-CNO method.
6. There are high correlations (typically, ≈ 0.99) between classical and latent estimates of person ability and item difficulty, obtained via DSM-L or IRT-based estimation methods.

Appendix 5.1: DSM-L Estimations via the JML-CNO Method

Described are the main stages in the estimation of person and item parameters in the framework of DSM-L, where the probability of correct item response is provided by the respective model. For example, under the two-parameter rational function model (RFM2), the probability of correct item response is:

$$P_i(D, b_i, s_i) = \frac{1}{1 + \left[\dfrac{b_i(1-D)}{D(1-b_i)}\right]^{s_i}}. \tag{A5.1}$$

Let $v_i = (b_i, s_i)$; $(i = 1, \ldots, n)$, so $v = (v_1, v_2, \ldots, v_n)$ represent the test parameters, and let X_{ij} be the binary (1/0) score of person j on item i in a test of n items ($i = 1, \ldots, n$) taken by N persons ($j = 1, 2, \ldots, N$). Thus, $\mathbf{X}_j = (X_{1j}, X_{2j}, \ldots X_{nj})$ is the response vector (pattern) of person j on the set of n test items. If D_j is the ability of that person, the likelihood for the person's response pattern to occur is:

$$L_j(\mathbf{X}_j | D_j, v) = \prod_{i=1}^{n} \left[P_i(D_j, b_i, s_i)\right]^{X_{ij}} \left[1 - P_i(D_j, b_i, s_i)\right]^{1-X_{ij}}. \tag{A5.2}$$

Also, let $\mathbf{D} = (D_1, D_2, \ldots, D_N)$ denote the vector of ability scores of all N persons, and $[\mathbf{X}]$ denote the $(n \times N)$ matrix of their response vectors. The likelihood of this matrix to occur is:

$$L([\mathbf{X}]|\mathbf{D}, v) = \prod_{j=1}^{N} L_j(\mathbf{X}_j | D_j, v) = \prod_{j=1}^{N} \prod_{i=1}^{n} \left[P_i(D_j, b_i, s_i)\right]^{X_{ij}} \left[1 - P_i(D_j, b_i, s_i)\right]^{1-X_{ij}}. \tag{A5.3}$$

Taking the natural logarithm on both sides of Equation A5.3, we obtain:

$$\ln L([\mathbf{X}]|\mathbf{D}, v) = \sum_{j=1}^{N} \sum_{i=1}^{n} \left\{X_{ij} \ln P_i(D_j, b_i, s_i) + (1 - X_{ij}) \ln\left[1 - P_i(D_j, b_i, s_i)\right]\right\}. \tag{A5.4}$$

To find the maximum of the likelihood function in Equation A5.4 is tantamount to finding the minimum of the negative of this function, $-\ln L([\mathbf{X}]|\mathbf{D}, v)$.

In the computer program DELTA (Atanasov & Dimitrov, 2018), written in MATLAB, the minimization of the target function, $-\ln L([\mathbf{X}]|\mathbf{D},v)$, is performed using the function *"fmincon"* implemented in MATLAB (e.g., https://www.mathworks.com/help/optim/ug/fmincon.html) (see also Coleman & Li, 1996). The *fmincon* function finds the constrained minimum of a scalar function of several variables starting with initial estimates in an iterative process. This procedure, generally referred to as *constrained nonlinear optimization* (CNO), is used under the design of *joint maximum-likelihood* (JML) iterations (hence, the name "JML-CNO" method). Specifically, under the restrictions of person D-scores and item parameters (D, b_i, and s_i), the optimization algorithm iterates over the following main steps:

Step 1. Selected are the initial values of the person D-scores, $D^{(0)}$. In DELTA, the classical D_w scores, computed at an initial stage of the procedure, are used as starting values of the person scores, $D^{(0)} = D_w$. Alternatively, one can use, say, the midpoint of the D-scale as a starting value of D (i.e., $D^{(0)} = 0.5$), but the convergence becomes much slower.

Step 2. At each step k, using the D-score estimates at the previous step ($k-1$), the item parameters $v = (v_1, v_2, \ldots, v_n)$, where $v_i = (b_i, s_i)$, are estimated:

$$v^k = \arg\min_{v} -\ln L\left(D^{(k-1)}, v\right).$$

Step 3. At each step k, person ability scores are estimated:

$$D^{(k)} = \arg\min_{D} -\ln L\left(D^{(k-1)}, v\right).$$

Step 4. Iterations of Steps 2 and 3 continue until $\left|v^{(k)} - v^{(k-1)}\right| < \varepsilon$ (default $\varepsilon = 0.0001$).

Appendix 5.2: R Code for the Estimation of Latent D-scores and Item Parameters

Step 1. Install the R packages listed in Chapter 4, Appendix 4.1 (Step 1).
  Step 2. Run the following R code:

```
library("DScoring")

# Load item response data
itemData = read.csv('item_scores.csv', header = FALSE)

# Latent estimation and export of item and person parameters under the RFM2 model
latent=DS.estimatePC(itemData)
latent$Persons$Dscore
latent$Items$Parameters
P = data.frame(latent$Items$Parameters, latent$Items$MAD)
colnames(P)<-c('b','s','MAD')
write.csv(P,'latent_parameters.csv')
D=data.frame(latent$Persons$Dscore,latent$Persons$SE)
colnames(D)<-c('DL','SE')
write.csv(D,'latent_DScores.csv')
```

Notes:
1. The input data file, which contains person scores (1/0) on the test items, must be in a "comma separated values" (.csv) format. Missing values must be replaced by zero prior to using the data file. In the R code here above, the name of the input data file is "item_scores.csv" but it could be a different name.
2. The analysis is performed under the two-parameter IRF model (RFM2; Equation 5.1).
3. The results are exported in two (.csv) files named as follows:

latent_DScores.csv: contains estimates of latent D-scores (DL) and their standard error (SE).

latent_parameters.csv: contains estimates of the item parameters under the latent RFM2, and an item fit statistic "MAD" (mean absolute difference) indicating (a) good item fit, if MAD ≤ 0.07; (b) tolerable item fit, if 0.07 < MAD < 0.10; and (c) poor item fit, if MAD ≥ 0.10 (for details, see Chapter 7).

4. The R code is provided also at https://github.com/amitko/Dscoring (folder: "samples/DSM-L").

Appendix 5.3: Rescaling of *D*-scores Obtained via Different Methods for the Same Data

Let D_X and D_Y denote D-scores on scales X and Y, respectively, obtained via different methods of latent estimation using the same data. In general, the D_X and D_Y scores are highly correlated, yet nonlinearly related. However, as these scores are values of random variables ranging from 0 to 1, their Z-scale of normal deviates are linearly related: $Z_{D_Y} = A \cdot Z_{D_X} + B$. Thus, the rescaling of D_X scores to $D_X^\star$ scores on scale Y can be performed in steps as follows:

Step 1. The D_X and D_Y scores are converted to Z-scale of normal deviates:

$$Z_{D_X} = \frac{1}{1.702} \ln\left(\frac{D_X}{1-D_X}\right) \text{ and } Z_{D_Y} = \frac{1}{1.702} \ln\left(\frac{D_Y}{1-D_Y}\right) \tag{A5.1}$$

Step 2. Using that the Z-scores are linearly related, $Z_{D_Y} = A \cdot Z_{D_X} + B$, the rescaling constants A and B are computed via the "mean-sigma" method (e.g., Hambleton et al., 1991, p. 131):

$$A = \sigma_{Z_Y}/\sigma_{Z_{D_X}} \text{ and } B = \text{mean}(Z_{D_Y}) - A \cdot \text{mean}(Z_{D_X}) \tag{A5.2}$$

Step 3. The Z_{D_X} scores are rescaled to $Z_{D_X}^\star$ scores (on the scale of Z_{D_Y} scores):

$$Z_{D_X}^\star = A \cdot Z_{D_X} + B. \tag{A5.3}$$

Step 4. The D_X scores are rescaled to $D_X^\star$ scores (on the D_Y scale):

$$D_X^\star = \frac{1}{1 + \exp\left(-1.702 Z_{D_X}^\star\right)}. \tag{A5.4}$$

Syntax Code in SPSS and R

The syntax codes in SPSS and R, provided here below, implement the four-step algorithm for the rescaling of D-scores obtained via different estimation methods for the same data. The SPSS data spreadsheet should contain two columns, labeled X and Y, where column X contains D-scores that have to be rescaled to the scale of D-scores located in column Y. Running the syntax will generate a third column, labeled XR, which contains the rescaled D-scores. The code in R reads a data file in comma-separated values (.csv) format, which contains the variables X and Y, and produces an output (.csv) file, which contains the values of X, Y, and the rescaled value, XR.

SPSS Code

```
COMPUTE ZX = LN(X/(1 - X))/1.702.
COMPUTE ZY = LN(Y/(1 - Y))/1.702.
COMPUTE ZX2 = ZX**2.
COMPUTE ZY2 = ZY**2.
aggregate outfile * mode addvariables
/MZX = mean(ZX)
/MZY = mean(ZY)
/MZX2 = mean(ZX2)
/MZY2 = mean(ZY2).
```

```
COMPUTE VZX = MZX2 - MZX**2.
COMPUTE VZY = MZY2 - MZY**2.
COMPUTE SD_ZX = SQRT(VZX).
COMPUTE SD_ZY = SQRT(VZY).
COMPUTE A = SD_ZY/SD_ZX.
COMPUTE B = MZY - A*MZX.
COMPUTE ZXR = A*ZX + B.
COMPUTE XR = 1/(1 + exp(-1.702*ZXR)).
EXECUTE.
DELETE VARIABLES ZX TO ZXR
```

R Code

Step 1. Install the R packages listed in Chapter 4, Appendix 4.1 (Step 1).
Step 2. Run the following R code:

```
library(DScoring)
Dscores<-read.csv("DATAXY.csv")
XR<-DS.equatingDScores(Dscores$X,Dscores$Y)
write.csv(data.frame(Dscores,XR),"result.csv")
```

References

Atanasov, D. V., & Dimitrov, D. M. (2018). *DELTA: A computer program for test scoring, equating, and item analysis under the D-scoring method.* Riyadh, KSA: National Center for Assessment at ETEC.

Birnbaum, A. (1968). Some latent trait models and their use in inferring an examinee's ability. Part 5. In F.M. Lord & M.R. Novick (Eds.), *Statistical Theories of mental test scores* (pp. 395–4790). Reading, MA: Addison-Wesley.

Brennan, R. L. (1998). Misconceptions at the intersection of measurement theory and practice. *Educational Measurement: Issues and Practice, 17*(1), 5–30.

Coleman, T.F., & Li, Y. (1996). An interior, trust region approach for nonlinear minimization subject to bounds. *SIAM Journal of Optimization, 6,* 418–445.

Dimitrov, D. M., & Atanasov, D. V. (2021). Latent D-scoring modeling: Estimation of item and person parameters. *Educational and Psychological Measurement, 81*(2), 388–404.

Hambleton, R. K., & Swaminathan, H. (1985). *Item response theory: Principles and applications.* Hingham, MA: Kluwer, Nijhoff.

Hambleton, R. K, Swaminathan, H., & Rogers, H. J. (1991). *Fundamentals of item response theory.* Newbury Park, CA: Sage.

Lord, F. M. (1980). *Applications of item response theory to practical testing problems.* Hillsdale, NJ: Erlbaum Publishers.

MathWorks, Inc. (2018). *MATLAB* (Version R2018a) [Computer software]. https://www.mathworks.com/products/new_products/release2018a.html

Ramsay, J. O., & Wilberg, M. (2017). A strategy for replacing sum scoring. *Journal of Educational and Behavioral Statistics, 42*(3), 282–307.

Ramsay, J. O., Wilberg, M., & Li, J. (2020). Full information optimal scoring. *Journal of Educational and Behavioral Statistics, 45*(3), 297–315.

Robitzsch, A. (2021). On the equivalence of the latent D-scoring model and the two-parameter logistic item response theory model. *Mathematics,* DOI: 10.3390/math9131465, retrieved from https://www.preprints.org/manuscript/202105.0699/v1.

6 DSM Test Equating

Introduction

In general, *equating of test scores* is a statistical procedure used to present the scores across test forms on a common scale so that they can be used interchangeably. To be equated, the tests must measure the same latent variable (ability, trait) with the same precision. The validity of score comparison across test forms must *not* depend on whether test X is equated to the scale of test Y or vice versa. These requirements, known together as "equity" in test equating, are presented by Lord (1980, p. 195) (e.g., see also Hambleton & Swaminathan, 1985, p.199). Some test equating procedures are presented in Chapters 1 and 2 in the context of classical test theory (CTT) and item response theory (IRT), respectively. In the context of the *D*-scoring method of measurement (DSM), equating of *D*-scores is performed using the *nonequivalent groups with anchor tests* (NEAT) design under which (a) the groups of examinees differ in ability levels and (b) the tests being equated differ in difficulty and contain a set of common (anchor) items (e.g., Kolen & Brennan, 2004). Hereafter, the term "rescaling" is used when item parameters for test X are presented on the scale of the respective item parameters for test Y, whereas the term "equating" is used when *D*-scores on test X are presented on the *D*-scale for test Y. In fact, in both cases we are dealing with rescaling, but "equating" is traditionally associated with test scores.

Rescaling of Item Parameters

Under the NEAT design for equating of *D*-scores on two tests, the same procedure is used to rescale item parameters in both DSM versions—classical (DSM-C) and latent (DSM-L). This procedure is described next for the rescaling of expected item difficulty, δ_i, in DSM-C, but it can be also used for the rescaling of b_i and s_i (upon a simple transformation of s_i) in DSM-L

DSM-C: Rescaling of Expected Item Difficulty

The goal is to transform the expected item difficulties, δ_i, of test X to $\delta_i^\star$ values on the scale of test Y. The procedure for δ_i rescaling, described here, is based on an approach to rescaling the proportion of correct responses, p_i, across two test forms with common items, introduced by Lord (1980, pp. 213–215; see also, Guo, Rudner, & Talento-Miller, 2009). It is *not* assumed that the p_i values of the common items are linearly related. Therefore, the p_i values are transformed to normalized z-scores which are linearly related. After rescaling the z-scores to $z^\star$ scores, they are transformed back to rescaled $p_i^\star$ values. In the context of DSM test equating, the rescaling of δ_i values under this approach is described next in algorithmic steps using the following notations (Dimitrov & Atanasov, 2021, p. 162):

$\delta_X = \delta_i$ values for the items of test X;
$\delta_{Xc} = \delta_i$ values for the common items of test X;
$\delta_{Yc} = \delta_i$ values for the common items of test Y.

The δ_X values are rescaled into $\delta_X^\star$ values on the scale of test Y in steps as follows:

Step 1. Convert δ_X, δ_{Xc}, and δ_{Yc} to z-scale of normal deviates:

$$z_{\delta_X} = \frac{1}{1.702}\ln\left(\frac{\delta_X}{1-\delta_X}\right); \; z_{\delta_{Xc}} = \frac{1}{1.702}\ln\left(\frac{\delta_{Xc}}{1-\delta_{Xc}}\right); \text{ and } z_{\delta_{Yc}} = \frac{1}{1.702}\ln\left(\frac{\delta_{Yc}}{1-\delta_{Yc}}\right).$$

Step 2. As the *z*-scores of the common items are linearly related, $z_{\delta_{Y_c}} = A \cdot z_{\delta_{X_c}} + B$, compute the scaling constants A and B using the "mean-sigma" method (Marco, 1977; e.g., see also Hambleton, Swaminathan, & Rogers, 1991, p. 131):

$A = \sigma_{z_{\delta_{Y_c}}} / \sigma_{z_{\delta_{X_c}}}$, where σ denotes *standard deviation*

$B = mean(z_{\delta_{Y_c}}) - A \cdot mean(z_{\delta_{X_c}})$

Step 3. For all items of test X, rescale the *z*-scores of δ_X to $z^{\star}_{\delta_X}$ scores as follows:

$z^{\star}_{\delta_X} = A \cdot z_{\delta_X} + B$

Step 4. For *all* items of test X, rescale δ_X to $\delta^{\star}_X$ as follows:

$$\delta^{\star}_X = \frac{1}{1 + \exp(-1.702 z^{\star}_{\delta_X})}.$$

It should be clarified that steps 4 and 1 are based on the approximations $\Phi(z) \approx \Psi(1.702z) = \frac{1}{1 + \exp(-1.702z)}$ and $z_\delta = \Phi^{-1}(\delta) \approx \frac{1}{1.702} \Psi^{-1}(\delta) = \frac{1}{1.702} \ln\left(\frac{\delta}{1-\delta}\right)$, respectively, where Φ is the normal cumulative distribution function and Ψ is the logistic function. This rescaling procedure can be performed using the syntax code in R provided in Appendix 6.1.

DSM-L: Rescaling of Item Parameters b_i and s_i

When DSM-L is used, the latent item parameters for *difficulty*, b_i, and *shape*, s_i, of test X are rescaled to $b^{\star}_i$ and $s^{\star}_i$ values, respectively, on the scale of test Y. Specifically, the rescaling of b_i is performed using the four-step algorithm for the rescaling of δ_i values, described here above, by simply replacing δ_i with b_i. The values of the shape parameter, s_i, are positive, but they can exceed 1, so this procedure cannot be applied directly for the rescaling of s_i values. The problem is solved by using a simple transformation "trick" that puts the transformed s_i values between 0 and 1, thus making it possible to use the four-step procedure for the rescaling of s_i. Specifically, this is done as follows (Dimitrov, 2022):

1. The transformation $t_i = \exp(-s_i)$ is used to make $0 < t_i < 1$.
2. The t_i values are rescaled to $t^{\star}_i$ values using the four-step procedure described earlier for the rescaling of δ_i values by replacing δ_i with t_i.
3. The rescaled values of s_i are obtained as follows: $s^{\star}_i = -\ln(t^{\star}_i)$.

The accuracy of rescaled $s^{\star}_i$ values was examined in a simulation study under a (3×3) design with three levels of difficulty for two tests X and Y and three ability levels for the respective two groups of examinees, with 5,000 observations per condition (Dimitrov, 2022). Specifically, the three levels of test difficulty, based on the average b_i value on the D-scale [0,1], are (a) *below average*: $\bar{b} = 0.4$, (b) *average*: $\bar{b} = 0.5$, and (c) *above average*: $\bar{b} = 0.6$. Likewise, the three ability levels are (a) *below average*: $\bar{D} = 0.4$, (b) *average*: $\bar{D} = 0.5$, and (c) *above average*: $\bar{D} = 0.6$. Estimates of "bias" for the rescaled $s^{\star}_i$ values across simulation conditions are provided in Table 6.1. The bias is practically negligible which lends support to the transformation-based procedure for rescaling of s_i values.

> **NOTE [6.1]** In statistics, "bias" refers to the systematic error associated with the estimation of a given parameter, π. If $\hat{\pi}_r$ are estimates of π obtained across R simulations ($r = 1, 2, ..., R$), the statistic for "bias" is computed as follows:
>
> $$\text{Bias}(\hat{\pi}) = \frac{\sum_{r=1}^{R}(\hat{\pi} - \pi)}{R}.$$

Table 6.1 Bias of rescaled values of the *shape* parameter, s_i, for simulated data under three ability levels of examinees and three difficulty levels of test items

Base group	Base test Y	New group	New test X	Bias	
				Mean	SD
$\bar{D} = 0.4$	$\bar{b} = 0.4$	$\bar{D} = 0.4$	$\bar{b} = 0.5$	0.00168	0.06555
$\bar{D} = 0.4$	$\bar{b} = 0.4$	$\bar{D} = 0.4$	$\bar{b} = 0.6$	−0.00028	0.06676
$\bar{D} = 0.5$	$\bar{b} = 0.4$	$\bar{D} = 0.5$	$\bar{b} = 0.5$	−0.00426	0.06747
$\bar{D} = 0.5$	$\bar{b} = 0.4$	$\bar{D} = 0.5$	$\bar{b} = 0.6$	0.00103	0.06744
$\bar{D} = 0.6$	$\bar{b} = 0.4$	$\bar{D} = 0.6$	$\bar{b} = 0.5$	−0.00297	0.07512
$\bar{D} = 0.4$	$\bar{b} = 0.6$	$\bar{D} = 0.6$	$\bar{b} = 0.6$	0.00080	0.07447
$\bar{D} = 0.4$	$\bar{b} = 0.4$	$\bar{D} = 0.5$	$\bar{b} = 0.4$	0.00248	0.06469
$\bar{D} = 0.4$	$\bar{b} = 0.4$	$\bar{D} = 0.6$	$\bar{b} = 0.4$	0.00069	0.06703
$\bar{D} = 0.4$	$\bar{b} = 0.5$	$\bar{D} = 0.5$	$\bar{b} = 0.5$	−0.00363	0.06929
$\bar{D} = 0.4$	$\bar{b} = 0.5$	$\bar{D} = 0.6$	$\bar{b} = 0.5$	−0.00126	0.06852
$\bar{D} = 0.4$	$\bar{b} = 0.6$	$\bar{D} = 0.5$	$\bar{b} = 0.6$	0.00064	0.07349
$\bar{D} = 0.4$	$\bar{b} = 0.5$	$\bar{D} = 0.6$	$\bar{b} = 0.6$	0.00169	0.06929

Equating of *D*-scores

Under the NEAT design, equating of *D*-scores is based on (a) rescaled δ_i values for the test items, when DSM-C is used, and (b) rescaled b_i and s_i values, when DSM-L is used. The respective procedures are described next.

Equating of Classical **D**-scores

In the framework of DSM-C, equating of classical *D*-scores, denoted D_w, is based on the principle of preequating which is used in IRT (e.g., Kolen and Brennan, 2004). Specifically, the equating of D_w scores on test X to $D_w^\star$ scores on the scale of test Y is performed as follows:

Step 1. The expected item difficulties, δ_i, of test X are rescaled to $\delta_i^\star$ values on the scale of test Y using the four-step procedure described in the previous section.

Step 2. The equated $D_w^\star$ scores are computed using the classical *D*-score formula (see Chapter 4, Equation 4.2) where δ_i is replaced with its rescaled value, $\delta_i^\star$; that is,

$$D_w^\star = \frac{\sum_{i=1}^{n} \delta_i^\star X_i}{\sum_{i=1}^{n} \delta_i^\star}, \tag{6.1}$$

where X_i is the person's binary (1/0) score on item *i*.

Equating of Latent **D**-scores

In DSM-L, the equating of latent *D*-scores on test X to $D^\star$ scores on the scale of test Y is performed using an approach developed by Dimitrov and Atanasov (2021). Under this approach, each latent *D*-score on test X is rescaled first at item level to a score $D_i^\star$ on the scale of test Y using that $P_i(D) = P_i(D_i^\star)$ (see Figure 6.1), that is:

$$P_i(D) = P_i(D_i^\star) = \frac{1}{1 + \left[\frac{b_i^\star(1-D_i^\star)}{D_i^\star(1-b_i^\star)}\right]^{s_i^\star}}, \tag{6.2}$$

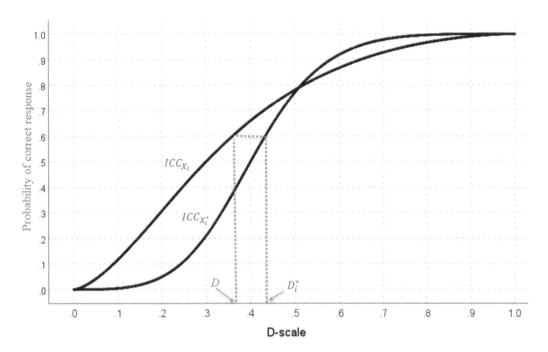

Figure 6.1 Item characteristic curves of an item in test X obtained before and after rescaling its parameters on the scale of test Y; (ICC_{X_i} prior to rescaling, and $ICC_{X_i^*}$ after rescaling).

After rescaling the D-score on test X to item-level equivalents, $D_i^{\star}$, for all n items, its equated $D^{\star}$ score on the scale of test Y is computed as the average of all $D_i^{\star}$ scores ($i = 1, \ldots, n$). The steps in the computational algorithm are as follows:

Step 1. Rescale the item parameters (b_i, s_i) of test X to their counterparts $(b_i^{\star}, s_i^{\star})$ on the scale of test Y using the rescaling procedure described in the previous section.

Step 2. Compute $P_i(D)$ and, using the rescaled $b_i^{\star}$, and $s_i^{\star}$ values, solve Equation 6.2 for $D_i^{\star}$ by first computing an intermediate ratio:

$$R_i = \frac{1 - P_i(D)}{P_i(D)} = \left[\frac{b_i^{\star}\left(1 - D_i^{\star}\right)}{D_i^{\star}\left(1 - b_i^{\star}\right)}\right]^{s_i^{\star}}. \tag{6.3}$$

and then find the solution as:

$$D_i^{\star} = \frac{b_i^{\star}}{b_i^{\star} + \left(1 - b_i^{\star}\right) R_i^{1/s_i^{\star}}}.$$

Step 3. After computing $D_i^{\star}$ for all n items, the equated $D^{\star}$ score on the scale of test Y is:

$$D^{\star} = \left(\frac{1}{n}\right) \sum_{i=1}^{n} D_i^{\star}. \tag{6.4}$$

Summary Points

1 *Equating of test scores* is a statistical procedure used to present the scores across test forms on a common scale so that they can be used interchangeably.
2 Under the NEAT design, (a) the two groups of examinees differ in ability levels and (b) the two tests differ in difficulty and contain a set of common (anchor) items.

3. In DSM-C, the rescaling of (nonlinearly related) δ_i values of the common items on two tests is based on their transformation to linearly related Z-scores under the standard normal distribution.
4. In DSM-L, the rescaling of the item parameters for *difficulty*, b_i, and *shape*, s_i, is based on the procedure for rescaling of δ_i values, upon a transformation of the shape parameter, $t_i = \exp(-s_i)$, to make $0 < t_i < 1$.
5. In DSM-C, the equating of D_w scores is based on the principle of preequating using the computation formula for D_w scores with the rescaled δ_i values.
6. In DSM-L, the equating of latent D-scores is performed via (a) rescaling the D-score on test X to item-level equivalents, $D_i^\star$ on the scale of test Y, and then (b) computing the rescaled D-score score as the average of $D_i^\star$ over all test items.

Appendix 6.1: R Code for Rescaling of Expected Item Difficulties

Step 1. Install the R packages listed in Chapter 4, Appendix 4.1 (Step 1).

Step 2. Run the following R code:

```
library("DScoring")


# Load the expected item difficulties ('deltas') of the base test
bt_deltas <- read.csv('base_test_deltas.csv',header = FALSE)


# Load the expected item difficulties ('deltas') of the new test
nt_deltas <- read.csv('new_test_deltas.csv',header = FALSE)


# Load the common items of the (base and new) tests
common <- read.csv('common.csv',header = FALSE)


# Compute the rescaling constants (A and B)
Const <- DS.equatingConstants(as.matrix(bt_deltas), as.matrix(nt_deltas),
as.matrix(common))
Const$A
Const$B


# Compute the rescaled 'deltas'
RescaledDeltas <- DS.equatingRescale(nt_deltas,Const)
RescaledDeltas
```

Notes:
1. There are three input (.csv) files in this application:
    "**base_test_deltas.csv**": consists of one column with the expected item difficulties (δ_{iY}) of the base test form, Y.
    "**new_test_deltas.csv**": consists of one column with the expected item difficulties (δ_{iX}) of the new test form, X, that have to be rescaled to the scale of the base test form, Y.
    "**common.csv**": consists of two columns with the location numbers of the common items in the base test (first column) and the new test (second column).
2. The rescaled values of the expected item difficulties of test form X (δ_{iX}) are exported in a (.csv) file named "**rescaled_delta.csv**".
3. The R code is provided also at https://github.com/amitko/Dscoring (folder: "samples/EQUATE").

References

Dimitrov, D. M. (2022). *DSM estimation and rescaling: Highlights and new procedures*. Research Report 03-2022. Riyadh, Saudi Arabia: National Center for Assessment at ETEC.

Dimitrov, D. M., & Atanasov, D. V. (2021). An approach to test equating under the latent D-scoring method. *Measurement: Interdisciplinary Research and Perspectives, 19*(3), 153–162.

Guo, F., Rudner, L., & Talento-Miller, E. (2009). *Scaling item difficulty estimates from nonequivalent groups*. GMAC R Research Report RR-09-03. Graduate Management Admission Council.

Hambleton, R. K., & Swaminathan, H. (1985). *Item response theory: Principles and applications*. Hingham, MA: Kluwer, Nijhoff.

Hambleton, R. K., Swaminathan, H., & Rogers, H. J. (1991). *Fundamentals of item response theory*. Newbury Park, CA: Sage.

Kolen, M. J., & Brennan, R. L. (2004). *Test equating, scaling, and linking: Methods and practice* (2nd ed.). New-York: Springer-Verlag.

Lord, F. M. (1980). *Applications of item response theory to practical testing problems*. Hillsdale, NJ: Erlbaum Publishers.

Marco, G. L. (1977). Item characteristic solution to three intractable testing problems. *Journal of Educational Measurement, 14*, 139–160.

7 Item and Person Fit

Testing for Item Fit

The evaluation of *item fit* is based on information about how closely the observed item responses "fit" their predicted values under an item response function (IRF) model. Item fit statistics in the context of IRT are discussed in Chapter 2. Such statistics, especially those involving chi-square distributions, are not directly applicable in the context of DSM due to IRT-DSM differences in IRF models (e.g., 2PL vs. RFM2) and type of scales (unlimited logit scale vs. bounded D-scale).

A couple of simulation studies on item fit in the context of DSM have examined the performance of item fit statistics which do not rely on distributional properties of the D-scores, such as *mean absolute difference* (MAD), *mean absolute error* (MAE), and *root-mean-square error* (RMSE) (e.g., Alqabbaa, 2021; Dimitrov & Luo, 2017).

The MAD, MAE, and RMSE statistics involve the probability of correct item response estimated via the respective IRF model in DSM (e.g., RFM2; see Chapter 5, Equation 5.1). These statistics quantify the discrepancy between empirical and model-based estimates of the probability of correct item response. Specifically:

$$\text{MAD}_i = \frac{\sum_{s=1}^{N} |X_{si} - P_{si}|}{N}, \tag{7.1}$$

where X_{si} is the binary (1/0) score of person s on item i, P_{si} is the person's probability of correct response on item i, and N is the number of persons who took the test.

$$\text{MAE}_i = \frac{\sum_{h=1}^{H} |O_{hi} - P_{hi}|}{H}, \tag{7.2}$$

where H is the number of *bins* (intervals) that cover the range of the D-scale (from 0 to 1), O_{hi} is the observed proportion of correct responses on item i for the examinees with D scores in bin h, and P_{hi} is the average probability of correct item response for the examinees with D scores in bin h. (This probability is estimated via the respective RFM, where the D-score is the midpoint of bin h.) Typically, the D-scale is divided into 10 bins ($n = 10$), with the range of each bin equal to 0.1, but other approaches to "binning" can be used to ensure enough examinees in each bin.

$$\text{RMSE}_i = \sqrt{\frac{\sum_{h=1}^{H}(O_{hi} - P_{hi})^2}{H}}, \tag{7.3}$$

where H, O_{hi}, and P_{hi} have the same meaning as with Equation 7.2.

In Equation 7.1 for MAD, $|X_{si} - P_{si}|$ is the absolute difference (residual) between the observed and expected item scores for each person. In Equation 7.2 for MAE, $|O_{hi} - P_{hi}|$ is the absolute difference (residual) associated with bin h ($h = 1, 2, \ldots, H$); that is, MAE is the mean of absolute errors. On the other hand, as shown in Equation 7.3, RMSE is the square root of the average of squared errors, thus confounding information about the average error with information about variation in the errors.

Based on a simulation study, Dimitrov and Luo (2017) found that the MAD statistic performed slightly better than the MAE and RSME statistics and recommended criteria for (a) *adequate fit* (type I error < 0.05), if MAD ≤ 0.07; (b) *tolerable fit*, if 0.07 < MAD < 0.10; and (c) *poor fit*, if MAD ≥ 0.10. Alqabbaa (2021) found that MAE and RSME in the context of DSM demonstrated similar results compared to their performance in the context of IRT.

Testing for Person Fit

In general, testing for *person fit* refers to statistical procedures used to evaluate the fit of a person's response pattern to the IRF model. In the context of IRT, two widely used person-fit statistics are presented in Chapter 2—the IRT-based Z3 statistic (Drasgow, Levin, & McLaughlin, 1987; Levine & Drasgow, 1988) and the nonparametric H^T statistic (Sijtsma, 1986). Dimitrov, Atanasov, and Luo (2020) modified the following two statistics to make them usable in the context of DSM: (a) the Z3 statistic, modified as Zd statistic, and (b) the U3 statistic (van der Flier, 1980, 1982), modified as Ud statistic. It was found that Zd and Ud are very efficient and perform better than U3 and H^T in detecting misfitting response patterns associated with simulated "guessing" and "cheating."

Zd *Person-Fit Statistic*

The Zd person-fit statistic is a modification of the IRT-based Z3 statistic. Specifically, the building element in the IRT-based formula for Z3 (see Chapter 2, Equation 2.35) is the probability of correct response $P_i(\hat{\theta}_s)$ of person s on item i, estimated via an IRT model. The modification of Z3 consists of replacing $P_i(\hat{\theta}_s)$ with DSM-based probability $P_i(\hat{D}_s)$ on the D-scale in the analytic terms of the Z3 formula (see Chapter 2, Equations 2.36–2.38). The resulting formula for Zd is:

$$Zd = \frac{l_0 - E(l_0 \mid \hat{D}_s)}{\left[\text{VAR}(l_0 \mid \hat{D}_s)\right]^{1/2}}, \tag{7.4}$$

where $\hat{D}_s$ is an estimate of the latent ability of person s on the D-scale, l_0 is the natural logarithm of the likelihood for the response pattern at $\hat{D}_s$, and $\text{VAR}(l_0 \mid \hat{D}_s)$ is the conditional variance of l_0 at $\hat{D}_s$. For a test of n binary items, l_0 is estimated through the equation:

$$l_0 = \sum_{i=1}^{n} \left\{ X_{si} \ln P_i(\hat{D}_s) + (1 - X_{si}) \ln\left[1 - P_i(\hat{D}_s)\right] \right\} \tag{7.5}$$

where X_{si} is the binary (1/0) score of person s on item i.

The expected value of l_0 is estimated as:

$$E(l_0 \mid \hat{D}_s) = \sum_{i=1}^{n} \left\{ P_i(\hat{D}_s) \ln P_i(\hat{D}_s) + \left[1 - P_i(\hat{D}_s)\right] \ln\left[1 - P_i(\hat{D}_s)\right] \right\}, \tag{7.6}$$

and the conditional variance of l_0 is estimated as:

$$\text{VAR}(l_0 \mid \hat{D}_s) = \sum_{i=1}^{n} P_i(\hat{D}_s)\left[1 - P_i(D_s)\right] \left[\ln \frac{P_i(\hat{D}_s)}{1 - P_i(D)}\right]^2. \tag{7.7}$$

Deterministic Guttman Model

The U3 statistic (van der Flier, 1980, 1982) and its DSM modification Ud, presented next, are defined under the *deterministic Guttman model* (Guttman, 1944, 1950) which states that:

$$(\theta_s < \delta_i) \leftrightarrow (P_{si} = 0) \text{ and } (\theta_s \geq \delta_i) \leftrightarrow (P_{si} = 1), \tag{7.8}$$

where P_{si} is the probability of correct response on item i with difficulty δ_i by person s with ability θ_s; ($i = 1, \ldots, n$; $s = 1, 2, \ldots, N$). Note that δ_i is item "difficulty" (not "easiness"); that is, if π_i is item "easiness" (proportion of correct item responses for the population), then $\delta_i = 1 - \pi_i$. Suppose that the items are ordered by difficulty (from easiest to most difficult) and the person's ability is greater than the difficulties of the first r items: $\delta_1 \leq \delta_2 \leq \ldots \leq \delta_r < \theta_s \leq \delta_{r+1} \ldots \leq \delta_n$. Under the deterministic Guttman model, the expected response pattern, referred to as *Guttman pattern* (GP), is a pattern with correct responses ($X = 1$) on the first r items and incorrect responses ($X = 0$) on the remaining ($n - r$) items. Conversely, a response pattern with incorrect responses on the first ($n - r$) items and correct responses on the last r items is called *reversed Guttman pattern* (RGP; Meijer & Sijtsma, 2001).

U3 *Person-Fit Statistic*

Van der Flier (1980, 1982) proposed a person-fit statistic U3 that measures the extent of fit between an observed response pattern and the expected *Guttman pattern* (GP):

$$U3 = \frac{\ln P(\mathbf{GP}) - \ln(\mathbf{X})}{\ln P(\mathbf{GP}) - \ln P(\mathbf{RGP})}, \tag{7.9}$$

where $\mathbf{X} = (X_1, X_2, \ldots, X_n)$ is the person's observed response pattern of item scores X_i (1/0), **GP** is the expected Guttman pattern for that person, **RGP** is the reversed Guttman pattern, and $\ln P(.)$ is the natural logarithm of the probability of the respective response pattern (**X**, **GP**, or **RGP**). The values of U3 can vary from 0 to 1, with U3 = 0 indicating perfect fit of the observed response pattern to the Guttman pattern (**X** = **GP**), and U3 = 1 indicating their total misfit (**X** = **RGP**). The closer U3 gets to 1, the higher the aberrance of the observed response vector **X** from the expected Guttman pattern.

For a person with r correct responses on a test of n binary items, Equation 7.9 for U3 becomes:

$$U3 = \frac{\sum_{i=1}^{r} \ln\left(\frac{\pi_i}{1-\pi_i}\right) - \sum_{i=1}^{n} X_i \ln\left(\frac{\pi_i}{1-\pi_i}\right)}{\sum_{i=1}^{r} \ln\left(\frac{\pi_i}{1-\pi_i}\right) - \sum_{i=n-r+1}^{n} \ln\left(\frac{\pi_i}{1-\pi_i}\right)}, \tag{7.10}$$

where π_i is estimated with the proportion of correct responses on item i for the persons who took the test (van der Flier, 1982, p. 295).

Ud *Person-Fit Statistic*

The Ud statistic is a modification of the U3 statistic for person fit under the DSM (Dimitrov et al., 2020). This modification consists of replacing π_i in Equation 7.10 with the probability of correct item response estimated under the two-parameter model, RFM2 (see Chapter 5, Equation 5.1). The computation of Ud is performed in three steps. First, the person's ability and item difficulty in the deterministic Guttman model are estimated under the RFM2. Second, under the ascending order of items by their location on the D-scale (item difficulty, b_i), the GP and RGP are based on the ordering $b_1 \leq b_2 \leq \ldots \leq b_r < D_s \leq b_{r+1} \ldots \leq b_n$. Third, Ud is computed via Equation 7.10, where π_i is replaced with the probability of correct item response estimated under the DSM model on the D-scale.

Zd *and* Ud *Cutoff Values*

There are different approaches to setting cutoff values of person-fit statistics for decisions on fit/misfit of response patterns (e.g., for a review, see Mousavi, Cui, & Rogers, 2019). As the theoretical distributions of the statistics Ud and Zd (as well as those of Z3, U3, and $s_i^\star$) are unknown, the setting of cutoff values is based on percentile ranks of

> **NOTE [7.1]** The three-parameter model, RFM3, is *not* appropriate for the computation of Ud because the ordering of item difficulties, s_i, is *not* valid under the RFM3, unless the pseudo-guessing parameter, $s_i^\star = -\ln\left(t_i^\star\right)$, is fixed to a prespecified value (e.g., see Chapter 5, NOTE [5.1]).

their empirical sampling distributions from simulated fitting responses. Such an approach, referred to as *quantile method*, was used by Dimitrov et al. (2020) in a simulation study with five conditions: (a) *type of response behavior*: guessing and cheating; (b) *sample size*: 1,000, 3,000, and 10,000 persons; (c) *test length*: 20, 40, and 80 items; (d) *percent misfitting items*: the most difficult 20%, 30%, and 40% of the items; and (e) *percent misfitting persons*: 20%, 30%, and 40%. Data were simulated over 500 replications per each combination of condition levels. Each data set consists of binary (1/0) scores generated under the RFM2 model on the D-scale. The results led to the identification of cutoff values for Zd and Ud as follows:

a   misfit (most likely due to guessing) is signaled if $Ud > 0.20$ and/or $Zd < -0.20$, and
b   misfit (most likely due to cheating) is signaled if $Ud > 0.30$ and/or $Zd < -2.00$.

Summary Points

1. The evaluation of *item fit* is based on information about how closely the observed item responses "fit" their predicted values under an item response function (IRF) model.
2. The item fit statistics MAD, MAE, and RMSE quantify the discrepancy between empirical and model-based estimates of the probability of correct item response.
3. The MAD statistic, which performed slightly better than MAE and RSME, is used to signal item fit/misfit under the following classification: (a) *adequate fit*: MAD ≤ 0.07, (b) *tolerable fit*: $0.07 <$ MAD < 0.10, and (c) *poor fit*: MAD ≥ 0.10.
4. Testing for *person fit* refers to statistical procedures used to evaluate the fit of a person's response pattern to the IRF model.
5. The Zd person-fit statistic, which is a modification of the IRT-based $Z3$ statistic, evaluates the discrepancy between the likelihood of a response pattern and its expected value on the D-scale.
6. The Ud statistic, which is a modification of the $U3$ statistic, evaluates the discrepancy between a response pattern and the Guttman response pattern. The values of Ud vary from 0 to 1, with (a) $Ud = 0$ indicating that the person's response pattern is exactly a Guttman pattern (i.e., perfect fit) and (b) $Ud = 1$ indicating that the person's response pattern is a reverse Guttman pattern (i.e., total misfit).
7. Using the Zd and Ud statistics, a workable empirical rule is that they signal (a) misfit, most likely due to guessing, if $Ud > 0.20$ and/or $Zd < -0.20$, and (b) misfit, most likely due to cheating, if $Ud > 0.30$ and/or $Zd < -2.00$.

References

Alqabbaa, M. (2021). *A Comparison between the use of latent D-Scoring method models and item response theory models with respect to item fit and person recovery parameter*. ProQuest Dissertations Publishing. https://www.proquest.com/
Dimitrov, D. M., Atanasov, D. V., & Luo, Y. (2020). Person-fit assessment under the D-scoring method. *Measurement: Interdisciplinary Research and Perspectives, 18*(3), 111–123.
Dimitrov, D. M., & Luo, Y. (2017). *Testing for item fit under the D-scoring model* (Research report RR-11-2017). Riyadh, Saudi Arabia: National Center for Assessment at ETEC.
Drasgow, F. Levin, M. V., & McLaughlin, M. E. (1987). Detecting inappropriate test scores with optimal and practical appropriateness indices. *Applied Psychological Measurement, 11*, 59–79.
Guttman, L. (1944). A basis for scaling qualitative data. *American Sociological Review, 9*, 139–150.
Guttman, L. (1950). The basis for scalogram analysis. In S.A. Stouffer, L. Guttman, E.A. Suchman, P.F., Lazarsfeld, S.A. Star, & J.A. Claussen (Eds.), *Measurement and prediction* (pp. 60–90). Princeton, NJ: Princeton University Press.
Levine, M. V., & Drasgow, F. (1988). Optimal appropriateness measurement. *Psychometrika, 53*, 161–176.
Meijer, R. R., & Sijtsma, K. (2001). Methodology review: Evaluating person fit. *Applied Psychological Measurement, 25*(2), 107–135.
Mousavi, A., Cui, Y., & Rogers, T. (2019). An examination of different methods of setting cutoff values in person fit research. *International Journal of Testing, 19*(1), 1–22.
Sijtsma, K. (1986). A coefficient of deviant response patterns. *Kwantitative Methoden, 7*, 131–145.
van der Flier, H. (1980). *Vergelijkbaarheid van individuele test prestaties [Comparability of individual test performance]*. Lisse, the Netherlands: Swets & Zeitlinger.
van der Flier, H. (1982). Deviant response patterns and comparability of test scores. *Journal of Cross Cultural Psychology, 13*, 267–298.

8 DSM Testing for Differential Item/Test Functioning

Introduction

Differential item functioning (DIF) occurs when respondents from different groups, but with the same level of ability measured by the test, differ in chances to endorse the response categories of the item. Testing for DIF of test items plays a key role in the examination of validity and fairness of assessments. In the context of IRT, testing for DIF is addressed in Chapter 2. Most approaches to testing for DIF in IRT are based on the discrepancy between the item characteristic curves (ICCs) of two groups—a majority group called *reference group* and a minority group, against which DIF is suspected, called *focal group*. Two types of DIF may occur: (a) *uniform* DIF—the ICCs of the two groups do *not* cross, and (b) *nonuniform* DIF—the ICCs of the two groups cross. Testing for DIF in the framework of the DSM is similar to testing for DIF in IRT in the sense that in both cases, the evaluation of DIF is based on the discrepancy between the IRFs of the reference and focal groups (e.g., Dimitrov, 2017; Raju, van der Linden, & Fleer, 1995). However, differences between the DSM- and IRT-based modeling do not allow for the direct application of IRT-based DIF statistics in the DSM context. For example, popular DIF indices in IRT, such as the compensatory DIF (CDIF) and noncompensatory DIF (NCDIF) indices (Raju et al., 1995), are derived via integrations of IRF differences over the range $(-\infty, +\infty)$ of the IRT logit scale, and therefore, such indices are not valid over the restricted range of the D-scale.

P–Z Method of Testing for DIF

Dimitrov and Atanasov (2022) proposed an approach to testing for DIF in the context of DSM referred to as *P–Z method* of testing for DIF. The results from their simulation study showed that the *P–Z* method performs very well on two key criteria in DIF testing—low Type I error (false positive) rate and high power on detecting DIF. Under the *P–Z* method, the probabilities of correct item response, P, of two groups are compared after converting them into Z-scale normal deviates (hence the name "*P–Z* method"). Specifically, testing for DIF is addressed by testing the null hypothesis:

$$H_o : P_{iR}(D) = P_{iF}(D), \tag{8.1}$$

where $P_{iR}(D)$ and $P_{iF}(D)$ are the probabilities of correct item response on item i for examinees in the *reference* (R) group and *focal* (F) group, respectively, who have the same ability level, D. DIF is signaled when H_o is rejected at a prespecified level of significance (e.g., 0.05). Conversely, there is *no* DIF when H_o is retained; that is, the ICCs of the two groups do not differ over the D-scale. As linear relationship between $P_{iR}(D)$ and $P_{iF}(D)$ is *not* assumed, the testing of H_o is performed by converting these probabilities into linearly related Z-scale normal deviates $Z_{iR}(D)$ and $Z_{iF}(D)$, respectively. Thus, H_o in Equation 8.1 translates into the following null hypothesis:

$$H_o : Z_{iR}(D) = Z_{iF}(D), \tag{8.2}$$

where $Z_{iR}(D)$ and $Z_{iF}(D)$ are linearly related. That is (omitting D for convenience):

$$Z_{iR} = A.Z_{iF} + B, \tag{8.3}$$

where the coefficients A and B represent the *slope* and *intercept*, respectively, of a straight line depicting the linear relationship.

DOI: 10.4324/9781003343004-8

Clearly, H_o in Equation 8.2 holds only when $A = 1$ and $B = 0$. Thus, testing for H_o is tantamount to testing the following pair of null hypotheses:

$$H_{0A}: A = 1 \text{ and } H_{0B}: B = 0. \tag{8.4}$$

By taking the variance and the mean of the terms on both sides of Equation 8.3, we obtain:

$$A = \frac{\sigma^2_{Z_{iR}}}{\sigma^2_{Z_{iF}}} \tag{8.5}$$

and

$$B = \mu_{Z_{iR}} - A . \mu_{Z_{iF}}. \tag{8.6}$$

Thus, H_{0A} and H_{0B} in Equation 8.4 hold simultaneously only when the following two null hypotheses hold simultaneously:

$$H_{0A}: \sigma^2_{Z_{iR}} = \sigma^2_{Z_{iF}} \tag{8.7}$$

and

$$H_{0B}: \mu_{Z_{iR}} = \mu_{Z_{iF}}. \tag{8.8}$$

In this way, testing for DIF is reduced to two routine statistical tests: (a) testing for equal variances, H_{0A}, and (b) testing for equal means, H_{0B}. Popular statistical packages provide both the F-statistic for H_{0A} and t-statistic for H_{0B}, with their p-values, under the statistical test for comparing the means of two independent samples. The following three scenarios may occur. First, H_{0A} is rejected (i.e., $A \neq 1$), which indicates the presence of *nonuniform* DIF. In this case, there is no need to proceed with testing H_{0B}. Second, H_{0A} is not rejected (i.e., $A = 1$) but H_{0B} is rejected, which indicates the presence of *uniform* DIF. Third, both H_{0A} and H_{0B} are retained, which indicates that there is *no* DIF.

The case of *nonuniform* DIF is illustrated in Figure 8.1, where the ICCs of the reference and focal groups cross and the DIF is (a) against the focal group, for examinees with ability score $D < 0.65$, and (b) against the reference group, for examinees with ability score $D > 0.65$. The linear relationship between the corresponding Z-scores

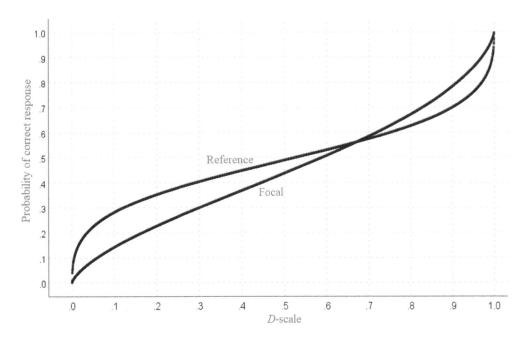

Figure 8.1 Nonuniform DIF—the ICCs of the reference and focal groups cross and the DIF is against (a) the focal group, for examinees with ability score $D < 0.65$, and (b) the reference group, for examinees with ability score $D > 0.65$.

(see Equation 8.3) is depicted in Figure 8.2. Clearly, the straight line of the relationship between Z_{iR} and Z_{iF} does not have a slope of 1 ($A \neq 1$) because it is not parallel to (or coincide with) the bisecting dotted line, which has a slope of 1.

The case of *uniform* DIF is illustrated in Figure 8.3, where the ICCs do not cross and the DIF is entirely against the focal group. In Figure 8.4, the corresponding straight line for the relationship between Z_{iR} and Z_{iF} is parallel to the bisecting dotted line (i.e., $A = 1$) but they do not coincide (i.e., $B \neq 0$). Note that if there is *no* DIF, the straight line of the relationship between Z_{iR} and Z_{iF} will coincide with the bisecting dotted line ($A = 1$ and $B = 0$).

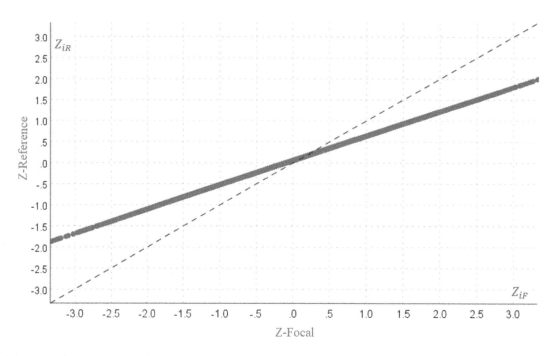

Figure 8.2 Nonuniform DIF—Z-scale normal deviates of the ICCs of the reference and focal groups depicted in Figure 8.1.

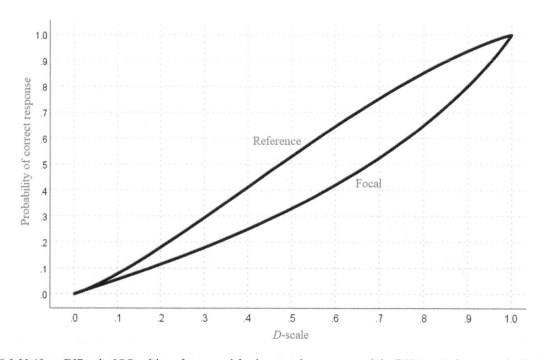

Figure 8.3 Uniform DIF—the ICCs of the reference and focal groups do not cross and the DIF is entirely against the focal group.

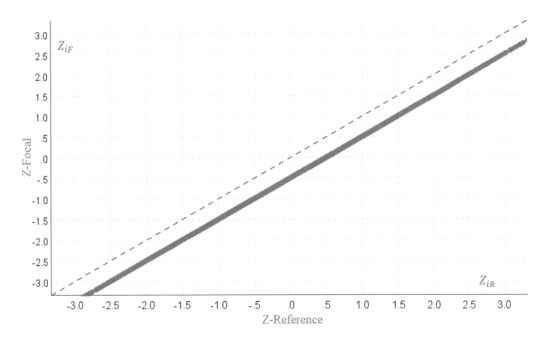

Figure 8.4 Uniform DIF—Z-scale normal deviates of the ICCs of the reference and focal groups depicted in Figure 8.3.

Computations associated with testing for DIF under the *P–Z* method are provided in steps, assuming that a test of *n* dichotomously scored items has been administered to a sample of examinees that belong to two (reference and focal) groups.

Step 1. The test items are calibrated separately for each group using a DSM model (say, RFM2; see Chapter 5, Equation 5.1).

Step 2. The item parameters for the reference group (b_{iR}, s_{iR}) and focal group (b_{iF}, s_{iF}) are presented on a common scale—e.g., using the procedure for rescaling of item parameters described in Chapter 6, with all test items treated as common items because the same test is administered to both groups.

Step 3. The probabilities of correct item responses (ICCs) of the respective item, *i*, are computed separately for the reference and focal groups (P_{iR} and P_{iF}, respectively) using their item parameters (b_{iR}, s_{iR}) and (b_{iF}, s_{iF}) after presenting them on a common scale (via Step 2).

Step 4. The Z_{iR} and Z_{iF} values corresponding to P_{iR} and P_{iF}, respectively, are computed using the formula for Z-score normal deviate, Z, of a probability *P*:

$$Z = \frac{1}{1.702} \ln\left(\frac{P}{1-P}\right), \tag{8.9}$$

where ln(.) denotes the natural logarithm.

Step 5. Given the Z_{iR} and Z_{iF} values, the null hypothesis for equal variances of two independent samples is tested: $H_{0A} : \sigma^2_{Z_{iR}} = \sigma^2_{Z_{iF}}$.

Step 6. If the null hypothesis H_{0A} (at Step 5) is retained at the prespecified level of significance (e.g., 0.05), then the null hypothesis for equal means is tested: $H_{0B} : \mu_{Z_{iR}} = \mu_{Z_{iF}}$.

NOTE [8.1] The procedures needed in *Step 5* (e.g., Levene's test for *equal variances*) and *Step 6* (Student's *t*-test for *equal means*) are described in books on basic statistics and implemented in popular software packages for statistical data analysis.

Differential Test Functioning

Differential test functioning (DTF), referred to also as *test bias*, occurs when the entire test is functioning differentially against a specific group (e.g., focal group). The P–Z method of testing for DIF is directly applicable to testing for DTF. In this case, instead of using the probabilities P_{iR} and P_{iF}, their averaged values over the entire set of n test items, P_{TR} and P_{TF}, respectively, are computed, that is,

$$P_{TR} = \frac{1}{n}\sum_{i=1}^{n} P_{iR} \tag{8.10}$$

and

$$P_{TF} = \frac{1}{n}\sum_{i=1}^{n} P_{iF}. \tag{8.11}$$

After transforming the probabilities P_{TR} and P_{TF} to Z-scale normal deviates, Z_{TR} and Z_{TF}, respectively, the testing for DTF is performed by testing the following null hypotheses

$$H_{0A}^{T}: \sigma_{Z_{TR}}^{2} = \sigma_{Z_{TF}}^{2} \quad \text{and} \quad H_{0B}^{T}: \mu_{Z_{TR}} = \mu_{Z_{TF}}. \tag{8.12}$$

The decision on DTF is (a) *nonuniform* DTF, if H_{0A}^{T} is rejected (the test characteristic curves of the reference and focal groups cross), (b) *uniform* DTF, if H_{0A}^{T} is retained and H_{0B}^{T} is rejected (the test characteristic curves of the two groups are different but do not cross), and (c) there is *no* DTF, if both H_{0A}^{T} and H_{0B}^{T} are retained (the test characteristic curves of the two groups coincide). Note also that DTF may not be signaled even in the presence of DIF for some items due to a certain "cancelation" of their DIF effects.

Effect Size for DIF and DTF

The computation and report of effect size for DIF are recommended for interpretation and decisions (retain or remove) on DIF items (e.g., DeMars, 2011; Nye & Drasgow, 2011). An *effect size* of DIF (or DTF) can be computed using the Cohen's effect size index, h, for the difference between two proportions, h (Cohen, 1988, p. 181):

$$h = 2\arcsin\sqrt{P_1} - 2\arcsin\sqrt{P_2}, \tag{8.13}$$

where $P_1 > P_2$.

When applied to DIF, the effect size h is computed over an interval, referred to hereafter as *h-interval*, where the item response function (IRF) of one group is consistently above the IRF of the other group. In the case of uniform DIF, the *h*-interval is the entire D-scale interval [0,1]. In the case of nonuniform DIF, there are two (or more) *h*-intervals in each of which the IRF of one group is consistently above the IRF of the other group. Thus, h is a "noncompensatory" effect size of DIF over *h*-interval(s)—the entire D-scale [0,1] or subintervals of the scale. The steps in computing an effect size h are as follows:

Step 1. Identify the *h*-interval for the computation of h.
Step 2. Compute the average value of probabilities of correct item response over the *h*-interval for the reference and focal groups, $\bar{P}_{iR}$ and $\bar{P}_{iF}$, respectively.
Step 3. Compute h using Equation 8.13, replacing P_1 with the larger value of $\bar{P}_{iR}$ and $\bar{P}_{iF}$, and P_2 with the smaller value of $\bar{P}_{iR}$ and $\bar{P}_{iF}$.

When applied to differential functioning of the entire test (DTF), the effect size h is computed in the same way using the *test response functions* (TRFs) of the reference and focal groups. In this case, the *h*-interval is an interval where the TRF of one group is consistently above the TRF of the other group— (a) the entire D-scale interval [0,1], in case of uniform DTF, or (b) a subinterval of the D-scale, in case of nonuniform DTF. Based on empirical analyses, Dimitrov (2022) suggested "rule of thumb" cutoffs for the classification of *h*-based effect size for DIF (or DTF): (a) *small*: $h \leq 0.1$, (b) *medium*: $0.1 < h < 0.2$, and (c) *large*: $h \geq 0.2$.

Some Practical Notes

It should be emphasized that DIF decisions on individual items (e.g., keep or remove them) should be based on a joint examination of P–Z test results, a graphical depiction of the IRFs for the reference and focal groups on a common scale, the effect size of DIF, and the purpose of testing for DIF. Flagging a test item based only on hypothesis testing is not a sufficient evidence to remove the test item (e.g., DeMars, 2011; Meade, 2010; Nye & Drasgow, 2011; Oshima, Raju, & Nanda, 2006). Furthermore, cancellations of DIF effects may occur (a) within individual items with nonuniform DIF, and/or (b) between items, some with DIF against the reference group and some others with DIF against the focal group. Cancelations of DIF can be practically useful if the goal is to minimize the differential functioning at the test level (e.g., see Stark, Chernyshenko, & Drasgow, 2006). However, this can be seen as a limitation if the DIF cancelation of some items is "hiding" information that is of interest to the researcher (e.g., "absolute" DTF).

Example 8.1

This real-data example illustrates a joint examination of pieces of DIF information that can be useful in reports and decisions on DIF. Specifically, testing for DIF on gender (references group = males, focal group = females) was performed using the computer program DELTA (Atanasov & Dimitrov, 2018). DELTA output results related to testing for DIF, based on the P–Z method, are shown in Table 8.1 for a set of 20 items. The DIF code in this table is interpreted as follows: 0 = No DIF, 1 = *nonuniform* DIF, and 2 = *uniform* DIF. For example, nonuniform DIF is signaled for item (question) "Q10" due to statistically significant F-statistic for the null hypothesis H_{0A} ($F = 4.83172$, $p = 0.00041$). For this item, the t-statistic for H_{0B} is not reported (NA) because there is no need to test H_{0B} when H_{0A} is rejected. On the other hand, uniform DIF is signaled for item "Q3" due to statistically significant t-statistic for H_{0B} ($t = -2.10576$, $p = 0.03942$); that is, H_{0A} is retained, but H_{0B} is rejected.

Another piece of DIF information, reported in the output of the computer program DELTA, consists of two types of figures for each item. The first type shows the ICCs of the two groups. For the two DIF items in Table 8.1, for example, the ICCs of item "Q10" are shown in Figure 8.1, and the ICCs of item "Q3" are shown in Figure 8.3. The second type of figure is depicting the difference between the ICCs of the two groups, $|P_{iR} - P_{iF}|$, over the h-interval(s) and shows the effect size of DIF for each h-interval. This is illustrated in Figure 8.5 for item "Q10" with DIF (a) against the focal group (females) over the ability interval (0, 0.65), with a medium effect size ($ES = 0.180$), and (b) against the reference group (males) over the ability interval (0.65, 1), with a small effect size ($ES = 0.096$). Provided also is the *mean probability difference* (MPD) between the ICCs over the two h-intervals.

It would be also useful to report DIF information as shown in Table 8.2, where the D-scale is divided into six ability levels, from "very low" ($0 \leq D \leq 0.2$) to "very high" ($0.8 \leq D \leq 1$), and the level of DIF (small, medium, or high) against the respective group is specified over these intervals.

Table 8.1 Testing for DIF via the P–Z method

Item label	DIF code	H_{0A}		H_{0B}	
		F-statistic	p-value	t-statistic	p-value
Q1	0	0.63209	0.21480	−1.33940	0.18549
Q2	0	1.07014	0.85393	−0.15178	0.87987
Q3	2	0.66098	0.26249	**−2.10576**	0.03942
Q4	0	1.18792	0.64021	−0.84875	0.39939
Q5	0	0.70456	0.34279	−1.76090	0.08335
Q6	0	1.50159	0.27118	−0.28124	0.77950
Q7	0	1.22389	0.58353	0.21796	0.82820
Q8	0	1.16838	0.67271	−0.33115	0.74169
Q9	0	0.72902	0.39167	−0.10523	0.91654
Q10	1	**4.83172**	**0.00041**	NaN	NaN
Q11	0	0.75688	0.45007	−0.22534	0.82248
Q12	0	0.93566	0.85667	0.02225	0.98232
Q13	0	0.99288	0.98452	−0.09933	0.92120
Q14	0	1.60381	0.20157	0.03512	0.97210
Q15	0	0.86664	0.69759	0.21314	0.83194
Q16	0	1.32998	0.43942	−1.24369	0.21845
Q17	0	0.50245	0.06411	−1.09417	0.27825
Q18	0	0.72909	0.39181	0.12456	0.90129
Q19	0	0.78520	0.51185	−1.12450	0.26528
Q20	0	1.20387	0.61457	−0.19600	0.84527

Note: Given in bold are items with statistically significant (F or t) values ($p < 0.05$).

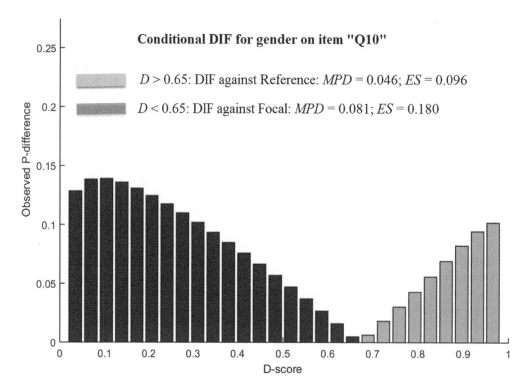

Figure 8.5 Nonuniform DIF (depicted in Figures 8.1 and 8.2) with estimates of (a) *MPD* = mean probability difference, and (b) *ES* = effect size.

Table 8.2 Regions of DIF (and its effect size) over the D-scale

DIF item	Ability level					
	Very low $0 \leq D \leq 0.2$	*Low* $0.2 < D < 0.4$	*Below average* $0.4 \leq D \leq 0.5$	*Above average* $0.5 \leq D \leq 0.6$	*High* $0.6 < D < 0.8$	*Very high* $0.8 \leq D \leq 1$
DIF against						
Q3	Females: *ES* = 0.268					
Q10	Females: *ES* = 0.180					Males: *ES* = 0.096

Note: Shaded are *h*-intervals with DIF against the focal group (females).

Summary Points

1 DIF occurs when respondents from different groups, but with the same level of ability measured by the test, differ in chances to endorse the respective response categories of the item.
2 Testing for DIF plays a key role in the examination of validity and fairness of assessments.
3 Two types of DIF may occur: (a) *uniform* DIF—the ICCs of the two groups do *not* cross, and (b) *nonuniform* DIF—the ICCs of the two groups cross.
4 In testing for DIF, the null hypothesis is that the ICCs of the reference and focal groups coincide over the D-scale, $H_o : P_{iR}(D) = P_{iF}(D)$. The presence of DIF is signaled when H_o is rejected at a prespecified level of significance (e.g., 0.05).
5 Under the P–Z method of testing for DIF, the (nonlinearly related) ICC probabilities of the reference and focal groups are transformed into (linearly related) Z-scores on the standard normal distribution scale, and thus, the null hypothesis becomes $H_o : Z_{iR}(D) = Z_{iF}(D)$.

6 Using the linear relationship $Z_{iR} = A.Z_{iF} + B$, the testing of $H_o : Z_{iR}(D) = Z_{iF}(D)$ is reduced to two basic statistical tests for independent samples: (a) *equal variances*, $H_{0A} : \sigma^2_{Z_{iR}} = \sigma^2_{Z_{iF}}$, and (b) *equal means*, $H_{0B} : \mu_{Z_{iR}} = \mu_{Z_{iF}}$.
7 Three outcomes of testing for DIF may occur: (a) *no* DIF, when both H_{0A} and H_{0B} are retained; (b) *nonuniform* DIF, when H_{0A} is rejected; in this case, there is no need to test for H_{0B}; and (c) *uniform* DIF, when H_{0A} is retained and H_{0B} is rejected.
8 *Differential test functioning* (DTF) occurs when the entire test is functioning differentially against a specific group. The P–Z method of testing for DIF is directly applicable to testing for DTF by replacing the probabilities P_{iR} and P_{iF} with their averaged values over the entire set of test items, P_{TR} and P_{TF}, respectively.
9 An *effect size* of DIF (or DTF) is computed using the Cohen's effect size index, h, for the difference between two proportions (see Equation 8.13).
10 DIF decisions on individual items (e.g., keep or remove them) should be based on a joint examination of P–Z test results, the ICCs of the reference and focal groups on a common scale, the effect size of DIF, and the purpose of testing for DIF.

Appendix 8.1: R Code for DIF Testing

Step 1. Install the R packages listed in Chapter 4, Appendix 4.1 (Step 1).
Step 2. Run the following R code:

```
library(DScoring)
itemData = read.csv("item_scores.csv",header=FALSE)
focalIndicator = read.csv("focal.csv",header=FALSE)
parameters = DS.parametersForGroups(itemData, focalIndicator)
DIF = DS.DIF(parameters$focal$parameters,parameters$reference$parameters)
write.csv(DIF$STATS,"dif_result.csv")
```

Notes:
1. There are two input (.csv) files in this application:
    "**item_scores.csv**": contains the person scores (1/0) on the test items. Missing values must be replaced by zero prior to using the data file. In the R code here above, the name of the input data file is "item_scores.csv" but it could be a different name.
    "**focal.csv**": consists of one column which contains (1/0) codes of two groups tested for DIF (1 = focal group; 0 = reference group).
2. The output file "**dif_result.csv**" has the structure of Table 8.1, where the column labeled "DIF" contains the coding of DIF: 0 = No DIF, 1 = nonuniform DIF, and 2 = uniform DIF.
3. The R code is provided also at https://github.com/amitko/Dscoring (folder: "samples/DIF").

References

Atanasov, D. V., & Dimitrov, D. M. (2018). DELTA: A computer program for test scoring, equating, and item analysis under the D-scoring method. Riyadh, Saudi Arabia: National Center for Assessment at ETEC.
Cohen, J. (1988). *Statistical power analysis for the behavioral sciences*. Hillsdale, NJ: Erlbaum.
DeMars, C. (2011). An analytic comparison of effect sizes for differential item functioning. *Applied Measurement in Education, 24*(3), 189–209.
Dimitrov, D. M. (2017). Examining differential item functioning: IRT-based detection in the framework of confirmatory factor analysis. *Measurement and Evaluation in Counseling and Development, 50*(3), 183–200.
Dimitrov, D. M. (2022). *Effect size of DIF under the D-scoring method* (Research report RR05-22). Riyadh, Saudi Arabia: National Center for Assessment at ETEC.
Dimitrov, D. M., & Atanasov, D. V. (2022). Testing for differential item functioning under the D-scoring method. *Educational and Psychological Measurement, 82*(1), 107–121.
Meade, A. (2010). A taxonomy of effect size measures for the differential functioning of items and scales. *Journal of Applied Psychology, 95*(4), 728–743.
Nye, C. D., & Drasgow, F. (2011). Effect size indices for analyses of measurement equivalence: Understanding the practical importance of differences between groups. *Journal of Applied Psychology, 96*(5), 966–980.

Oshima, T. C., Raju, N. S., & Nanda, A. O. (2006). A new method for assessing the statistical significance in the differential functioning of items and tests (DFIT) framework. *Journal of Educational Measurement, 43*(1), 1–17.

Raju, N. S., van der Linden, W. J., & Fleer, P. F. (1995). IRT-based internal measures of differential functioning of items and tests. *Applied Psychological Measurement, 19*(4), 353–368.

Stark, S., Chernyshenko, O. S., & Drasgow, F. (2006). Detecting differential item functioning with CFA and IRT: Toward a unified strategy. *Journal of Applied Psychology, 91*(6), 1292–1306.

9 DSM for Polytomous Items

Introduction

The classical and latent versions of DSM are designed for dichotomously scored items, such as *multiple-choice* (MC) *items* with one correct option and incorrect options (distractors). In many testing scenarios, however, some (or all) test items require polytomous scoring using more than two scoring categories. Such items, referred to as *constructed response* (CR) *items*, are thought to be more appropriate for measuring knowledge and skills that require higher-level cognitive processing (e.g., Ercikan et al., 1998; Wainer & Thissen, 1993). There are different item response theory (IRT) models for CR items, such as the *graded response model* (GRM; Samejima, 1969, 1996), *nominal response model* (Bock, 1972), *rating scale model* (Andrich, 1978), *partial credit model* (Masters, 1982), and *generalized partial credit model* (Muraki, 1992) (e.g., see also Nering & Ostini, 2011, for a comprehensive presentation of polytomous IRT models). Presented in the following is an approach to D-scoring of polytomous items and its comparison to the GRM in IRT.

Graded Response Model

The IRT GRM (Samejima, 1969, 1996) works for polytomous items with ordered categories ($x = 0, 1, \ldots, m$). The analytic form of the GRM is:

$$P_{ix}^{\star}(\theta) = \frac{\exp(D\alpha_i(\theta - \tau_{ix}))}{1 + \exp(D\alpha_i(\theta - \tau_{ix}))} \tag{9.1}$$

where $P_{ix}^{\star}(\theta)$ is the probability of an examinee with ability θ on the latent trait measured by the test to score in a category x or above on item i, α_i is the *item discrimination* parameter, and τ_{ix} is the *difficulty* parameter for category x, referred to also as *category boundary* or *threshold*. That is, τ_{ix} is the difficulty of scoring in category x or above, rather than scoring below category x. With ($m + 1$) ordered categories, there are m category thresholds, $\tau_{i1}, \tau_{i2}, \ldots, \tau_{im}$.

The analytic function $P_{ix}^{\star}(\theta)$ in Equation 9.1 is referred to as *cumulative category response function* (CCRF). The probability of an examinee with ability θ to score in category x, denoted here $P_{ix}(\theta)$, is obtained as follows:

$$P_{ix}(\theta) = P_{ix}^{\star}(\theta) - P_{i,x+1}^{\star}(\theta), \tag{9.2}$$

where $x = 1, 2, \ldots, m - 1$. The probabilities at the two extreme categories are computed as follows: (a) at $x = 0$, $P_{i0}(\theta) = 1 - P_{i1}^{\star}(\theta)$, and (b) at $x = m$, $P_{im}(\theta) = P_{im}^{\star}(\theta)$. The analytic function $P_{ix}(\theta)$ in Equation 9.2, with the additional formulas for the two extreme categories, is referred to as a *score category response function* (SCRF).

Figure 9.1 shows the CCRFs for an item with four ordered categories (0, 1, 2, 3) indicating, say, levels of proficiency. The GRM parameters of this item are its discrimination, $\alpha_i = 1.309$, and three cumulative category thresholds, $\tau_{i1} = -2.496$, $\tau_{i2} = 0.999$, and $\tau_{i3} = 3.675$. In this case, $P_{i,1}^{\star}$ is the probability of a person with ability θ on the logit scale to score in category 1 or higher rather than at category 0, $P_{i,2}^{\star}$ is the probability of scoring in category 2 or higher, and $P_{i,3}^{\star}$ is the probability of scoring in category 3, which is the highest category in this case. The SCRFs of this item are shown in Figure 9.2. The threshold τ_{ix} indicates the location on the IRT scale where the probability of a person scoring at or above category x is 0.5; ($x = 1, 2, 3$). It also represents the location on the scale where the person has equal chances of scoring at category x or its preceding category ($x - 1$).

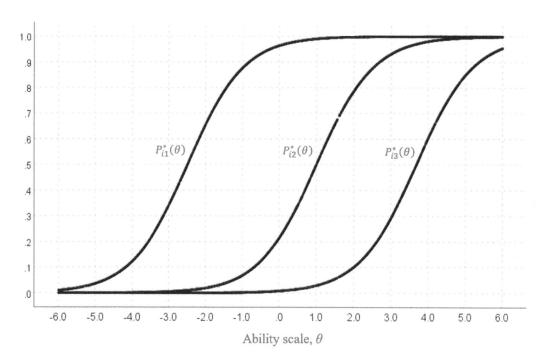

Figure 9.1 Cumulative category response functions (CCRFs) on the GRM logit scale in IRT for categories 0, 1, 2, and 3 of a polytomous item i (parameters for $i = 7$ in Table 9.2).

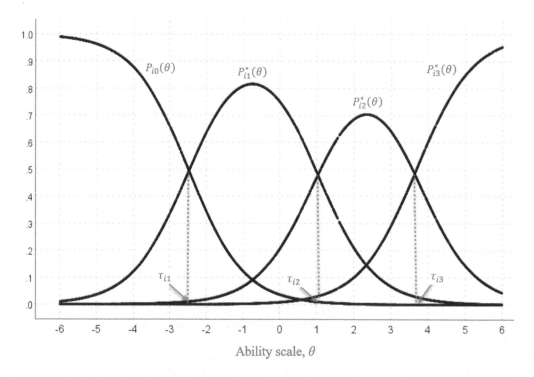

Figure 9.2 Score category response functions (SCRFs) on the GRM logit scale in IRT for categories 0, 1, 2, and 3 of a polytomous item i (parameters for $i = 7$ in Table 9.2).

D-scoring of Polytomous Items

Polytomous items with ordered categories can be analyzed under DSM to produce results on the D-scale (Dimitrov & Luo, 2019). The first step is to recode the polytomous category scores into binary scores (1/0) to allow for DSM scoring and analysis. Specifically, a polytomous item with $(m + 1)$ ordered categories ($x = 0, 1, \ldots,$

Table 9.1 Binary scores of four "virtual" items generated by a polytomous item with five category scores (0, 1, 2, 3, 4)

Polytomous item	Category score	Binary scores on "virtual" items			
		$X_{i,1}$	$X_{i,2}$	$X_{i,3}$	$X_{i,4}$
i	4	1	1	1	1
	3	1	1	1	0
	2	1	1	0	0
	1	1	0	0	0
	0	0	0	0	0

NOTE [9.1] The hierarchical dependency among virtual items generated by a polytomous item, as shown in Table 9.1, is not expected to hamper the estimation of D-scores because the DSM-C scoring does not assume local independence. Also, as shown in a simulation study, the DSM-L scoring is fairly robust in this scenario of recoding polytomous items (Luo & Dimitrov, 2018).

m) generates m "virtual" items with binary scores (1/0): $X_{i,1}, X_{i,2}, ..., X_{i,m}$. A person who scores at category x of a polytomous item i receives a score of 1 on the virtual item $X_{i,x}$ and all preceding virtual items. If a person has a score of 0 on a polytomous item ($x = 0$), all virtual items generated by that polytomous item are given a score of 0. This rule is illustrated in Table 9.1 for a polytomous item i with five ordered categories (0, 1, 2, 3, 4) that generate four virtual items, $X_{i,1}$, $X_{i,2}$, $X_{i,3}$, and $X_{i,4}$.

After recoding the ordered category items into virtual binary items, DSM can be used under its classical or latent scoring versions. Under DSM-C, weighted scores, D_w, are computed using Equation 4.2 in Chapter 4. The probability of correct item response, $P_i(D_w)$, is estimated using, say, the RFM2 as a nonlinear regression model, where the D_w score is a predictor (see Chapter 4, Equation 4.3). Under DSM-L, latent D-scores are estimated using the respective model, and the probability of correct response, $P_i(D)$, is estimated via the same model (e.g., RFM2; see Chapter 5, Equation 5.1). Furthermore, DSM-based category characteristic curves (CCRF and CSRF) can be developed as shown for the case of GRM (Equations 9.1 and 9.2) but using probabilities that are estimated under the respective DSM model. This is illustrated in the next example.

Example 9.1

The approach to DSM analysis of polytomous items, outlined here above, is illustrated here for 15 polytomous items with four ordered categories each (0, 1, 2, 3), and the results are compared to those obtained under the GRM in IRT. Data were simulated using the GRM with generating item parameters shown in Table 9.2 and ability scores, θ, of 1,000 examinees randomly selected from the standard normal distribution, $\theta \sim N(0,1)$. As each of the 15 polytomous items with four ordered categories generated three "virtual" binary items, 45 binary items were obtained and analyzed in the framework of DSM-L using the two-parameter model (RFM2; see Chapter 5, Equation 5.1). The resulting item parameters (b_i, s_i) are shown in Table 9.3.

The latent D-scores, estimated via the RFM2 for 45 virtual items, were highly correlated with the ability scores, θ, estimated via the GRM in IRT for the 15 polytomous items ($r_{D\theta} = 0.936$). This indicates high consistency between ability scores obtained via the GRM on polytomous items and D-scores obtained via the latent RFM2 on the corresponding virtual binary items. Also, the ordering of GRM category thresholds, τ_{ix}, for any polytomous item in Table 9.2 is the same as the ordering of the location parameters b_{ix} on the D-scale for its corresponding three virtual items in Table 9.3. Furthermore, the category response functions (CCRF and SCRF) obtained under the GRM and the D-scoring exhibit similar behavior, although they are not directly comparable as they are obtained using different IRF models and different scales.

For the data in this example, Figures 9.1 and 9.2, shown earlier, depict the GRM-based CCRFs and SCRFs, respectively, of the polytomous "item 7" in Table 9.2 (discrimination $\alpha_7 = 1.309$ and thresholds $\tau_{71} = -2.496$, $\tau_{72} = 0.999$, and $\tau_{73} = 3.675$). As shown in Table 9.3, the RFM2-based item parameters of the three virtual binary items generated by "item 7," denoted $X_{7,1}$, $X_{7,2}$, and $X_{7,3}$, are ($b_{71} = 0.10000$, $s_{71} = 0.80772$), ($b_{72} = 0.47855$, $s_{72} = 1.70054$), and ($b_{73} = 0.83146$, $s_{73} = 2.15181$). Using these item parameters and estimates of the latent D-scores,

Table 9.2 GRM item parameters used to simulate data on 15 polytomous items with four ordered categories each

Item	Discrimination	Cumulative category thresholds		
	α_i	τ_{i1}	τ_{i2}	τ_{i3}
1	1.466	−3.218	−1.092	0.526
2	1.708	−1.516	−0.665	0.466
3	1.710	−1.783	0.402	2.424
4	1.289	−4.444	−0.838	1.442
5	1.828	−1.584	−0.490	0.146
6	0.875	0.113	0.145	2.678
7	1.309	−2.496	0.999	3.675
8	1.787	−0.973	−0.852	0.251
9	0.805	−1.547	1.583	3.417
10	1.510	−0.914	−0.343	1.919
11	2.316	0.115	1.102	3.053
12	1.623	−3.009	2.324	4.328
13	1.655	−0.510	0.671	0.830
14	1.366	−2.900	−0.973	−0.041
15	1.533	−2.361	−1.433	0.239

Note: The threshold τ_{ix} ($x = 1, 2, 3$) indicates the location on the GRM logit scale where the probability of a person scoring at or above category x is 0.5. It also represents the location on the logit scale where the person has equal chances of scoring at category x or its preceding category ($x - 1$).

Table 9.3 RFM2 item parameters of 45 "virtual" binary items generated by 15 polytomous items with four ordered categories each

Item	b_{ix}	s_{ix}	Item	b_{ix}	s_{ix}
$X_{1,1}$	0.01036	1.33671	$X_{9,1}$	0.06600	0.80164
$X_{1,2}$	0.10454	1.33892	$X_{9,2}$	0.54848	1.28730
$X_{1,3}$	0.37664	1.86503	$X_{9,3}$	0.76489	1.53285
$X_{2,1}$	0.07466	1.46516	$X_{10,1}$	0.14018	1.56305
$X_{2,2}$	0.17286	1.71112	$X_{10,2}$	0.22398	1.74761
$X_{2,3}$	0.39602	1.88289	$X_{10,3}$	0.64955	2.18467
$X_{3,1}$	0.04201	1.30712	$X_{11,1}$	0.33431	2.53840
$X_{3,2}$	0.35277	1.80875	$X_{11,2}$	0.54785	2.72907
$X_{3,3}$	0.75421	2.41641	$X_{11,3}$	0.89023	2.28856
$X_{4,1}$	0.01000	1.56415	$X_{12,1}$	0.01049	1.17698
$X_{4,2}$	0.14365	1.18810	$X_{12,2}$	0.74102	2.27095
$X_{4,3}$	0.62072	1.55274	$X_{12,3}$	0.94979	1.55567
$X_{5,1}$	0.05228	1.24749	$X_{13,1}$	0.19858	1.73092
$X_{5,2}$	0.18782	1.55587	$X_{13,2}$	0.41685	2.13797
$X_{5,3}$	0.30892	1.84288	$X_{13,3}$	0.44994	2.11815
$X_{6,1}$	0.31376	1.36001	$X_{14,1}$	0.01462	1.21197
$X_{6,2}$	0.31639	1.35101	$X_{14,2}$	0.12378	1.27054
$X_{6,3}$	0.75682	1.28252	$X_{14,3}$	0.28116	1.42285
$X_{7,1}$	0.10000	0.80772	$X_{15,1}$	0.01853	1.18520
$X_{7,2}$	0.47855	1.70054	$X_{15,2}$	0.05786	1.10959
$X_{7,3}$	0.83146	2.15181	$X_{15,3}$	0.33870	1.65078
$X_{8,1}$	0.12822	1.72395			
$X_{8,2}$	0.14345	1.85517			
$X_{8,3}$	0.34241	1.91991			

Notes: $X_{i,x}$ = binary item generated by polytomous item i and category x; s_{ix} = item *shape* parameter; b_{ix} = item *difficulty* parameter; ($i = 1, \ldots, 15$; $x = 1, 2, 3$).
Highlighted for visual clarity are triplets of "virtual" binary items associated with odd-number polytomous items (1, 3, 5, 7, 9, 11, 13, 15).

RFM2-based probability $P_{7k}^{\star}$ ($k = 1, 2, 3$) is computed for each of the three binary items $X_{7,1}$, $X_{7,2}$, and $X_{7,3}$ as follows (see Chapter 5, Equation 5.1):

$$P_{7k}^{\star}(D) = \frac{1}{1 + \left[\dfrac{b_{7k}(1-D)}{D(1-b_{7k})}\right]^{s_{7k}}}; (k = 1, 2, 3). \tag{9.3}$$

The item response functions $P^\star_{71}(D)$, $P^\star_{72}(D)$, and $P^\star_{73}(D)$, obtained via Equation 9.3, represent CCRFs of the polytomous "item 7" on the D-scale (see Figure 9.3). The corresponding CSRFs, shown in Figure 9.4, are computed as follows:

$$P_{70}(D) = 1 - P^\star_{71}(D),$$

$$P_{71}(D) = P^\star_{71}(D) - P^\star_{72}(D),$$

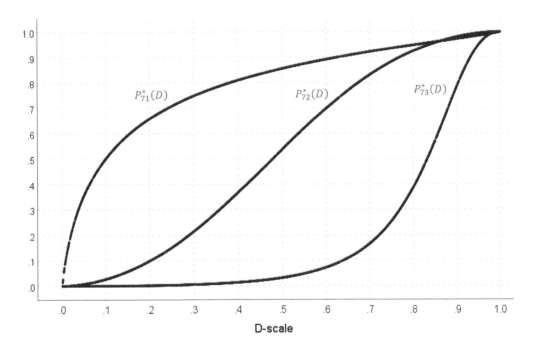

Figure 9.3 Cumulative category response functions (CCRFs) on the D-scale for categories 1, 2, and 3 of polytomous item 7 via its virtual items $X_{7,1}$, $X_{7,2}$, and $X_{7,3}$ (parameters in Table 9.3).

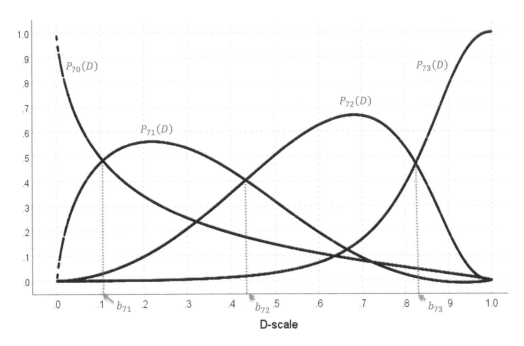

Figure 9.4 Score category response functions (SCRFs) on the D-scale for categories 0, 1, 2, and 3 of polytomous item 7 via its virtual items $X_{7,1}$, $X_{7,2}$, and $X_{7,3}$ (parameters in Table 9.3).

NOTE [9.2] The GRM-based CCRFs in Figure 9.1 look parallel as the item discrimination α_i does not vary across scoring categories under the GRM. In contrast, the DSM-based CCRFs in Figure 9.3 have different slopes at the locations of the virtual items on the D-scale, thus providing information about the discrimination power for each scoring category of the polytomous item.

$P_{72}(D) = P^\star_{72}(D) - P^\star_{73}(D)$, and

$P_{73}(D) = P^\star_{73}(D)$.

Summary Points

1. CR *items* require polytomous scoring using more than two scoring categories.
2. The IRT GRM is designed for polytomous items with ordered categories ($x = 0, 1, \ldots, m$). Its analytic form (Equation 9.1) involves parameters of person *ability*, θ; *item discrimination*, α_i; and *category thresholds*, $\tau_{i1}, \ldots, \tau_{im}$.
3. The CCRF (Equation 9.1) presents the probability of an examinee with ability θ on the latent trait measured by the test to score in a category x or above on the scale of the respective item.
4. The SCRF (Equation 9.2) presents the probability of an examinee with ability θ on the latent trait measured by the test to score exactly in category x.
5. For DSM-based scoring of polytomous items with ordered categories, each polytomous item with ($m + 1$) ordered categories ($x = 0, 1, \ldots, m$) generates m "virtual" items with binary scores: $X_{i,1}, X_{i,2}, \ldots, X_{i,m}$. If a person scores at category x of a polytomous item i, this person receives a score of 1 on the virtual item $X_{i,x}$ and all preceding virtual items. If a person has a score of 0 on a polytomous item, all virtual items generated by that polytomous item are given a score of 0.
6. Under the GRM model in IRT (Equation 9.1), there is one discrimination parameter, α_i, for the item. In contrast, the DSM-based CCRFs have different slopes at the locations of the "virtual" items, thus providing information about the discrimination power of the polytomous item across its scoring categories on the D-scale.
7. Results from empirical studies, such as those presented with Example 9.1, showed that (a) the D-scores, estimated for "virtual" items generated by polytomous items, are highly correlated with the ability scores, θ, obtained via the GRM in IRT, and (b) the category response functions (CCRF and SCRF) obtained under the GRM and D-scoring exhibit similar behavior although they are not directly comparable due to differences in their IRF models and scales.

References

Andrich, D. (1978). Application of a psychometric rating model to ordered categories, which are scored with successive integers. *Applied Psychological Measurement, 2*, 581–594.

Bock, R. D. (1972). Estimating item parameters and latent ability when responses are scored in two or more nominal categories. *Psychometrika, 37*, 29–51.

Dimitrov, D. M., & Luo, Y. (2019). A note on the D-scoring method adapted for polytomous test items. *Educational and Psychological Measurement, 79*(3), 545–557.

Ercikan, K., Schwarz, R. D., Julian, M. W., Burket, G. R., Weber, M. M., & Link, V. (1998). Calibration and scoring of tests with multiple-choice and constructed-response item types. *Journal of Educational Measurement, 35*, 137–154.

Luo, Y., & Dimitrov, D. M. (2018). *Robustness of the D-scoring model to violation of IRT assumptions*. Research Note-4-2018, Riyadh, Saudi Arabia: National Center for Assessment.

Masters, G. N. (1982). A Rasch model for partial credit scoring. *Psychometrika, 47*, 149–174.

Muraki, E. (1992). A generalized partial credit model: Applications of an EM algorithm. *Applied Psychological Measurement, 16*(2), 159–176.

Nering, M. L., & Ostini, R. (2011). *Handbook of polytomous item response theory models*. New York: Taylor & Francis.

Samejima, F. (1969). Estimation of latent ability using a response pattern of graded scores. *Psychometrika Monograph* (pp. 1–97), Vol. 17, No. 17. Richmond, VA: Psychometric Society.

Samejima, F. (1996). The graded response model. In W.J. van der Linden & R.K. Hambleton (Eds.), *Handbook of modern item response theory*. New York: Springer.

Wainer, H., & Thissen, D. (1993). Combining multiple-choice and constructed-response test scores: Toward a Marxist theory of test construction. *Applied Measurement in Education, 6*(2), 103–118.

10 DSM for Standard Setting

Introduction

The *standard setting* is a complex process of establishing cut-scores on assessment scales to classify examinees into two groups (e.g., mastery/nonmastery) or more than two groups—e.g., below basic, basic, proficient, and advanced. The derivation of cut-scores is based on judgments of content experts (panelists) guided by the methodology of the selected standard-setting method. There is a variety of standard-setting approaches, with the most popular to date being the Angoff's (1971) method (e.g., Clauser, Margolis, & Case, 2006; Hambleton, 2001; Hambleton & Plake, 1995; Plake & Cizek, 2012) and the *Bookmark method* (Lewis et al., 1999; Mitzel et al., 2001) (see also, Cizek, 2001; Karantonis & Sireci, 2006; Lewis et al., 2012; Lin, 2006). Other methods of standard setting are the *Mapmark* method (Schulz & Mitzel, 2005, 2011), *Item-Mapping* method (Wang, 2003), *Body of Work method* (Cizek & Bunch, 2007; Hambleton & Pitoniak, 2006; Wyse et al., 2014), *Item-Descriptor (ID) Matching* method (Ferrara, Perie, & Johnson, 2008; Ferrara & Lewis, 2012), *Benchmark method* (Phillips, 2012), and some alternative methods (Zwick et al., 2001). It should be noted that there is *no* single ("best") approach to setting standards for a variety of assessment scenarios and policy guidelines. In general, the ongoing efforts for improving existing methods of standard setting and developing new ones are motivated by the need to address problems related to the consistency and accuracy of cut-scores produced by such methods and the validity of examinees' classifications into targeted levels of performance.

Some Popular Standard Setting Methods

This section provides a brief description and comments on the popular *Angoff's* (1971) method, the *Bookmark method*, and the relatively new *ID matching method* (Ferrara & Lewis, 2012; Ferrara, Perie, & Johnson, 2008). The focus is on issues that are addressed with the *response vector for mastery* (RVM) method of standard setting presented in this chapter.

Angoff Method

Under the Angoff's (1971) method and its modifications, content experts (panelists) are required to conceptualize the *minimally proficient (borderline) examinee*—the examinee whose proficiency level is just high enough to justify a given classification (e.g., see Cizek & Bunch, 2007). Then, the panelists are asked to review each test item and estimate the probability with which the borderline examinee would answer correctly the item. The sum of such probabilities over the test items is an estimate of the true score for the borderline examinee, which is then mapped on the test characteristic curve to obtain the cut-score ("theta") on the item response theory (IRT) logit scale. Problems with this method stem from (a) the panelists' error-prone conceptualizations of a borderline examinee and (b) probability judgments for correct response on each test item by the borderline examinee. As noted by Berk (1986), "judges have the sense that they are pulling the probabilities from thin air" (p. 147) (see Chang, 1999; Ricker, 2006; van der Linden, 1982).

Bookmark Method

Under the Bookmark method, the test items are sorted by increasing difficulty in an *ordered item booklet* (OIB), and the panelists are asked to place a bookmark at the point between the items in the booklet at which the probability of correct response by the borderline examinee drops below a prespecified value referred to as *response probability* (RP). The most frequently used *RP* value is 0.67 (denoted *RP*67), that is, 67% (or 2/3) chances of correct item response (e.g., Huynh, 1998, 2006), but other *RP*s (e.g., 0.50 and 0.80) have also been used (e.g., Beretvas, 2004; Wang, 2003). The cut-score is the point on the IRT scale that corresponds to the selected *RP* of a correct response for the item located just before the bookmark. In some cases, the cut-score is set equal to the midpoint between the bookmarked item and the previous item.

Although the Bookmark method is considered a better alternative to the Angoff's (1971) method and its variants, there are serious doubts about the conceptualization of key concepts and understanding of the bookmark procedure by participating panelists (e.g., Baldwin, 2018; Davis-Becker, Buckendahl, & Gerrow, 2011; Ferrara & Lewis, 2012; Lewis et al., 2012; Skaggs & Tessema, 2001; Williams & Schulz, 2005; Zieky, 2001). Main problems with the Bookmark method relate to the conceptualization of the borderline examinee, the choice of an *RP* value, the probability judgment for placing the bookmark, item disordinality, and restricted focus on item difficulty. Provided next are some details on these issues.

Conceptualizing the borderline examinee: As with the Angoff method, a major validity hurdle with the Bookmark method is the proper and consistent conceptualization of the borderline examinee by the panelists. There is no persuasive research evidence on the panelists' ability to create a valid mental model of the borderline examinee at the training stage (or other rounds) of the Bookmark procedure. The Bookmark approach to this task is challenged by researchers seeking for alternative solutions, such as the ID Matching method (Ferrara & Lewis, 2012; Ferrara, Perie, & Johnson, 2008).

The RP choice: Research on the Bookmark method shows that the choice of *RP* values (e.g., 0.67, 0.50, or 0.80) systematically affects the resulting cut-score (e.g., Baldwin, 2018; Baldwin et al., 2019; Beretvas, 2004; Hauser et al., 2005; Lewis et al., 2012; Williams & Schulz, 2005; Wyse, 2011). For example, in a study using three *RP* values (1/2, 2/3, and 4/5), Beretvas (2004) found that the ordering of the bookmark difficulty locations changes depending on the *RP* used. In a different study, investigating the destabilizing role of the *RP* choice, Baldwin (2018) noted that, "the implications of these findings are alarming—after all, if panelists are unable to adjust their judgments to reflect the choice of *RP, what do their judgments actually mean?*" (p. 483). Also, based on rigorous analytic derivations in that study, he demonstrated that "the often-repeated claim that the .67 [*RP*] value corresponds with the maximum information for a correct response, which is believed to be beneficial in some way, is mistaken" (Baldwin, 2018, p. 481).

Item disordinality: The term "item disordinality" refers to the disagreement among Bookmark panelists on the order of items within the OIB (e.g., Lewis & Green, 1997; Skaggs & Tessema, 2001). Such a disagreement typically occurs when the panelists differ in education curricula and/or judgments on item difficulty. Item disordinality is particularly problematic when it occurs near the cut-scores produced by individual panelists. As noted by Lewis and Green (1997), item disordinality issues arise in virtually all applications of the Bookmark method. In another study, Davis-Becker et al. (2011) compared cut-score results of experts using OIBs with results of experts placing bookmarks in test forms where the items were randomly ordered by difficulty, and they found similar recommendations on cut-scores under both conditions.

Narrow focus on item difficulty: The Bookmark panelists focus on item difficulty to mark an item within the OIB. As noted by Zieky (2001), "this does not allow participants to distinguish purposefully among the items above the bookmark, or among the items below the bookmark on the basis of importance, curricular relevance, or necessity for performance on the job" (p. 35). This issue, not fully addressed in the extant research on the Bookmark method, has a negative impact on the substantive meaning of the cut-score—namely, the cut-score does not reflect adequately the substantive structure of the dimension(s) measured by the test.

ID Matching Method

The *Item-Descriptor* (ID) *Matching method* (Ferrara & Lewis, 2012; Ferrara et al., 2008) involves three key elements—OIB, *item response demands* (IRDs), and *performance level descriptors* (PLDs). Specifically, (a) the OIB contains all test items sorted from the easiest to the most difficult based on IRT scale location, just like under the Bookmark method; (b) the IRDs of an item represent the content knowledge, skills, and cognitive processes required by the item; and (c) the PLDs describe the knowledge and skills that the examinees in a particular performance level are expected to be able to demonstrate (Lewis & Green, 1997; Perie, 2008; Ferrara, et al., 2008).

Under the ID Matching method, the panelists match the IRDs of each item and the PLDs. This results in (a) one sequence of items that most closely match the PLDs in a given performance level, (b) another sequence of items that match the PLDs of the next (higher) performance level, and (c) a "threshold region" with items that do not match clearly either of the PLDs of the two adjacent performance levels. The cut-score is located between the scale values of the first and last items in the threshold region. Typically, the cut-score is obtained by (a) asking the panelists to identify the first item in the sequence of items in the threshold region whose IRDs match more closely the PLDs of the higher performance level and use the scale value of this item as a cut-score or (b) computing the cut-score as the midpoint between the scale locations of the first and last item in the threshold region (e.g., Ferrara & Lewis, 2012).

The ID Matching does not require panelists to conceptualize a borderline examinee and make probability judgments (e.g., using $RP67$). As stated by Ferrara et al. (2008)

> "this simplifies the cognitive complexity of the panelists' judgmental task, relative to the Bookmark method. In ID Matching, panelists can focus on matching the knowledge and skill requirements of each item to the knowledge and skills articulated in performance level descriptors."
>
> (p. 2)

Response Vector for Mastery (RVM) Method

Motivation

Along with the advantages of the ID Matching over the Bookmark method, some problems remain under both methods. Specifically, the location of cut-scores on the IRT scale under both methods is affected by the RP-based item ordering in the OIB and their dependence on a single test item, whereas the estimation of ability scores in IRT is based on the likelihood of *response vectors* (RVs) of binary scores on all test items. These issues are avoided in the RVM method of standard setting (Dimitrov, 2022). Specifically, the RVM of standard setting is designed to (a) free the panelists from psychometric conceptualizations and judgments; (b) avoid the use of OIB and related problems; (c) produce cut-scores based on response vectors of item scores, instead of using a single OIB item; and (d) produce cut-scores on the D-scale (or, on the IRT logit scale, if needed).

Response Vector Units

Under the RVM method, the cognitive judgmental task for the panelists is not performed for ordered items in an OIB but, instead, for items grouped into *response-vector units* (RVUs) on substantive basis. Along with avoiding issues with the OIB, grouping the items into such RVUs preserves the substantive structure of the test. This is important because the items of standardized tests are usually grouped into domains and subdomains. For each RVU, the panelists are asked to mark the items that they consider as sufficient (if answered correctly) for mastering the respective unit. This task requires matching of IRDs and PLDs but the matching is performed on substantively grouped items in an RVU, instead of individual items in an OIB. The validity of an RVM produced by panelists depends on the clarity and completeness of the IRDs and PLDs—a critical condition for the quality of any standard-setting method (e.g., see Egan et al., 2009; Ferrara, Swaffield, & Mueller, 2009; Mills & Jaeger, 1998; Skorupski & Hambleton, 2005).

RVM Cut-Scores

The computation of cut-scores is based on the RVM of test items and their parameters. This is illustrated here for the cases of classical D-scoring (DSM-C), latent D-scoring (DSM-L), and IRT-based scoring on the logit scale.

Case 1. Under DSM-C, the cut-score associated with a given RVM of items is computed using the formula for classical D_w scores (see Chapter 4, Equation 4.2), that is:

$$D_{w\_cut} = \frac{\sum_{i=1}^{n} \delta_i X_i}{\sum_{i=1}^{n} \delta_i}, \tag{10.1}$$

where X_i is the binary (1/0) score on item i in the RVM obtained via expert judgments, and δ_i is the expected item difficulty; ($i = 1, ..., n$).

Example 10.1

The RVM-based computation of D_{w_cut} scores is illustrated in Table 10.1 for a test of 15 items grouped into three response vector units, RVUs (e.g., domains). It is assumed that (a) panelists have "circled" the items that they believe (if answered correctly) are sufficient for mastery of the respective RVU and (b) the expected item difficulties, δ_i, are known (e.g., from an item bank). The resulting RVMs of the three RVUs render the RVM for the entire test. The cut-score for each RVM (and eventually for the entire test) is computed via Equation 10.1. For example, the cut-score for the entire test ($D_{w\_c} = 0.601$) can be used for a "mastery/nonmastery" classification of examinees, whereas the cut-scores of the three RVUs can be used to provide diagnostic feedback on the examinees' performance by test domains.

Case 2. Under the DSM-L, the latent cut-score, D_c, that corresponds to an RVM obtained via expert judgments is computed as a maximum-likelihood estimator of that RVM, using the item parameters of the DSM-L model—e.g., b_i and s_i of the RFM2 (Chapter 5, Equation 5.1). Thus, D_c is the MLE solution of the log-likelihood function:

$$\ln L(\mathbf{RVM} \mid D) = \sum_{i=1}^{n} \left\{ X_i \ln[P_i(D)] + (1 - X_i) \ln[1 - P_i(D)] \right\}, \tag{10.2}$$

where $\mathbf{RVM} = (X_1, X_2, \ldots, X_n)$ is the expert-based RVM of binary (1/0) scores of n test items, $L(\mathbf{RVM} \mid D)$ is the likelihood of the RVM, $\ln(.)$ is the natural logarithm, and $P_i(D)$ is the probability of correct item response estimated under the DSM-L model (e.g., RFM2). For this case, Appendix 10.1 provides an R code for the computation of a latent cut-score, D_c, which corresponds to a given RVM.

Case 3. In IRT framework, the RVM-based computation of a cut-score, θ_c, on the logit scale is similar to the computation of a cut-score under DSM-L. That is, θ_c is obtained as a maximum-likelihood estimator of the expert-based RVM using the item parameters of the IRT model (e.g., 2PL). That is, θ_c is the MLE solution of the log-likelihood function

$$\ln L(\mathbf{RVM} \mid \theta) = \sum_{i=1}^{n} \left\{ X_i \ln[P_i(\theta)] + (1 - X_i) \ln[1 - P_i(\theta)] \right\}, \tag{10.3}$$

where the notations are the same as those in Equation 10.2, except that $P_i(\theta)$ is the probability of a correct item response estimated under an IRT model (e.g., 2PL, see Chapter 2, Equation 2.4).

Table 10.1 Computation of cut-scores for "mastery" for a test of 15 items grouped in three response vector units (RVUs)

RV unit (RVU)	Item	Response vector for mastery (RVM)	δ_i	Computation of the cut-score corresponding to the RVM	D_w cut-score
RVU1	1	0	0.421		0.549
	2	0	0.463	$D_{w\_c1} = \dfrac{\delta_3 + \delta_4}{\delta_1 + \delta_2 + \delta_3 + \delta_4 + \delta_5}$	
	③	1	0.730		
	④	1	0.800		
	5	0	0.373		
RVU2	6	0	0.422		0.644
	⑦	1	0.730	$D_{w\_c2} = \dfrac{\delta_7 + \delta_8 + \delta_{10}}{\delta_6 + \delta_7 + \delta_8 + \delta_9 + \delta_{10} + \delta_{11}}$	
	⑧	1	0.540		
	9	0	0.275		
	⑩	1	0.665		
	11	0	0.370		
RVU3	⑫	1	0.525		0.609
	13	0	0.612	$D_{w\_c3} = \dfrac{\delta_{12} + \delta_{14}}{\delta_{12} + \delta_{13} + \delta_{14} + \delta_{15}}$	
	⑭	1	0.821		
	15	0	0.253		
TOTAL Test				$D_{w\_c} = \dfrac{\delta_3 + \delta_4 + \delta_7 + \delta_8 + \delta_{10} + \delta_{12} + \delta_{14}}{\delta_1 + \delta_2 + \cdots + \delta_{14} + \delta_{15}}$	0.601

Notes: δ_i = expected item difficulty.
For each RVU, the panelists have come to an agreement that answering correctly the "circled" items is sufficient for mastery of the respective RVU. D_w cut-scores on the D-scale are computed for each RVU and for the entire test.

Example 10.2

This example illustrates RVM-based computations of latent cut-scores under (a) the RFM2 model in DSM-L and (b) the 2PL model in IRT, with simulated data for a test of 20 items. The item parameters, estimated under the RFM2 (b_i, s_i) and 2PL (α_i, β_i) are given in Table 10.2. The RVM of binary scores is hypothetical.

Table 10.2 Response vector for "mastery" and estimates of item parameters under the two-parameter models in DSM-L and IRT for simulated data on 20 binary items

Item	RVM	DSM-L (RFM2)		IRT (2PL)	
		b_i	s_i	α_i	β_i
1	1	0.66	1.50	0.69	2.48
2	0	0.33	1.03	0.60	-0.18
3	1	0.59	1.25	0.53	2.03
4	1	0.25	0.92	0.56	-0.80
5	0	0.89	1.46	0.61	5.88
6	1	0.56	1.31	0.58	1.69
7	0	0.04	0.71	0.67	-2.75
8	1	0.34	1.11	0.66	-0.12
9	1	0.39	1.21	0.68	0.23
10	0	0.13	0.83	0.62	-1.78
11	1	0.50	1.22	0.59	1.11
12	0	0.52	1.35	0.66	1.21
13	1	0.15	0.86	0.63	-1.53
14	0	0.41	1.21	0.66	0.40
15	1	0.39	1.14	0.63	0.25
16	0	0.48	1.19	0.56	0.97
17	1	0.20	0.92	0.59	-1.22
18	1	0.47	1.26	0.61	0.88
19	0	0.48	1.42	0.76	0.88
20	1	0.57	1.21	0.50	1.87

Note: From "The response vector for mastery method of standard setting," by D. M. Dimitrov, 2022, *Educational and Psychological Measurement*, 82(4), p. 728. Copyright 2021 by Sage Publications. Reprinted with permission.

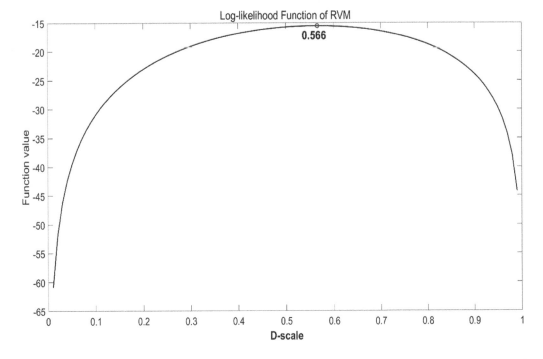

Figure 10.1 A cut-score (0.566) on the *D*-scale estimated for the RVM and item parameters (b_i and s_i) of 20 simulated items calibrated under the RFM2 model (see Table 10.2).

Note: From "The response vector for mastery method of standard setting," by D. M. Dimitrov, 2022, *Educational and Psychological Measurement*, 82(4), p. 729. Copyright 2021 by Sage Publications. Reprinted with permission.

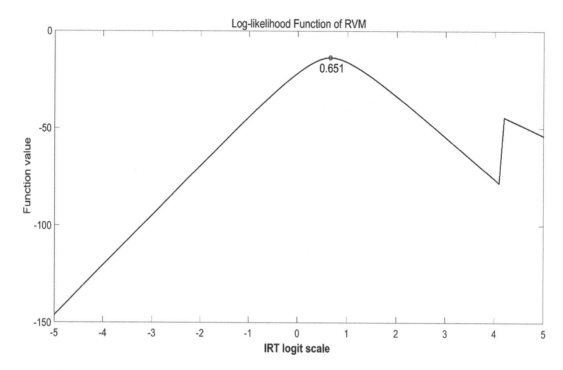

Figure 10.2 A cut-score (0.651) on the IRT logit scale estimated for the RVM and item parameters (α_i and β_i) of 20 simulated items calibrated under the 2PL model in IRT (see Table 10.2).

Note: From "The response vector for mastery method of standard setting," by D. M. Dimitrov, 2022, *Educational and Psychological Measurement, 82*(4), p. 730. Copyright 2021 by Sage Publications. Reprinted with permission.

Under DSM-L, the cut-score, D_c, is the MLE solution of the log-likelihood function in Equation 10.2, where the **RVM** and the item parameters (b_i, s_i) for the estimation of $P_i(D)$ are given in Table 10.2. It was found that $D_c = 0.566$; that is, the cut-score is slightly above the mean of the D-scale (0.5). The likelihood function in this case is depicted in Figure 10.1.

Under the 2PL model in IRT, the cut-score, θ_c, is the MLE solution of the log-likelihood function in Equation 10.3, where the **RVM** and the item parameters (α_i, β_i) for the estimation of $P_i(\theta)$ are given in Table 10.2. It was found that $\theta_c = 0.651$, which is slightly above the mean of the logit scale ($\theta = 0$). The likelihood function in this case is depicted in Figure 10.2.

Described next are some practical considerations related to the choice of RVUs, computation of cut-scores, and limitations of the RVM method for standard setting.

The Choice of RVUs

The RVUs should be obtained via partitioning the content structure of the test into substantively meaningful units that (a) are relatively short (e.g., 5–10 items) and (b) can be evaluated for "mastery" based on relevant descriptors. For each RVU, the panelists should identify items that (if answered correctly) are sufficient to evidence mastery of the unit. The response vectors for mastery by units render directly a response vector for targeted "mastery" for the entire test.

Computation of Cut-Scores

When the goal is to place cut-scores on the D-scale, their computation as classical D_{w_cut} scores is simple, transparent, and dependable. Specifically, the D_{w_cut} score is obtained directly as a scalar product of two vectors—the expert-based **RVM** and the vector of expected item difficulties, δ (see Equation 10.1 and Table 10.1). The estimation of δ_i values can be easily performed via bootstrapping that is available in widely used statistical packages such as R, SPSS, and STATA. For very large samples of examinees (e.g., $N > 10{,}000$), a quick and quite accurate estimation of the expected item difficulty is $\hat{\delta}_i = 1 - p_i$, where p_i is the proportion of correct responses of the item. Furthermore, as shown in Chapter 5, classical D_w scores and latent D_b scores on the *base D-scale* are highly correlated ($r \approx 0.99$) and differ in a very small range.

Under DSM-L, a latent estimation of a cut-score on the *D*-scale, using the RVM method, is obtained as an MLE solution of the log-likelihood function in Equation 10.2 (e.g., see Figure 10.1). The computation can be performed using the R code in Appendix 10.1. If an RVM-based cut-score on the IRT scale is targeted, its computation is performed via maximizing the log-likelihood function in Equation 10.3 (e.g., see Figure 10.2). IRT-based procedures of MLE are implemented in R, MALTAB, and other software packages.

With the understanding that there is *no* single ("best") approach to setting standards for a variety of assessment scenarios and policy guidelines, the RVM method is an efficient approach to standard setting with unique features of transparency, simplicity, dependability, and separability of panelists' judgments and psychometric estimations of cut-scores on the *D*-scale (or IRT scale). Of course, the validation of RVM-based cut-scores needs to be further examined from a variety of perspectives, including modern approaches to validating "mastery" classifications (e.g., Kane, 1994, 2001; Grabovsky & Wainer, 2017).

Summary Points

1. The *standard setting* is a complex process of establishing cut-scores on assessment scales to classify examinees into two or more groups (e.g., by targeted levels of performance).
2. The derivation of cut-scores for standard setting is based on judgments of content experts (panelists) guided by the methodology of the selected standard-setting method.
3. Problems with the *Angoff's* (1971) method of standard setting relate to (a) the panelists' error-prone conceptualizations of a borderline examinee and (b) probability judgments for correct response on each test item by the borderline examinee.
4. Problems with the *Bookmark method* of standard setting relate to (a) the conceptualization of the borderline examinee, (b) the choice of an *RP* value, (c) the probability judgment of placing the bookmark, (d) item disordinality, and (e) restricted focus on item difficulty.
5. The *Item-Descriptor* (ID) *Matching method* of standard setting involves OIB, IRDs, and PLDs. Unlike the bookmark method, the ID matching method does not require panelists to conceptualize a borderline examinee and make probability judgments, but potential issues with using the OIB remain.
6. Under the RVM method of standard setting, the cognitive judgmental task for the panelists is not performed for ordered items in an OIB but, instead, for items grouped into RVUs on substantive basis to preserve the substantive structure of the test. For each RVU, the panelists are asked to mark the items that they consider as sufficient (if answered correctly) for mastering the respective unit.
7. Main features of the RVM method for standard setting are that (a) the RVM does not require panelists to conceptualize a borderline examinee and make probability judgments, (b) the RVM avoids problems related to the OIB (e.g., item disordinality), (c) the RV units reflect more adequately the structure of the test compared to focusing on a single item, and (d) the estimation of RVM cut-scores is aligned with the estimation of examinees' ability levels (e.g., using MLE on a response vector) in the framework of DSM or IRT.

Appendix 10.1: R Code for the Computation of a Latent Cut-Score, D_c, Corresponding to a Given RVM

Step 1. Install the R packages listed in Chapter 4, Appendix 4.1 (Step 1).

Step 2. Run the following R code:

```
library("DScoring")
itemParameters = read.csv("parameters.csv",header = FALSE)
responseVector = read.csv("response_vector.csv",header = FALSE)
RVM = DS.RVM_cutScore(responseVector,itemParameters)
RVM$cutScore
```

Notes:
1. There are two input (.csv) files in this application:
   "parameters.csv": consists of two columns with the RFM2 item parameters for *difficulty*, b_i (first column), and *shape*, s_i (second column), and
   "response_vector.csv": consists of one horizontal raw with the given RVM—a sequence of 1/0 values.
2. The execution of the R code renders the value of the cut-score on the *D*-scale.

References

Angoff, W. H. (1971). *Scales, norms, and equivalent scores.* In R.L. Thorndike (Ed.), *Educational Measurement* (2nd ed., pp. 508–600). Washington, DC: American Council on Education.

Baldwin, P. (2018). Some problems with the analytical argument in support of RP67 in the context of the Bookmark standard setting method. *Applied Psychological Measurement, 43*(6), 481–492.

Baldwin, P., Margolis, M., Clauser, B. E., Mee, J., & Winward, M. (2019). The choice of response probability in Bookmark standard setting: An experimental study. *Educational Measurement: Issues and Practices, 39*(1), 37–44.

Beretvas, S. N. (2004). Comparison of Bookmark difficulty locations under different item response models. *Applied Psychological Measurement, 28*(1), 25–47.

Berk, R. A. (1986). A consumer's guide to setting performance standards on criterion-referenced tests. *Review of Educational Research, 56*(1), 137–172.

Chang, L. (1999). Judgmental item analysis of the Nedelsky and Angoff standard-setting methods. *Applied Measurement in Education, 12*(2), 151–165.

Cizek, G. J. (2001). *Setting performance standards.* Mahwah, NJ: Lawrence Erlbaum Associates.

Cizek, G. J., & Bunch, M. B. (2007). *Standard stetting: A guide to establishing and evaluating performance standards on test.* Thousand Oaks, CA: Sage.

Clauser, B. E., Margolis, M. J., & Case, S. M. (2006). Testing for licensure and certification in the professions. In R.L. Brennan (Ed.) *Educational Measurement* (4th ed., pp. 701–731). Westport, CT: Praeger Publishers.

Davis-Becker, S. L., Buckendahl, C., & Gerrow, J. (2011). Evaluating the bookmark standard setting method: The impact of random item ordering. *International Journal of Testing, 11*(1), 24–37.

Dimitrov, D. M. (2022). The response vector for mastery (RVM) method of standard setting. *Educational and Psychological Measurement, 82*(4), 719–746.

Egan, K. L., Ferrara, S., Schneider, M. C., & Barton, K. E. (2009). Writing performance level descriptors and setting performance standards for assessments of modified achievement standards: The role of innovation and importance of following conventional practice. *Peabody Journal of Education, 84*, 552–577.

Ferrara, S., & Lewis, D. M. (2012). The item-descriptor (ID) matching method. In G.J. Cizek (Ed.), *Setting performance standards: Foundations, methods, and innovations* (2nd ed., pp. 255–282). New York: Routledge.

Ferrara, S., Perie, M., & Johnson, E. (2008). Matching the judgmental task with standard setting panelist expertise: The item-descriptor (ID) matching procedure. *Journal of Applied Testing Technology, 9*(1), 1–22.

Ferrara, S., Swaffield, S., & Mueller, L. (2009). Conceptualizing and setting performance standards for alternate assessments. In W.D. Schafer & R.W. Lissitz (Eds.), *Alternate assessments based on alternate achievement standards: Policy, practice, and potential* (pp. 93–111). Baltimore, MD: Brookes.

Grabovsky, I., & Wainer, H. (2017). The cut-score operating function: A new tool to aid in standard setting. *Journal of Educational and Behavioral Statistics, 42*(3), 251–263.

Hambleton, R. K. (2001). Setting performance standards on educational assessments and criteria for evaluating the process. In G.J. Cizek (Ed.), *Setting performance standards* (pp. 89–115). Mahwah, NJ: Lawrence Erlbaum Associates.

Hambleton, R. K., & Pitoniak, M. J. (2006). Setting performance standards. In R.L. Brennan (Ed.), *Educational measurement* (4th ed.). Westport, CT: American Council on Education/Praeger Publishers.

Hambleton, R. K., & Plake, B. S. (1995). Using an extended Angoff procedure to set standards on complex performance assessments. *Applied Measurement in Education 8*, 41–55.

Hauser, R. M., Edley, C. F., Jr., Koenig, J. A., & Elliott, S. W. (2005). *Measuring literacy: Performance levels for adults.* Washington, DC: National Academies Press.

Huynh, H. (1998). On score locations of binary and partial credit items and their applications to item mapping and criterion-referenced interpretation. *Journal of Educational and Behavioral Statistics, 23*(1), 35–56.

Huynh, H. (2006). A clarification on the response probability criterion RP67 for standard settings based on bookmark and item mapping. *Educational Measurement: Issues and Practice, 25*(2), 19–20.

Kane, M. T. (1994). Validating the performance standards associated with passing scores. *Review of Educational Research, 64*(3), 425–461.

Kane, M. T. (2001). So much remains the same: Conception and status of validation in setting standards. In G.J. Cizek (Ed.), *Setting performance standards.* Mahwah, NJ: Lawrence Erlbaum Associates.

Karantonis, A., & Sireci, S. G. (2006). The bookmark standard-setting method: A Literature review. *Educational Measurement: Issues and Practice, 25*(1), 4–12.

Lewis, D. M., & Green, R. (1997, June). *The validity of PLDs.* Paper presented at the National Conference on Large Scale Assessment, Colorado Springs, CO.

Lewis, D. M., Mitzel, H. C., Green, D. R., & Patz, R. J. (1999). *The bookmark standard setting procedure.* Monterey, CA: McGraw-Hill.

Lewis, D. M., Mitzel, H. C., Mercado, R. L., & Schulz, E. M. (2012). The bookmark standard setting procedure. In G.J. Cizek (Ed.), *Setting performance standards: Foundations, methods, and innovations* (2nd ed., pp. 225–254). New York: Routledge.

Lin, J. (2006). The bookmark procedure for setting cut-scores and finalizing performance standards: Strengths and weaknesses. *The Alberta Journal of Educational Research, 52*(1), 36–52.

Mills, C. N., & Jaeger, R. M. (1998). Creating descriptions of desired student achievement when setting performance standards. In L. Hansche (Ed.), *Handbook for the development of performance standards.* Washington, DC: U.S. Department of Education and Council of Chief State School Officers.

Mitzel, H. C., Lewis, D. M., Patz, R. J., & Green, D. R. (2001). *The bookmark procedure: Psychological perspectives.* In G.J. Cizek (Ed.), Setting performance standards: Concepts, methods, and perspectives (pp. 249–281). Mahwah, NJ: Lawrence Erlbaum.

Perie, M. (2008). A guide to understanding and developing PLDs. *Educational Measurement: Issues and Practice, 27*(4), 15–29.

Phillips, G. W. (2012). The benchmark method of standard setting. In G.J. Cizek (Ed.), *Setting performance standards: Foundations, methods, and innovations* (2nd ed., pp. 323–346). New York: Routledge.

Plake, B. S., Cizek, G. J. (2012). Variations on a theme: The modified Angoff, extended Angoff, and Yes/No standard setting methods. In G.J. Cizek (Ed.), *Setting performance standards: Foundations, methods, and innovations* (2nd ed., pp. 181–200). New York, NY: Routledge.

Ricker, K. L. (2006). Setting cut-scores: A critical review of the Angoff and modified Angoff methods. *The Alberta Journal of Educational Research, 52*(1), 53–64.

Schulz, E. M., & Mitzel, H. C. (2005, April). *The mapmark standard setting method.* Paper presented at the annual meeting of the National Council on Measurement and Education, Montreal, Canada.

Schulz, E. M., & Mitzel, H. C. (2011). A mapmark method of standard setting as implemented for the National Assessment Governing Board. *Journal of Applied Measurement, 12*(2), 165–193.

Skaggs, G., & Tessema, A. (2001, April). *Item disordinality with the bookmark standard setting procedure.* Paper presented at the National Council for Measurement in Education annual meeting, Seattle.

Skorupski, W. P., & Hambleton, R. K. (2005). What are panelists thinking when they participate in standard-setting studies? *Applied Measurement in Education, 18*(3), 233–256.

Wang, N. (2003). Use of the Rasch IRT model in standard setting: An item mapping method. *Journal of Educational Measurement, 40*, 231–252.

van der Linden, W. J. (1982). A latent trait method for determining intrajudge inconsistency in the Angoff and Nedelsky techniques of standard-setting. *Journal of Educational Measurement, 19*, 295–308.

Williams, N. J., & Schulz, E. M. (2005, April). *An investigation of response probability (RP) values used in standard setting.* Annual meeting of the National Council on Measurement in Education, Montreal, Quebec, Canada.

Wyse, A. E. (2011). The similarity of bookmark cut scores with different response probability values. *Educational and Psychological Measurement, 71*(6), 963–985.

Wyse, A. E., Bunch, M., Deville, C., & Viger, S. G. (2014). Body of work standard-setting method with construct maps. *Educational and Psychological Measurement, 74*(2), 236–262.

Zieky, M. J. (2001). So much has changed: How the setting of cutscores has evolved since the 1980s. In G.J. Cizek (Ed.), *Setting performance standards: Concepts, methods, and perspectives* (pp. 249–281). Mahwah, NJ: Erlbaum.

Zwick, R., Senturk, D., Wang, J., & Loomis, S. C. (2001). An investigation of alternative methods for item mapping in the National Assessment of Educational Progress. *Educational Measurement: Issues and Practice, 20*(2), 15–25.

11 DSM for Multistage Testing

Introduction

In traditional tests, referred to as *linear tests*, all examinees are supposed to answer all test items. In this case, difficult items are not useful for low-ability examinees, and, on the other hand, easy items are not useful for high-ability examinees in terms of accuracy of their ability scores. This is because, as shown by Birnbaum (1968) in the context of the 3PL of IRT, an item provides its maximum contribution to the estimation of an ability level which is (a) slightly above the item difficulty, β_i, when the pseudo-guessing parameter is positive ($c_i > 0$), and (b) equal to β_i, when $c_i = 0$ (see also, Chapter 2). This problem is avoided with *computerized adaptive tests* (CATs)—computer-based tests (CBTs) that use an algorithmic sequential administration of selected items that match the ability level of each examinee (e.g., Lord, 1980; Wainer, 1990). However, CATs are based on complex algorithms for item selection and the examinees cannot review their item responses.

Multistage Tests

Multistage tests (MSTs) were developed to minimize the disadvantages of linear and item-level adaptive tests while preserving their main advantages (e.g., Mead, 2006; Hendrickson, 2007; van der Linden & Glas, 2010; Yan, Lewis, & von Davier, 2014a). An MST consists of preassembled groups of items (*modules*) that are built up in stages. The test delivery unit in MST is called a "panel." For example, the (1-2-3) panel configuration depicted in Figure 11.1 consists of one module at the initial stage, Stage 1; two modules at the second stage, Stage 2; and three modules at the final stage, Stage 3. Typically, modules are designed and assembled prior to administration, which allows test developers to control the content balance (e.g., when items are grouped into content domains) and the testing process. Furthermore, an MST allows the examinees to review their item responses within each module, which is not possible with item-level CATs. An MST can be implemented in separate administrations as a computer-based test or a paper-and-pencil test, using similar statistical analyses at each step in both cases. It is also possible to have continuously administered MST, but this mode of administration entails numerous challenges in monitoring the testing process, item calibration, scoring, and test assembly (e.g., see Yan, von Davier, & Lewis, 2014).

MST Structure

The module at Stage 1, referred to also as a *routing test*, typically contains items with a broad range of difficulty to allow for dependable initial estimation of the examinees' ability levels and their routing to an appropriate module at Stage 2. In Figure 11.1, the routing test is module M1. The next stage, Stage 2, consists of two modules, where the items in module M2 are easier than those in module M3. The final stage consists of three modules (M4, M5, and M6) at three levels of item difficulty ordered from the easiest (M4) to the most difficult (M6). The one-way arrows that connect two modules in a routing sequence are called *paths*. Each complete path is referred to also as a *track*. For example, the MST panel in Figure 11.1 contains six paths and four tracks (complete paths): *Track* A = (M1-M2-M4), *Track* B = (M1-M2-M5), *Track* C = (M1-M3-M5), and *Track* D = (M1-M3-M6). Taken together, the modules in one track generate a test form, and each examinee takes only one test form. In general, an MST design (number of stages, modules, levels of difficulty, etc.) is guided by the purpose of the test (e.g., Zenisky & Hambleton, 2014).

Routing Rules

Consider again the MST structure in Figure 11.1. An examinee's performance on the first-stage module, M1, is used to estimate his/her ability level and determine which module at the second stage includes items with

DOI: 10.4324/9781003343004-11

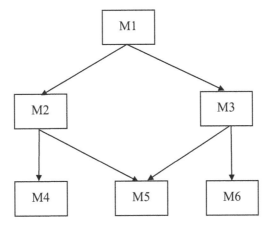

Figure 11.1 MST panel configuration (1-2-3) design.

difficulty values that best match this ability level and thus will lead to the most precise measurement (Lord, 1980). After completing the initial module, each examinee is routed to a module at Stage 2 (M2 or M3). Then, after completing the respective module at Stage 2, the examinee is routed to a module at Stage 3 (M4, M5, or M6).

In general, the routing rules are described as *static* or *dynamic*. Static routing rules are determined before an MST is administered, and most often, the routing decision is based on comparing the examinee's score on module(s) to a predetermined threshold score for the module(s). In contrast, dynamic routing rules use algorithms that operate in real time and predict the performance of an examinee on sets of items prior to their administration. Referring to modules as those in Figure 11.1, Weissman (2014) provided an example of a dynamic routing rule:

"suppose person i has completed module 1 and a point estimate $\hat{\theta}_{i1}$ has been obtained. Let $I^{M2}(\theta)$ be the information function for module 2 and $I^{M3}(\theta)$ be the information function for module 3. A possible routing rule could be as follows: given provisional estimate $\hat{\theta}_{i1}$, if $I^{M2}(\hat{\theta}_{i1}) \geq I^{M3}(\hat{\theta}_{i1})$, route person i to module 2; otherwise, route to module 3."

(p. 166)

In a comparative study on routing methods, Weissman, Belov, and Armstrong (2007) found that static routing methods based on thresholds for number-correct (NC) scores are preferable to dynamic information-based methods. Han (2020) presented an approach to routing for short-length tests, referred to as *intersectional routing*.

> **NOTE [11.1]** The scoring method used in the routing of examinees may be different from the scoring method of their performance on a complete MST path. For example, the routing rule can be based on thresholds for classical NC scores (number-correct responses), whereas the subsequent scoring on complete paths might be based on the maximum-likelihood estimation of latent scores, θ, in the context of IRT.

Scoring and Equating

Typically, current approaches to MST scoring are based on classical NC scores or IRT estimates of ability (trait). With IRT scoring, the assumption of local independence must be tested for items within modules and between modules. In case of dependency among items within a module, they can be treated as a polytomous item, and the total test score may be obtained using a polytomous IRT model, but conditional independence between the modules must hold (Wainer, 1990). Nonparametric approaches to MST scoring have also been developed to avoid limitations of IRT-based methods, such as strong model assumptions and model fit. One promising method in this regard is the so-called tree-based MST (e.g., Yan et al., 2014a). This method uses a tree-based regression algorithm to predict the scores of examinees based on the MST paths that they follow and the modules of items they answer. The regressions do not involve latent trait or true scores but, instead, classical NC scores are used (e.g., see

Yan, Lewis, & von Davier, 2014b). It is important to note that the MST routing and scoring strategy depends on whether the goal is to (a) estimate a person's latent trait level in proficiency testing (e.g., using MLE-based scoring in IRT) or (b) classify people into criterion-based categories (e.g., mastery/nonmastery).

Under any MST design, the routing rules must be comparable across test administrations, and persons' scores must be comparable across different paths and different test forms over time. This is achieved via proper linking and equating in the framework of MST. A comprehensive treatment of MST scoring and linking, including methods based on classical sums of scores, is presented, for example, by Haberman and von Davier (2014).

Test Assembly

MST *panels* are the primary units of test assembly and administration (e.g., a 1-2-3 panel configuration is shown in Figure 11.1). The assembly of parallel panels, based on the availability of a sufficiently large item bank, is a key task in practical implementations of MST. As Zheng et al. (2014) stated:

> "MST assembly consists of grouping items into modules and modules into panels optimally according to three goals: (1) to make information curves of *modules* in a stage sufficiently *distinct* to provide adaptivity between stages, (2) to make information curves of corresponding *pathways* across panels sufficiently *similar* to achieve parallel panels, and (3) to meet all nonstatistical constraints for every pathway in each panel."
>
> (p. 88)

In this (IRT-based) context, a target *test information function* (TIF) for each module is often used as a statistical aspect of the assembly of panel (e.g., see the section on TIF in Chapter 2).

Typically, the algorithms used in automated test assembly (ATA) specify a criterion function based on a target TIF and optimize the criterion under a set of constraints. The assembly of parallel panels is based on solutions of mathematical "optimizations under constraints" that produce distinct subsets of items and constraints to be assigned to different stages of the panel. An efficient approach to finding such solutions is referred to as a *shadow-test assembler* (van der Linden, 2010; van der Linden & Diao, 2014). Typically, test assembly is conducted prior to MST administration. A relatively new approach, referred to as *on-the-fly MST* (OMST) assembly paradigm, provides dynamic assembly of the modules at each stage for each examinee on the fly (e.g., Zheng et al., 2014; see also Han & Guo, 2014). Under the OMST method, after an examinee completes a randomly selected module at the initial stage (Stage 1), an individualized module is assembled for that examinee based on his/her provisional ability score using a constrained CAT item selection method, such as the *shadow test* method or the *maximum priority index* (MPI) method (Cheng & Chang, 2009).

MST Using *D*-scoring

This section describes an approach to MST using DSM. This approach, referred to as *MST-D method*, was introduced by Dimitrov (2017) in the framework of classical *D*-scoring (DSM-C). The MST-D approach follows the general MST principles, but its procedures (routing rules, scoring, equating, and test assembly) are based on the classical D_w scores of persons and the expected difficulty of items, δ_i ("*delta*"), on the *D*-scale. MST-D is under implementation for large-scale assessments at the National Center for Assessment (NCA), Saudi Arabia (e.g., Dimitrov, 2017; Al-Mashari & Dimitrov, 2018; Han, Dimitrov, & Al-Mashari, 2019; AlGhamdi & Dimitrov, 2022). The selection of a specific MST-D design is guided by the purpose of the test. For example, the MST-D design shown in Figure 11.2 is used in computer-based administrations of a general aptitude test at the NCA.

Under MST-D, the modules are preassembled to ensure (a) balance across content domains of the test, and (b) targeted levels of expected item difficulty, δ_i, on the *D*-scale ($0 < \delta_i < 1$). In practical applications with large-scale assessments at the NCA, the items are taken from an item bank with precalibrated items (δ_i values on a common scale). In Figure 11.2, for example, the initial routing module at Stage 1 (S1R) is formed of items with a wide range of difficulty ($0.20 \leq \delta_i \leq 0.90$) on the *D*-scale. There are three modules at the second stage: (a) S2E: Stage 2—easy module, (b) S2M: Stage 2—medium-difficulty module, and (c) S2D: Stage 2—difficult module. The modules at Stage 3 parallel those at Stage 2: (a) S3E: Stage 3—easy module, (b) S3M: Stage 3—medium-difficulty module, and (c) S3D: Stage 3—difficult module. The *mean* value, $\bar{\delta}$, of item difficulties and their range are shown in the box for each module. The MST-D routing rules and scoring procedures are based on a simulation study on the efficiency of the method under different conditions of routing and scoring (Han et al., 2019). The MST-D method is implemented in the new version of the simulated data generator for multistage testing (MSTGen; Han, 2013, 2022).

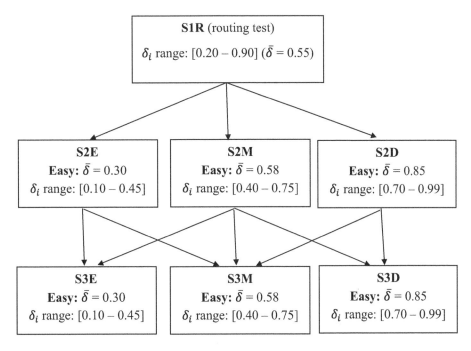

Figure 11.2 MST-D panel configuration (1-3-3) design used for computer-based administrations of a general aptitude test.

MST-D Routing and Scoring

In many IRT-based CAT/MST applications, item/module selection is based on the expected *item information function*, given θ, or based on the distance between θ and item difficulty parameter, β. The logic of the latter approach is used as a routing rule in MST-D. Specifically, a person with a score D at a certain stage is routed to the module at the next stage that minimizes the distance between the person's D-score and the average difficulty, $\bar{\delta}$, of the items in the module. (D-scores and $\bar{\delta}$ are on the same scale.) Routing based on this approach, referred to as *MinDδ* criterion (Han et al., 2019), is illustrated next in reference to the MST-D design in Figure 11.2:

1. The initial routing module, S1R, is taken by all examinees, and the D-score of each examinee is computed under DSM-C (Chapter 4, Equation 4.2):

$$D_{w1} = \frac{\sum_{i=1}^{n_1} \delta_i X_i}{\sum_{i=1}^{n_1} \delta_i}, \qquad (11.1)$$

where n_1 is the number of items in the initial routing module (S1R), X_i is the examinee's score on item i, and δ_i is the expected item difficulty.

2. Using the *MinDδ* criterion, an examinee with a score D_{w1} is routed to a module at the second stage that has the closest *mean difficulty*, $\bar{\delta}$, to the person's score D_{w1}.

3. At Stage 2, the D-score of each examinee is computed for the set of items in the examinee's modules at Stage 2 and Stage 1 together, that is:

$$D_{w2} = \frac{\sum_{i=1}^{n_2} \delta_i X_i}{\sum_{i=1}^{n_2} \delta_i}, \qquad (11.2)$$

where n_2 is the number of items in S1R and the respective module at Stage 2 taken together, X_i is the examinee's score on item i, and δ_i is the expected item difficulty for these n_2 items.

4 The final test score, D_{w3}, is based the examinee's performance on all items in the track (complete path) of modules at all three stages, relative to the total difficulty of the items in the *hardest track* (S1R-S2D-S3D), that is:

$$D_{w3} = \frac{\sum_{i=1}^{n_3} \delta_i X_i}{\sum_{h=1}^{n_h} \delta_h}, \qquad (11.3)$$

where n_3 is the number of items in S1R and the respective two modules at Stage 2 and Stage 3 taken together, X_i is the examinee's score on item i, δ_i is the expected item difficulty for these n_3 items, and δ_h is the difficulty of item h in the hardest track of n_h items.

> **NOTE [11.2]** In the right-hand side of Equation 11.3 for the final test score, the numerator is based on the *specific track* taken by an examinee, whereas the denominator, which is the sum of item difficulties in the *hardest track* (S1R-S2D-S3D), is the same for all examinees. Thus, a perfect test score ($D_{w3} = 1$) will receive only an examinee who has taken the hardest track and answered correctly all items in that track. The final test scores, obtained via different tracks, are comparable on the D-scale as the expected item difficulties of all test items are presented (*a priori*) on a common scale (e.g., taken from a precalibrated item bank).

MST-D Test Assembly

Under current applications of MST-D in large-scale assessments (e.g., AlGhamdi & Dimitrov, 2022), the assembly of test panels is conducted prior to test administration. This is performed using a computer-based *system of automated test assembly under D-scoring* (SATA-D; Atanasov & Dimitrov, 2018). SATA-D operates via interface with a large item bank of precalibrated items (δ_i values on a common scale). The algorithm for assembly of modules is based on "optimizations under constraints" using the *shadow-test* method (van der Linden, 2010; van der Linden & Diao, 2014). The optimization target is the *minimized standard error of estimate*, $minSE(D_w)$, over the D-scale (see Chapter 4, Equation 4.8). For each module type (stage and level of difficulty), the following constraints are specified in a configuration file:

1 Number of modules to be generated.
2 Number of items in the module.
3 *Range* of δ_i values and their *mean*, $\bar{\delta}$, in the module (with tolerable variation, e.g., 0.01).
4 Frequency distribution of δ_i values for the module items across 10 bins on the D-scale, specified in a separate input file.
5 Frequency distribution of the module items across content domains of the test, specified in a separate input file.
6 ID of items that should be "forced" in the module (if necessary, say, to ensure content representation), specified in a separate input file.
7 ID of Items that should be "excluded" from the module (if necessary, say, for security reason), specified in a separate input file.

> **NOTE [11.3]** The specification of the *mean*, *range*, and *frequency distribution* of δ_i values for a module of a given type ensures "δ-equivalency" of the selected modules of that type. This, coupled with the specification of content balance of the modules at all stages and levels of difficulty, ensures the parallelism of panels for MST-D.

Example 11.1

This example provides results from an application of MST-D on the *General Ability Test* (GAT) of the National Center for Assessment at ETEC in Saudi Arabia. The test is administered to high school graduates for college admission. The test consists of two parts—verbal (GAT-V) and quantitative (GAT-Q). The MST-D structure of the test is shown in Figure 11.2. The test assembly, routing rules, and scoring were performed under the MST-D design described in the previous section. The data in this example come from an administration of the test to a large sample of 21,790 examinees. Provided are frequency distributions and test scores of the examinees by seven tracks (complete paths) under this MST-D application (AlGhamdi & Dimitrov, 2022). The distribution of examinees by tracks under the MST-D is shown in Table 11.1. As can be logically expected, (a) there are more examinees in track T1 compared to tracks T2 and T3, (b) there are more examinees in track T7 compared to tracks T5 and T6, and (c) most of the examinees fall in the "medium-difficulty" track, T4 (S1R–S2M–S3M).

When MST-D results are reported, the final *D*-scores are multiplied by 100 to present them on a scale from 0 to 100 for easiness of interpretation. In this example, the mean *D*-scores of examinees by tracks (rounded to the nearest integer on a scale from 0 to 100) are shown in Figure 11.3. As can be seen, there is logical monotonic increase of the mean *D*-scores from the "easiest" tack, T1 (S1R–S2E–S3E), to the "most difficult" track, T7

Table 11.1 Frequency distribution of examinees by seven tracks (MST-D in Figure 11.2)

Track label	Path (sequence of modules)	Verbal part		Quantitative part	
		Count	%	Count	%
T1	S1R–S2E–S3E	5,896	27.05	7,146	2.79
T2	S1R–S2E–S3M	1,273	5.84	1,391	6.38
T3	S1R–S2M–S3E	748	3.43	1,196	5.49
T4	S1R–S2M–S3M	8,266	37.93	7,276	33.38
T5	S1R–S2M–S3D	409	1.87	297	1.36
T6	S1R–S2D–S3M	673	3.09	1,660	7.62
T7	S1R–S2D–S3D	4,525	20.76	2,824	12.96

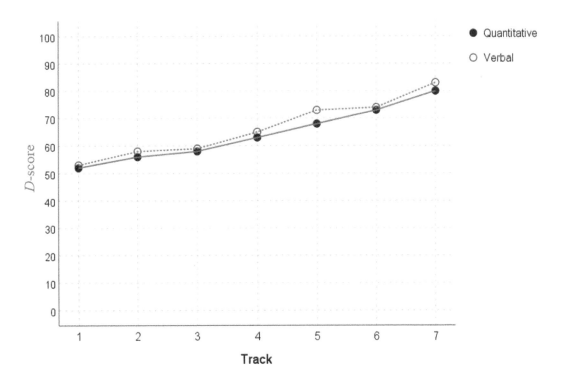

Figure 11.3 Mean *D*-scores of examinees (on a scale from 0 to 100) by tracks under the MST-D design in Figure 11.2 (see also Table 11.1).

(S1R–S2D–S3D); that is, from the group of examinees with the lowest test performance to the group of examinees with the highest test performance. These results attest to logical trends in the examinee's performance and appropriateness of routing rules under the MST-D design.

Summary Points

1. *Multistage tests* (MSTs) were developed to minimize the disadvantages of the linear and item-level adaptive tests while preserving their main advantages.
2. An MST consists of preassembled groups of items (*modules*) that are built up in stages. The modules are designed and assembled prior to administration, which allows test developers to control the content balance and the testing process.
3. The module at Stage 1, referred to also as a *routing test*, typically contains items with a broad range of difficulty to allow for dependable initial estimation of the examinees' ability levels and their routing to subsequent stages of the MST.
4. The one-way arrows that connect two modules in a routing sequence are called *paths*. Each complete path is referred to also as a *track* of the MST. Taken together, the modules in one track generate a test form, and each examinee takes only one test form.
5. *Static routing rules* are determined before the MST is administered, and the routing decision is based on comparing the examinee's score on module(s) to a predetermined threshold score for the module(s). In contrast, *dynamic routing rules* use algorithms that operate in real time and predict the performance of an examinee on sets of items prior to their administration.
6. MST *assembly* consists of grouping items into modules and modules into panels optimally according to pre-specified goals. Typically, the algorithms used in automated test assembly specify a criterion function based on a target test information function and optimize the criterion under a set of constraints.
7. The scoring method used in the routing of examinees (e.g., classical number-correct scores) may be different from the scoring method of their performance on a complete MST path (e.g., MLE-based scoring on the IRT scale).
8. The assembly of parallel panels is based on solutions of mathematical "optimizations under constraints" that produce distinct subsets of items and constraints to be assigned to different stages of the panel (e.g., using the *shadow-test assembler* method).
9. Under MST using classical D-scoring (MST-D), modules are preassembled to *minimize the standard error of estimate*, $minSE(D_w)$, under a set of prespecified restrictions designed to ensure parallelism of panels.
10. Under MST-D, the routing of examinees is based on the "$MinD\delta$" criterion, according to which an examinee at a given stage is routed to a next-stage module with the closest *mean difficulty*, δ, to the examinee's D-score on the items in the module at the given stage and all preceding modules.
11. The final MST-D score is based on the examinee's performance on all items in his/her track (complete path) of modules at all stages, relative to the total expected difficulty of the items in the *hardest track* (see Equation 11.3).

References

AlGhamdi, H., & Dimitrov, D. M. (2022, September). *Piloting of multistage testing under D-scoring method*. Paper presented at the 8th Conference of the International Association for Computerized Adaptive Testing, Frankfurt am Main, Germany.

Al-Mashari, F., & Dimitrov, D. M. (2018, April). *Multistage testing application at the National Center for Assessment in Saudi Arabia*. Paper presented at the Annual Meeting of the National Council of Measurement in Education, New York.

Atanasov, D. V., & Dimitrov, D. M. (2018). *SATA-D: A System for Automated Test Assembly on the D-scale*. Riyadh, Saudi Arabia: National Center for Assessment at ETEC.

Birnbaum, A. (1968). Some latent trait models and their use in inferring an examinee's ability. Part 5. In F.M. Lord & M.R. Novick (Eds.). *Statistical theories of mental test scores* (pp. 395–4790). Reading, MA: Addison-Wesley.

Cheng, Y., & Chang, H.-H. (2009). The maximum priority index method for severely constrained item selection in computerized adaptive testing. *British Journal of Mathematical and Statistical Psychology, 62*, 369–383.

Dimitrov, D. M. (2017). *A pseudo-simulation of multistage testing with data from a large-scale assessment at the NCA* (RR-02–2017). Riyadh, Saudi Arabia: National Center for Assessment at ETEC.

Mead, A. D. (2006). An introduction to multistage testing. *Applied Measurement in Education, 19*, 185–187.

Haberman, S. J., & von Davier, A. A. (2014). Considerations of parameter estimation, scoring, and linking in multistage testing. In D. Yan, A.A von Davier, & C. Lewis (Eds.), *Computerized multistage testing: Theory and applications* (pp. 229–248). Boca Raton, FL: CRC Press.

Han, K. T. (2013). MSTGen: Simulated data generator for multistage testing. *Applied Psychological Measurement, 37*(8), 666–668.

Han, K. T. (2022). *User's manual: MSTGen*. Reston, VA: Graduate Management Admission Council.

Han, K. T. (2020). Framework for developing multistage testing with intersectional routing for short-length tests. *Applied Psychological Measurement, 44*(2) 87–102.

Han, K. T., Dimitrov, D. M., & Al-Mashari, F. (2019). Developing multistage tests using D-scoring method. *Educational and Psychological Measurement, 79*(5), 988–1008.

Han, K. T., & Guo, F. (2014). Assembling optimal modules on-the-fly. In D. Yan, A. von Davier, & C. Lewis (Eds.), *Computerized multistage testing: Theory and applications* (pp. 115–131). Boca Raton, FL: CRC Press.

Hendrickson, A. (2007). An NCME instructional module on multistage testing. *Educational Measurement: Issues and Practice, 26*, 44–52.

Lord, F. M. (1980). Applications of item response theory to practical testing problems. Hillsdale, NJ: Lawrence Erlbaum.

van der Linden, W. J. (2010). Constrained adaptive testing with shadow tests. In W.J. van der Linden & C.A.W. Glas (Eds.) *Elements of computerized adaptive testing* (pp. 31–55). New York: Springer.

van der Linden, W. J., & Diao, Q. (2014). Using a universal shadow-test assembler with multistage testing. In D. Yan, A.A. von Davier, and C. Lewis (Eds.), *Computerized multistage testing: Theory and applications* (pp. 101–118). Boca Raton, FL: CRC Press.

van der Linden, W. J., & Glas, C. A. W. (Eds.). (2010). *Elements of computerized adaptive testing*. New York: Springer.

Wainer, H. (1990). *Computerized adaptive testing: A primer*. Hillsdale, NJ: Lawrence Erlbaum.

Weissman, A. (2014). IRT-based multistage testing. In D. Yan, A.A von Davier & C. Lewis (Eds.) *Computerized multistage testing: Theory and applications* (pp. 153–168). Boca Raton, FL: CRC Press.

Weissman, A., Belov, D. I., & Armstrong, R. D. (2007). Information-based versus umber-correct routing in multistage classification tests. Research Report RR-07-05. Newton, PA: Law School Admission Council.

Yan, D., Lewis, C., & von Davier, A. A. (2014a). Overview of computerized multistage tests. In D. Yan, A.A von Davier, & C. Lewis (Eds.), *Computerized multistage testing: Theory and applications* (pp. 3–20). Boca Raton, FL: CRC Press.

Yan, D., Lewis, C., & von Davier, A. A. (2014b). A tree-based approach for multistage testing. In D. Yan, A.A. von Davier, & C. Lewis (Eds.), *Computerized multistage testing: Theory and applications* (pp. 169–188). Boca Raton, FL: CRC Press.

Yan, D., von Davier, A. A., & Lewis, C. (Eds.). (2014). *Computerized multistage testing: Theory and applications*. Boca Raton, FL: CRC Press.

Zheng, Y., Wang, C., Culbertson, J., & Chang, H. H. (2014). Overview of test assembly methods in multistage testing. In D. Yan, A.A. von Davier, & C. Lewis (Eds.), *Computerized multistage testing: Theory and applications* (pp. 87–99). Boca Raton, FL: CRC Press.

Zenisky, A. L., & Hambleton, R. K. (2014). Multistage test design: Moving research results into practice. In D. Yan, A.A. von Davier, & C. Lewis (Eds.) *Computerized multistage testing: Theory and applications* (pp. 21–37). Boca Raton, FL: CRC Press.

12 DSM-IRT Connections

Introduction

A key element of the DSM framework is the analytic modeling of *item response functions* (IRFs). At the initial stage of DSM development, IRFs were modeled in a classical framework (DSM-C) using a two-parameter logistic regression (2PLR) model with the classical D_w score, computed *a priori*, as a predictor (Dimitrov, 2018a). However, the 2PLR model was found to underestimate the IRFs at the top end of the D-scale (e.g., Han, Dimitrov, & Al-Mashari, 2019). To address this problem, Dimitrov (2018b, 2020) developed an alternative model of IRFs on the D-scale, referred to as *rational function model* (RFM), which is currently used in research and practical applications of the (classical and latent) DSM. Three RFM models (RFM1, RFM2, and RFM3) are presented in Chapters 4 and 5 for classical and latent DSM, respectively. Presented in the following are (a) the derivation of RFMs, (b) some DSM-IRT connections, and (c) rescaling of D-scores, obtained via different estimation methods, to a common scale referred to as *base D-scale*.

Derivation of IRF Models on the D-scale

Dimitrov (2018b) approached the development of rational function models (RFMs) by (a) mapping the original form of the Rasch (1960) model on the restricted D-scale (0, 1), thus obtaining a one-parameter RFM (RFM1); (b) adding to RFM1 a *shape* parameter, s_i, to obtain a two-parameter RFM (RFM2); and (c) adding to RFM2 a *pseudo-guessing* parameter, c_i, to obtain a three-parameter RFM (RFM3). Some details are provided next.

One-Parameter RFM

The original form of the Rasch (1960) model for the probability of item success is (e.g., see also, Hambleton, Swaminathan, & Rogers, 1991, p. 81):

$$P_i = \frac{\theta^\star}{\theta^\star + b_i^\star}, \tag{12.1}$$

where P_i is the probability of correct response on item i, with difficulty $b_i^\star$, for a person with ability level $\theta^\star$ on the latent ability (trait) measured by the test.

Alternatively, the model in Equation 12.1 is presented as follows:

$$P_i = \frac{1}{1 + \frac{b_i^\star}{\theta^\star}}. \tag{12.2}$$

Theoretically, the person and item parameters $\theta^\star$ and $b_i^\star$, respectively, can vary from $-\infty$ to $+\infty$. To rescale them on the bounded D-scale (from 0 to 1), Dimitrov (2018b) used the following transformations:

$$\theta^\star = \frac{D}{1-D} \text{ and } b_i^\star = \frac{b_i}{1-b_i}. \tag{12.3}$$

By replacing $\theta^\star$ and $b_i^\star$ in Equation 12.2 with their transformed ratios in Equation 12.3, the following RFM1 on the D-scale is obtained:

$$P_i = \frac{1}{1 + \frac{b_i(1-D)}{D(1-b_i)}}, \tag{12.4}$$

where D is the person ability level and b_i is the item difficulty (i.e., the location on the D-scale where the probability of correct item response is $P_i = 0.5$), with both D and b_i restricted to range on a D-scale from 0 to 1 ($0 \le D \le 1$; and $0 \le b_i \le 1$).

Thus, the RFM1 is obtained from the Rasch model, with the person ability level presented as "ability odds" $[D/(1-D)]$ and the item difficulty level as "difficulty odds" $[b_i/(1-b_i)]$ on a bounded scale from 0 to 1 (0 = total failure; 1 = total success]. In fact, the ratio of "ability odds" to "difficulty odds" represents the odds ratio for item success, $P_i/(1-P_i)$. Indeed, using the expression for P_i in Equation 12.4, a simple algebra shows that:

$$\frac{P_i}{1-P_i} = \frac{D/(1-D)}{b_i/(1-b_i)} \tag{12.5}$$

Note also that item characteristic curves (ICCs) produced by the RFM1 do not cross (e.g., see Chapter 4, Figures 4.2 and 4.3).

Two-Parameter RFM

To allow for crossing ICCs, a second parameter, referred to as *shape* parameter, s_i, is added to the RFM1, thus obtaining RFM2 on the D-scale:

$$P_i = \frac{1}{1+\left[\dfrac{b_i(1-D)}{D(1-b_i)}\right]^{s_i}}. \tag{12.6}$$

Under the RFM1 and RFM2, the IRF $P_i(D)$ is a continuous function that increases monotonically from 0 to 1 when the ability D increases from 0 to 1 on the D-scale, that is, $\lim_{D \to 0} P_i(D) = 0$ and $\lim_{D \to 1} P_i(D) = 1$. Therefore, the IRF at the ends of the D-scale is defined as follows: $P_i(0) = 0$ and $P_i(1) = 1$. ICCs obtained under the RFM2 are illustrated in Chapter 4, Figure 4.1. (Note that higher values of the *shape* parameter, s_i, produce steeper ICCs.)

Three-Parameter RFM

To account for pseudo-guessing, a third item parameter, c_i, is added to the RFM2, thus obtaining RFM3 on the D-scale:

$$P_i = c_i + \frac{1-c_i}{1+\left[\dfrac{b_i(1-D)}{D(1-b_i)}\right]^{s_i}}. \tag{12.7}$$

The transition from RFM2 to RFM3 is analogous to that from 2PL to 3PL models in item response theory (IRT) (e.g., see Chapter 2, Equation 2.7).

Connecting the RFM2 and 2PL Models

The previous section outlined the derivation of IRF models in DSM based on the Rasch (1960) model (Dimitrov, 2018b). A different perspective and elaboration on DSM-IRT connections was provided by Robitzsch (2021) related to the mathematical equivalence between the latent RFM2 model and the 2PL model in IRT. First, he presented the RFM2 in Equation 12.6 in the following equivalent form (Robitzsch, 2021, p. 5, Equation 10):

$$P_i(D) = \frac{1}{1+\exp\left[-s_i\left(\ln\dfrac{D}{1-D} - \ln\dfrac{b_i}{1-b_i}\right)\right]}, \tag{12.8}$$

where exp(.) and ln(.) denote *exponent* and *natural logarithm*, respectively.

Then, using the transformation $\alpha_i = s_i$ and the logit transformations $\theta = \ln\dfrac{D}{1-D}$ and $\beta_i = \ln\dfrac{b_i}{1-b_i}$, the RFM2 in Equation 12.7 becomes the 2PL model in IRT:

$$P_i(\theta) = \frac{1}{1 + exp\left[-\alpha_i(\theta - \beta_i)\right]},\tag{12.9}$$

where θ is the person's ability, α_i is the item discrimination, and β_i is the item difficulty on the IRT logit scale.

Conversely, the 2PL model in IRT is equivalently transformed into the RFM2 model using the transformation $s_i = \alpha_i$ and the logistic transformations $D = \Psi(\theta) = 1/\left[1 + \exp(-\theta)\right]$ and $b_i = \Psi(\beta_i) = 1/\left[1 + \exp(-\beta_i)\right]$ (see Figure 12.1). Mathematically, the logistic function $D = \Psi(\theta)$ is the *inverse function* of the logit function $\theta = \ln\left[D/(1-D)\right]$. As shown in Figure 12.1, the logistic transformation $D = \Psi(\theta)$ maps the unlimited IRT interval $(-\infty, +\infty)$ onto the bounded D-scale $(0, 1)$, that is:

$$\lim_{\theta \to -\infty} \Psi(\theta) = 0 \text{ and } \lim_{\theta \to +\infty} \Psi(\theta) = 1$$

As Robitzsch (2021) noted, the RFM2 and 2PL models are statistically equivalent at the population level. Furthermore, the transformations of RFM2 to 2PL (and, conversely, 2PL to RFM2) entail the following relationships between the density function of D-scores, $g(D)$, and the density function of θ scores, $f(\theta)$:

$$g(D) = \frac{1}{D(1-D)} f\left(\ln \frac{D}{1-D}\right) \tag{12.10}$$

and, conversely,

$$f(\theta) = \Psi(\theta)\left[1 - \Psi(\theta)\right] g\left[\Psi(\theta)\right]. \tag{12.11}$$

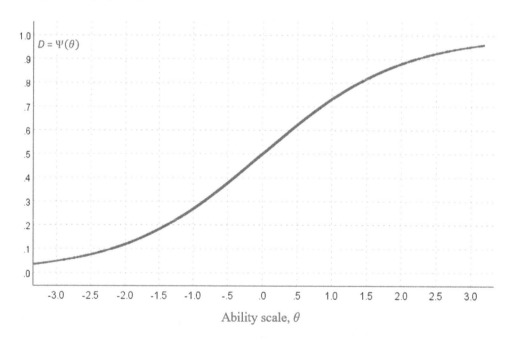

Figure 12.1 Relationship between IRT "theta" scores and their logistic transformation on the D-scale.

NOTE [12.1] Equations 12.10 and 12.11 are based on the *density transformation theorem* (e.g., Abadir & Magnus, 2007). Specifically, let (a) X be a continuous random variable with density function f_X and (b) $Y = h(X)$ be a random variable with a density function g_Y. Suppose that the inverse function $X = h^{-1}(Y)$ is differentiable for all values of Y. Then, the density function g_Y is related to the density function f_X as follows:

$$g_Y = f_X\left[h^{-1}(Y)\right] / \left[h^{-1}(Y)\right]', \tag{12.12}$$

where $\left[h^{-1}(Y)\right]'$ is the first derivative of the inverse function $h^{-1}(Y)$.

Logit-Normal Distribution

The logit-normal distribution is obtained via Equation 12.10 when the IRT ability scores are normally distributed. By definition, a variable Y has a *logit-normal distribution*, $\text{LogitN}(\mu,\sigma^2)$, if its logit transformation, $X = \ln[Y/(1-Y)]$, follows the normal distribution $N(\mu,\sigma^2)$. Thus, using the known analytic form of $N(\mu,\sigma^2)$ and the density transformation theorem (see NOTE [12.1]), the density distribution of Y, $g(Y)$, is derived from the normal density for X as follows:

$$g(Y) = \frac{1}{Y(1-Y)\sigma\sqrt{2\pi}} \exp\left\{-\frac{1}{2}\left[\frac{\ln\left(\frac{Y}{1-Y}\right) - \mu}{\sigma}\right]^2\right\}, \qquad (12.13)$$

where π is the known mathematical constant ($\pi \approx 3.14159$), $\ln(.)$ is the natural logarithm, and the variable Y takes values from 0 to 1 ($0 < Y < 1$).

Equation 12.13 is derived from Equation 12.12 when $X = \ln[Y/(1-Y)]$ and $f_X \sim N(\mu,\sigma^2)$. For the relationship between D-scores and normally distributed IRT scores, $\theta = \ln[D/(1-D)]$, the density distribution of D-scores is obtained from Equation 12.13 by replacing Y with D. In the special case of standard normal distribution, $\theta \sim N(0, 1)$, the density distribution of D-scores is:

$$g(D) = \frac{1}{D(1-D)\sqrt{2\pi}} \exp\left\{-\frac{1}{2}\left[\ln\left(\frac{D}{1-D}\right)\right]^2\right\}. \qquad (12.14)$$

Figure 12.2 shows the *probability density functions* (PDFs) of two logit-normal distributions on the D-scale (a) PDF1: $\text{LogitN}(\mu = 0,\ \sigma^2 = 1)$, obtained via Equation 12.14, and (b) PDF2: $\text{LogitN}(\mu = 1,\ \sigma^2 = 1)$, obtained via Equation 12.13 with $\mu = 1$ and $\sigma = 1$; ($Y = D$; $0 < D < 1$).

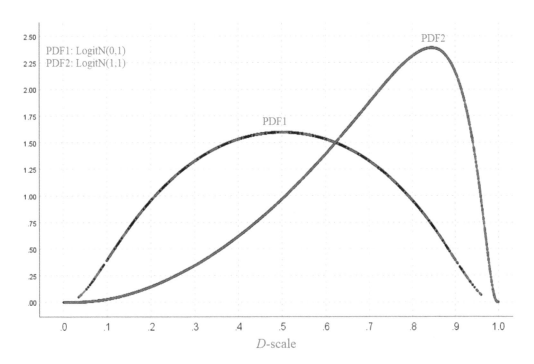

Figure 12.2 Probability density functions (PDFs) of two logit-normal distributions on the D-scale (a) PDF1: LogitN ($\mu = 0$, $\sigma^2 = 1$), and (b) PDF2: LogitN ($\mu = 1$, $\sigma^2 = 1$).

Conditional Standard Errors

The *conditional standard error* of latent D-scores, $SE(D)$, derived from the test information function on the D-scale, $I(D)$, has the following analytic form (e.g., Chapter 5, Equation 5.12):

$$SE(D) = \frac{1}{\sqrt{I(D)}} = \frac{D(1-D)}{\sqrt{\sum_{i=1}^{n} s_i^2 P_i(D)\left[1 - P_i(D)\right]}} \tag{12.15}$$

Under the transformation $D = \Psi(\theta) = 1/[1 + \exp(-\theta)]$, Robitzsch (2021) derived the following relationship between $SE(D)$ and the IRT-based conditional standard error, $SE(\theta)$:

$$SE(D) = SE[\Psi(\theta)] = \sqrt{\Psi(\theta)[1 - \Psi(\theta)]} SE(\theta) \tag{12.16}$$

NOTE [12.2] $SE(\theta)$ increases when θ gets large positive or large negative values on the IRT logit scale (e.g., see Chapter 2, Figure 2.5), whereas $SE(D)$ decreases sharply toward the ends of the D-scale (e.g., see Chapter 5, Figure 5.2). That is, the latent ability of low-performing and high-performing examinees is estimated more accurately on the D-scale compared to the IRT logit scale. Analytically, the term $\sqrt{\Psi(\theta)[1 - \Psi(\theta)]}$ in Equation 12.16 tends to 0 when θ tends to $-\infty$ or $+\infty$ and reaches its highest value of 0.5 when $\theta = 0$. Hence, under the conditions of mathematical equivalence of the RFM2 and 2PL models, Equation 12.16 yields the following relationship: $0 \leq SE(D) \leq 0.5 SE(\theta)$.

Multidimensional Latent D-scoring

Although the latent D-scoring models are unidimensional (e.g., RFM2; see Equation 12.6), Robitzsch (2021) extended the connection between the RFM2 and 2PL models to the case of multidimensional latent variables. He illustrated the reparametrizing of the two-dimensional IRT model:

$$P_i(X_i = 1 \mid \theta_1, \theta_2) = \frac{1}{1 + \exp(-\alpha_{i1}\theta_1 - \alpha_{i2}\theta_2 + \beta_i)}, \quad (\theta_1, \theta_2) \sim F, \tag{12.17}$$

where F is a bivariate distribution of the latent variables θ_1 and θ_2 to a two-dimensional latent D-scoring model with the following analytic form:

$$P_i(X_i = 1 \mid D_1, D_2) = \frac{1}{1 + \left(\frac{1-D_1}{D_1}\right)^{s_{i1}} \left(\frac{1-D_2}{D_2}\right)^{s_{i2}} \left(\frac{b_i}{1-b_i}\right)}, \quad (D_1, D_2) \sim G, \tag{12.18}$$

where G is a bivariate distribution of the latent variables D_1 and D_2; $(0 < D_k < 1)$; $k = 1, 2$.

It can be easily seen that the DSM model in Equation 12.18 is obtained from the IRT model in Equation 12.17 upon the following transformations:

$$\theta_k = \ln\left(\frac{D_k}{1 - D_k}\right), (k = 1, 2). \tag{12.19}$$

$$\beta_i = \ln\left(\frac{b_i}{1 - b_i}\right), \text{ and} \tag{12.20}$$

$$\alpha_{ik} = s_{ik}. \tag{12.21}$$

Conversely, the IRT model in Equation 12.17 is obtained from the DSM model in Equation 12.18 using the transformations

$$D_k = \Psi(\theta_k) = 1/[1 + \exp(-\theta_k)], \quad (k = 1, 2) \tag{12.22}$$

$$b_i = \Psi(\beta_i) = 1/[1+\exp(-\beta_i)], \text{ and} \qquad (12.23)$$

$$s_{ik} = \alpha_{ik}. \qquad (12.24)$$

For practical purposes, given the availability of software for multidimensional IRT models, the transformations in Equations 12.22–12.24 can be used to obtain D-scores on two latent variables, D_1 and D_2, on a bounded scale: $0 < D_k < 1$, ($k = 1, 2$).

Rescaling of Latent D-scores

The theoretical connections between latent D-scoring models and IRT models are valid at the population level, taking into account the relationship between the density distributions of D-scores and θ scores (Equations 12.10 and 12.11). For sample data, transforming IRT scores, θ, via the logistic transformation $D = \Psi(\theta) = 1/[1+\exp(-\theta)]$ produces scores on the D-scale (0, 1) denoted here as D_θ scores. One practical task is to rescale such D_θ scores to the *base D-scale*. As described in Chapter 5, the *base D-scale* is formed by latent D-scores, D_B, obtained via the JML-CNO method (see Chapter 5, Appendix 5.1). The rescaling of D_θ scores to the *base D-scale* can be performed as described in Chapter 5 (Appendix 5.3). Assuming that latent D_B scores are not available, the classical D_w scale can be used as a "proxy" of the *base D-scale*.

Example 12.1

The data in this example are the same used in Chapter 5 (Examples 1 and 2)—binary item scores on a teacher certification test of 71 items administered to 2,662 examinees. The following sets of scores were computed for these data:

1. D_w: classical D-scores (see Chapter 4, Equation 4.2) used as "proxy" of the *base D-scale*.
2. θ: IRT scores obtained under the 2PL model (see Chapter 2, Equation 2.4).
3. D_θ: latent D-scores obtained via the logistic transformation $D_\theta = 1/[1+\exp(-\theta)]$.
4. D_B: latent D-scores on the *base D-scale* (used here only for verification purposes).

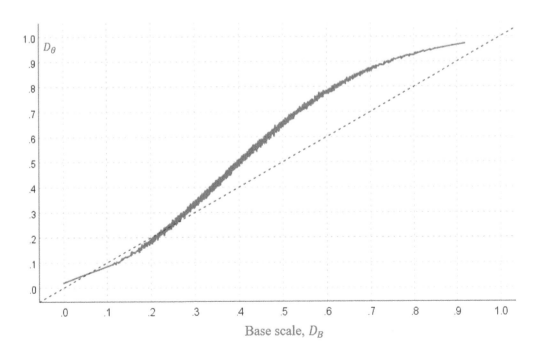

Figure 12.3 Relationship between latent D_B scores (*base D-scale*) and D_θ scores obtained from IRT ability scores, θ, using the logistic transformation $D_\theta = 1/[1+\exp(-\theta)]$.

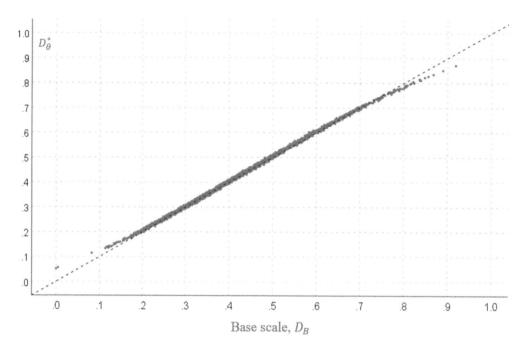

Figure 12.4 Relationship between latent D_B scores (*base D-scale*) and D_θ^* scores obtained via rescaling D_θ scores on the scale of classic D_w scores.

The D_θ scores were rescaled to D_θ^* scores on the D_w scale via the procedure described in Chapter 5, Appendix 5.3. For example, using the syntax code in SPSS (or R) with input variables $X = D_\theta$ and $Y = D_w$, the resulting output variable, denoted XR, contains the rescaled D_θ^* scores. Figure 12.3 shows the relationship between the D_θ scores (*prior* to rescaling) and latent D_B scores. As expected, the D_θ and D_B scores were highly correlated ($r = 0.992$) and nonlinearly related. The relationship between the rescaled scores, D_θ^*, and the latent D_B scores is depicted in Figure 12.4. The D_θ^* and D_B scores are almost perfectly correlated ($r = 0.999$) and their differences are very small, ranging from 0 to 0.050 in absolute value (*Mean* = 0.004, *SD* = 0.003) on the D-scale.

The rescaling procedure described in Chapter 5, Appendix 5.3, illustrated in Example 12.1 for the rescaling of D_θ scores, was previously used for the rescaling of latent D_{hmc} scores, obtained via the Hamiltonian Monte Carlo (HMC) algorithm (see Chapter 5, Example 5.2). Yet another illustration of this procedure is provided next for the rescaling of latent scores obtained in the framework of confirmatory factor analysis (CFA).

Example 12.2

A one-factor CFA was fitted to the data used in Example 12.1. The latent factor scores, η, were saved and then mapped onto a "D-scale" (0, 1) using the transformation $D_\eta = 1/[1+\exp(-\eta)]$. To rescale the D_η to D_B scores on the *base D-scale*, the following sets of scores were computed:

1 D_w: classical D-scores (see Chapter 4, Equation 4.2) used as "proxy" of the *base D-scale*.
2 η: CFA-based latent scores.
3 D_η: latent "D-scores" obtained via the logistic transformation $D_\eta = 1/[1+\exp(-\eta)]$.
4 D_B: latent D-scores on the *base D-scale* (used here only for verification purposes).

The D_η scores were rescaled to D_η^* scores on the D_w scale as described in Chapter 5, Appendix 5.3, using the SPSS (or R) syntax with input variables $X = D_\eta$ and $Y = D_w$. The output variable, denoted XR, contains the rescaled D_η^* scores. Figure 12.5 shows the relationship between the D_η scores (*prior* to rescaling) and latent D_B scores. The D_η and D_B scores are highly correlated ($r = 0.998$) and nonlinearly related. The relationship between the rescaled scores, D_η^*, and D_B scores is depicted in Figure 12.6. The D_η^* and D_B scores are almost perfectly correlated ($r = 0.999$) and their differences range from 0 to 0.050 in absolute value (*Mean* = 0.004, *SD* = 0.004).

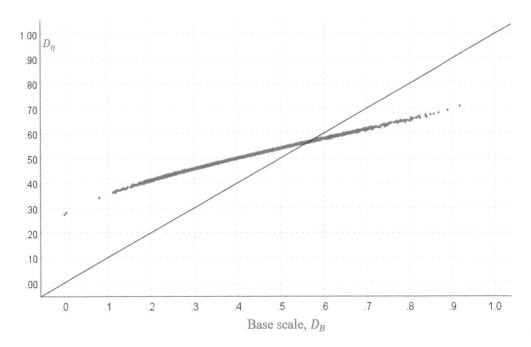

Figure 12.5 Relationship between latent D_B scores (*base D-scale*) and $D\eta$ scores obtained from CFA-based latent scores, η, via the logistic transformation $D\eta = 1/[1 + exp(-\eta)]$.

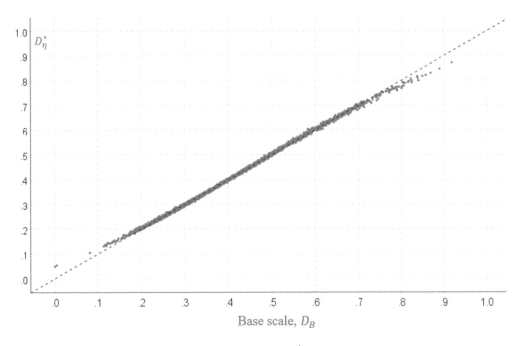

Figure 12.6 Relationship between latent D_B scores (*base D-scale*) and $D_\eta^\star$ scores obtained via rescaling $D\eta$ scores on the scale of classic D_w scores.

Appendix 12.1 provides a syntax code in Mplus (Muthén & Muthén, 1998–2012) for CFA-based computation of latent factor scores, η, and expected item difficulties, δ_i, for unidimensional data of binary scores (1/0). One practical implication is that, after obtaining the factor scores, η, and δ_i values of the items, one can (a) use the transformation $D\eta = 1/[1 + exp(-\eta)]$; (b) compute the classical D_w scores, using Equation 4.2 (in Chapter 4); and (c) rescale the $D\eta$ scores to the scale of D_w scores, as shown in Example 12.2, to place the $D\eta$ scores on the *base D-scale*.

Example 12.3

In this example, a one-factor CFA, fitted to the data used in Examples 12.2, is used to illustrate the rescaling of an *optimal linear combination* (OLC) of binary item scores X_i to the *base D-scale*, D_B. Specifically, the OLC is obtained as follows (Bartholomew, 1996; e.g., see also Raykov, Gabler, & Dimitrov, 2016):

$$Z = (\lambda_1/v_1)X_1 + (\lambda_2/v_2)X_2 + \cdots + (\lambda_n/v_n)X_n, \qquad (12.25)$$

where λ_i is the factor loading, and v_i is the error variance associated with X_i in a one-factor CFA model with uncorrelated errors; ($i = 1, 2, ..., n$).

The OLC in Equation 12.25 is a "weighted" score, Z, with *maximal reliability* (Bartholomew, 1996). By dividing each weight, $w_i = \lambda_i/v_i$, to the sum of all weights, $w_i^* = w_i / \sum w_i$, the Z scores are transformed into scores on the bounded scale (0,1), referred to here as D-*scores with maximal reliability* and denoted D_{mr}, that is, $D_{mr} = w_1^* X_1 + w_2^* X_2 + w_n^* X_n$. Technically, using the standardized factor loadings, λ_i, the respective error variances are: $v_i = 1 - \lambda_i^2$; ($i = 1, ..., n$).

The D_{mr} scores were rescaled to D_{mr}^* scores on the classical D_w scale as described in Chapter 5, Appendix 5.3, using the SPSS (or R) syntax with input variables $X = D_{mr}$ and $Y = D_w$. The output variable, denoted XR, contains the rescaled D_{mr}^* scores. Figure 12.7 shows the relationship between the D_{mr} scores (*prior to rescaling*) and latent D_B scores (*base D-scale*), computed for verification purposes. The D_{mr} and D_B scores are highly correlated ($r = 0.998$) and nonlinearly related. The relationship between the rescaled scores, D_{mr}^*, and D_B scores is depicted in Figure 12.8. The D_{mr}^* and D_B scores are almost perfectly correlated ($r = 0.999$) and their differences range from 0 to 0.023 in absolute value (*Mean* = 0.004, *SD* = 0.003).

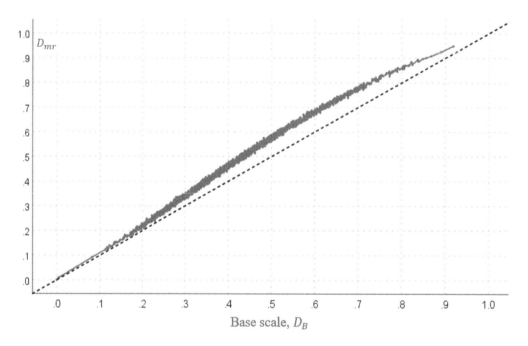

Figure 12.7 Relationship between latent D_B scores (*base D-scale*) and D_{mr} scores with maximal reliability obtained in the framework of CFA.

NOTE [12.3] When latent D_B scores on the *base D-scale* are not available, it is practically efficient to use the classical D_w scores as a "base" for the rescaling of latent D-scores obtained via different methods. The D_w scores do not require assumptions of latent modeling, and they are easy to compute, given the expected item difficulties, δ_i (Chapter 4, Equation 4.2). As described in Chapter 4, δ_i estimates can be obtained via bootstrapping. Alternatively, if IRT item parameters (e.g., α_i and β_i, in the 2PL model) are available, δ_i can be estimated as a function of those parameters (see Chapter 4, Equation 4.1; see also Appendix 12.1).

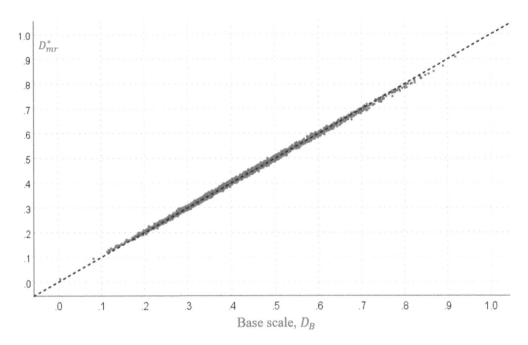

Figure 12.8 Relationship between latent D_B scores (*base D-scale*) and $D_{mr}^\star$ scores obtained via rescaling D_{mr} scores on the scale of classic D_w scores.

Summary Points

1. The RFM1 is derived from the Rasch model (Equation 12.2) by transforming its person ability and item difficulty parameters as follows:

    $\theta^\star = D/(1-D)$ and $b_i^\star = b_i/(1-b_i)$. Then (a) a *shape* parameter, s_i, for discrimination, is added to the RFM1 to obtain RFM2 and (b) a pseudo-guessing parameter, c_i, is added to the RFM2 to obtain RFM3.

2. The 2PL model in IRT (Equation 12.9) is mathematically equivalent to the RFM2 model in DSM-L. Specifically, the 2PL model can be obtained from the RFM2 using the transformations: $\alpha_i = s_i$, $\theta = \ln[D/(1-D)]$, and $\beta_i = \ln[b_i/(1-b_i)]$. Conversely, the RFM2 can be obtained from the 2PL model using the inverse transformations: $\alpha_i = s_i$, $D = \Psi(\theta) = 1/[1+\exp(-\theta)]$ and $b_i = \Psi(\beta_i) = 1/[1+\exp(-\beta_i)]$.

3. The equivalence of the RFM2 and 2PL models entails a specific relationship between the density functions of the respective ability scores D and θ (see Equations 12.10 and 12.11) according to the *density transformation theorem* (see NOTE [12.1]).

4. A variable Y has a *logit-normal distribution*, $\text{LogitN}(\mu, \sigma^2)$, if its logit transformation, $X = \ln[Y/(1-Y)]$, follows the normal distribution $N(\mu, \sigma^2)$.

5. Under the logistic transformation $D = \Psi(\theta) = 1/[1+\exp(-\theta)]$, the standard errors $SE(D)$ and $SE(\theta)$ are related as shown in Equation 12.16.

6. The connection between the RFM2 and 2PL models can be extended to the case of multidimensional latent variables (see Equations 12.17 and 12.18).

7. When latent D_B scores on the *base D-scale* are not available, it is practically efficient to use the classical D_w scores as a "base" for the rescaling of latent D-scores obtained via different methods (see Examples 12.1–12.3).

Appendix 12.1: CFA-Based Computation of Latent Factor Scores and Expected Item Difficulties for Unidimensional Data of Binary Scores: Procedure and Syntax Code in Mplus

Relating CFA and IRT Parameters

Consider a one-factor CFA model with binary items as indicators of the latent factor (ability) measured by the test (e.g., Bollen, 1989; Jöreskog, 1969; Kline, 1998). Each binary item score variable, Y_i, is treated as a coarse representation of an underlying latent continuous variable, denoted $y_i^\star$, which is assumed normally distributed. The location on the continuum of $y_i^\star$ above which the examinees provide a correct answer of the item is referred to as *threshold*, denoted here, τ_i. In other words, τ_i is the latent cutting point between the response categories (0 and 1) of a binary item, that is:

$$Y_i = \begin{cases} 0, & \text{if} \quad y_i^\star < \tau_i \\ 1, & \text{if} \quad y_i^\star \geq \tau_i. \end{cases} \tag{A12.1}$$

If η is the latent ability measured by the test under the one-factor CFA model, the continuous latent response variables are explained by the latent trait variable, η, as follows:

$$y_i^\star = \lambda_i \eta + \varepsilon_i, \tag{A12.2}$$

where λ_i is the regression coefficient (factor loading) and ε_i is the random error term.

The CFA-based item parameters λ_i and τ_i relate to the item parameters under the 2PL model in IRT as follows (Lord & Novick, 1968; Takane & de Leeuw, 1987; Muthén & Asparouhov, 2002):

$$\alpha_i = D\lambda_i / \sqrt{1-\lambda_i^2} \quad \text{and} \quad \beta_i = \tau_i / \lambda_i, \tag{A12.3}$$

where D is the scaling constant, α_i is the item discrimination, and β_i is the item difficulty under the 2PL model in IRT (e.g., see Chapter 2, Equation 2.4).

In Mplus, the estimation of α_i and β_i in the framework of CFA is based on the normal-ogive IRT model, where the scaling constant ($D = 1.702$) is incorporated. Thus, Equation A12.3 becomes:

$$\alpha_i = \lambda_i / \sqrt{1-\lambda_i^2} \quad \text{and} \quad \beta_i = \tau_i / \lambda_i. \tag{A12.4}$$

The syntax code in Mplus (Muthén & Muthén, 1998–2012), given here below, tends the estimation of expected item difficulty, δ_i, using Equations 3.5 (Chapter 3), where the error function, *erf*(X), is computed via the Hastings (1955) approximation in Equation 3.4 (Chapter 3), with α_i and β_i obtained via Equation A12.4.

Mplus Syntax Code

```
TITLE: CFA-based computation of expected item difficulty ('delta');
DATA: FILE IS    MYDATA.csv.
VARIABLE: NAMES ARE Y1-Y10;
                USEVARIABLES ARE Y1-Y10;
            CATEGORICAL ARE Y1-Y10;
MODEL:      ETA BY Y1*           (L1)
                            Y2-Y10         (L2-L10);
                [Y1$1-Y10$1]           (T1-T10);
                ETA@1;
MODEL CONSTRAINT:
                NEW(A1-A10, B1-B10, delta1-delta10,
                X1-X10, erf1-erf10);
    DO(1,10) A# = L#/SQRT(1-L#**2);
    DO(1,10) B# = sqrt(T#**2)/L#;
    DO(1,10) X# = A#*B#/SQRT(2+2*A#**2);
    DO(1,10) erf# = 0.5*(1- 1/(1 + 0.278393*X#
                + 0.230389*X#**2 + 0.000972*X#**3
                + 0.078108*X#**4)**4);
```

```
            DO(1,10) delta# = 0.5 + (T#/sqrt(T#**2))*erf#;
  ANALYSIS: BOOTSTRAP = 1000;
  SAVEDATA: FILE = ETASCORES.csv;
                    SAVE = FSCORES;
```

Notes:
1. The data file, MYDATA.csv, contains binary scores of 10 items, but different number of items can be used in practical applications.
2. The output file ETASCORES.csv contains the 1/0 scores of the items, the scores of the latent factor η (ETA), and their standard error, $SE(\eta)$, in the last column.
3. Estimates of the expected item difficulty, δ_i, are provided with the Mplus output, denoted as DELTA 1, DELTA 2, ..., DELTA 10 (in the results section "New/Additional Parameters" of the Mplus output).

References

Abadir, K. M., & Magnus, J. R. (2007). A statistical proof of the transformation theorem. In G.D.A. Phillips & E. Tzavalis (Eds.). *The refinement of econometric estimation and test procedures* (pp. 319–325). Cambridge University Press.

Bartholomew, D. J. (1996). *The statistical approach to social measurement.* New York: Academic Press.

Bollen, K. A. (1989). *Structural equations with latent variables.* New York: Wiley.

Dimitrov, D. M. (2018a). The delta scoring method of tests with binary items: A note on true score estimation and equating. *Educational and Psychological Measurement, 78*(5), 805–825.

Dimitrov, D. M. (2018b). *Rational function models on the D-scoring scale.* Research Report RR-12-2018. Riyadh, Saudi Arabia: National Center for Assessment at ETEC.

Dimitrov, D. M. (2020). Modeling of item response functions under the D-scoring method. *Educational and Psychological Measurement, 80*(1), 126–144.

Hambleton, R. K, Swaminathan, H., & Rogers, H. J. (1991). *Fundamentals of item response theory.* Newbury Park, CA: Sage.

Han, K. T., Dimitrov, D. M., Al-Mashari, F. (2019). Developing multistage tests using D-scoring method. *Educational and Psychological Measurement, 79*(5), 988–1008.

Hastings, C., Jr. (1955). *Approximations for digital computers.* Princeton, NJ: Princeton University Press.

Jöreskog, K. G. (1969). A general approach to confirmatory maximum likelihood factor analysis. *Psychometrika, 34*, 183–202.

Kline, R. B. (1998). Principles and practice of structural equation modeling. New York: Guildwood.

Lord, F. M., & Novick, M. R. (1968). *Statistical theories of mental test scores.* Reading, MA: Addison-Wesley.

Muthén, B. O., & Asparouhov, T. (2002). *Latent variable analysis with categorical outcomes: Multiple-group and growth modeling in Mplus* (Mplus Web Note No. 4). Retrieved from www.statmodel.com.

Muthén, L. K., & Muthén, B. O. (1998–2012). *Mplus user's guide* (7th ed.). Los Angeles, CA: Author.

Rasch, G. (1960). *Probabilistic models for some intelligence and attainment tests.* Copenhagen: Danish Institute for Educational Research.

Robitzsch, A. (2021). On the equivalence of the latent D-scoring model and the two-parameter logistic item response theory model. *Mathematics*, DOI: 10.3390/math9131465, retrieved from https://www.preprints.org/manuscript/202105.0699/v1.

Raykov, T., Gabler, S., & Dimitrov, D. M. (2016). Maximal reliability and composite reliability: Examining their difference for multi-component measuring instruments using latent variable modeling. *Structural Equation Modeling, 23*(3), 384–391.

Takane, Y., & de Leeuw, J. (1987). On the relationship between item response theory and factor analysis of discretized variables. *Psychometrika, 52*, 393–408.

13 Summary Notes

Motivation

The development of the D-*scoring method of measurement* (DSM) was motivated by efforts in the field of measurement to address the drawbacks of the traditional classical test theory (CTT) and item response theory (IRT) and enhance their connection from methodological and practical perspectives. Some researchers have emphasized problems with using unweighted sum scores in CTT, as well as problems with IRT score estimations over the unlimited numeric line $(-\infty, +\infty)$, calling for "optimal" scoring via weighted scores on a bounded metric, such as from 0 to 100 (e.g., Ramsay & Wilberg, 2017; Ramsay, Wilberg, & Li, 2020). Other researchers have also discussed the advantages of using bounded scales, such as the *true domain scale* (e.g., Brennan, 1998; Hambleton & Swaminathan, 1985). Some testing companies are combining CTT and IRT procedures to achieve transparency and clarity in the computation and interpretation of test scores, while maintaining psychometric dependability. However, an effective bridging of CTT and IRT would require that they share the same scale and some important psychometric features, which is a deficiency with the traditional CTT and IRT.

The DSM is designed to combine merits of the traditional CTT and IRT, *not* to replace them, in a unified framework of classical and latent scoring of test data and their psychometric analysis. This is achieved by bridging the traditional CTT and IRT on a bounded scale by (a) extending the traditional CTT to acquire some IRT features in a classical framework and (b) performing latent (IRT-like) calibration and analysis on the bounded scale of the extended CTT framework. The two DSM versions, classical (DSM-C) and latent (DSM-L), share the same scale and important psychometric features. The DSM is implemented in the practice of large-scale assessments at the National Center for Assessment of the Education & Training Evaluation Commission in Saudi Arabia (https://etec.gov.sa/en). There is a rising interest in DSM by testing companies and academic programs in other countries as well.

DSM-C and CTT

Under DSM-C, the person's score on a test is a weighted sum of the binary (1/0) scores on the test items, where the item "weight" is based on the expected item difficulty, δ ("*delta*"), hence the name "*Delta*-scoring" ("*D*-scoring," for short). Unlike the traditional CTT test scores, the weighted DSM-C scores, D_w, form an interval scale on a bounded metric [0,1]. Furthermore, the D_w scores serve as independent variable (predictor) in nonlinear regression models of item response functions (IRFs), namely, one-, two-, and three-parameter rational function models (RFM1, RFM2, and RFM3; see Chapter 4). In summary, DSM-C provides key psychometric extensions of the traditional CTT such as (a) scoring based on the examinee's response pattern and expected item difficulties, (b) interval scoring scale on a bounded metric, (c) person scores and item difficulties presented on the same scale, (d) classical (regression-based) models of item response functions, and (e) conditional standard error of test scores. At the same time, DSM-C preserves important features of the traditional CTT such as transparency, computational simplicity, clarity of interpretations, and easy-to-meet assumptions. Moreover, DSM-C test scores, D_w, are model independent as they are computed *prior* to being used as a predictor in the respective regression-based model of IRF.

DSM-C and DSM-L

DSM-L can be seen as a latent analog of DSM-C as they share the same scale, same analytic models of IRFs, and produce similar results. However, the DSM-L and DSM-C differ in approaches to estimation (latent vs. classical) of person and item parameters, standard error of estimates, and other psychometric features (see Chapter 5).

Under DSM-L, the IRF model (e.g., RFM2) is a latent model for simultaneous estimation of person and item parameters using IRT estimation approaches [e.g., maximum-likelihood estimation (MLE) or Bayesian] on a bounded scale (0, 1). Regardless of the estimation method, latent D-scores and classical D_W scores are highly correlated ($r \approx 0.99$). The scale of latent D-scores obtained via the *JML-CNO* method of estimation is referred to as *base D-scale*. Such D-scores, denoted D_B, are not only highly correlated with the classical D_W scores, but their absolute difference is very small (typically, < 0.10). As shown in Chapter 12, the classical D_W scale can be used as a proxy of the *base D-scale* (when D_B scores are not available) for efficient rescaling of latent D-scores obtained via different estimation methods. Furthermore, the conditional standard errors of D-scores behave in the same way under DSM-C and DSM-L (decreasing towards the ends of the scale), but DSM-L produces smaller errors in the middle range of the D-scale. Both D_W and base D_B scores, their standard errors, and comprehensive item analysis are provided by the computer program DELTA (Atanasov & Dimitrov, 2018).

Whether to use DSM-C or DSM-L (or both) should depend on the purpose and restricting conditions of the application. For example, when the purpose is to select items that produce a targeted test information function (TIF), DSM-L would be more appropriate because its TIF is a sum of the item information functions. This allows to evaluate the contribution of each item to the targeted TIF, whereas the TIF additive property does not hold under DSM-C (see Chapter 5, NOTE [5.3]). On the other hand, DSM-C has proven its practical value in terms of computational simplicity, transparency, and efficiency in scoring and equating of multiple test forms, multistage testing, and standard-setting procedures. Furthermore, unlike DSM-L, DSM-C works well even with relatively small samples and does not require the strong assumptions of unidimensionality, local independence, and model-data fit.

DSM-L and IRT

As shown in Chapter 12, the DSM-L rational function models (RFM1, RFM2, and RFM3) are based on the derivation of the RFM1 from the original Rasch model, $P_i(\theta^*) = \theta^*/(\theta^* + b_i^*)$, via the transformations: $\theta^* = D/(1-D)$ and $b_i^* = b_i/(1-b_i)$ (Dimitrov, 2018). Independently, Robitzsch (2021) showed that the RFM2 is mathematically equivalent (at population level) to the 2PL model in IRT upon the logit transformations $\theta = \ln[D/(1-D)]$ and $\beta_i = \ln[b_i/(1-b_i)]$ or, inversely, the transformations $D = \Psi(\theta) = 1/[1+\exp(-\theta)]$ and $b_i = \Psi(\beta_i) = 1/[1+\exp(-\beta_i)]$, keeping the discrimination parameters equal ($s_i = \alpha_i$). Such equivalency supports the psychometric validity of DSM-L and provides means for research and practical applications. For example, when IRT scores, θ, are available, one can use the logistic transformation $D = \Psi(\theta)$ to obtain latent scores on the D-scale (0, 1) and to rescale them on the *base D-scale*, as shown in Chapter 12. Furthermore, the IRT key property of "invariance up to linear transformation" translates in the context of DSM-L as "invariance up to nonlinear transformation" across samples.

Although the transformations $D = \Psi(\theta)$, $b_i = \Psi(\beta_i)$, and $s_i = \alpha_i$, which map IRT person and item parameters on the D-scale, can be useful in research and some practical applications, this is not to suggest that we can just use IRT, instead of DSM-L, and then transform the IRT parameters to their DSM-L counterparts for equivalent inferences. Several considerations come into play in this regard.

1. Issues that occur with IRT estimations over the unlimited interval ($-\infty$, $+\infty$) do not go away with *post-hoc* transformations, whereas such issues (e.g., nonconvergence and local maxima) do not occur with DSM-L estimations on the bounded D-scale.
2. As Brennan (1998) noted, "different scaling procedures often do not converge to the same result because different methodologies involve different assumptions" and "the role of scaling in drawing inferences about test scores is one of the most neglected aspects of validation" (p. 8).
3. Statistics such as those for person fit and differential item functioning (DIF), which are derived over the IRT logit scale, are not directly applicable on the D-scale. For example, the compensatory DIF (CDIF) and noncompensatory DIF (NCDIF) indices for DIF in IRT (Raju et al., 1995), derived via integrations of IRF differences over the ($-\infty$, $+\infty$) scale, are not valid over the bounded D-scale [0,1]. As another example, as shown by Dimitrov, Atanasov, and Luo (2020), two popular person-fit statistics, developed in IRT, perform better on the D-scale [0.1] after their adjustment in the framework of DSM: (a) the $Z3$ statistic (Drasgow, Levin, & McLaughlin, 1987; Levine & Drasgow, 1988) and (b) the $U3$ statistic (Van der Flier, 1980, 1982) (see Chapter 7).
4. The rescaling of item parameters in IRT is based on linear relationships that hold under the assumption of perfect model fit at the population level. The rescaling of item parameters under DSM-L does not require such

linear relationships and, instead, uses a procedure based on transforming nonlinearly related item parameters to linearly related z-score normal deviates (see Chapter 6). This procedure applies to parameters restricted from 0 to 1, and therefore, it is not applicable for rescaling of IRT item parameters.

5 Advantages of DSM-L as a latent "mirror" of the classical DSM-C, both sharing the same analytic modeling of item response functions, will be lost with "detours" via IRT.

Some key properties of the traditional CTT, DSM-C, DSM-L, and IRT are listed in Table 13.1.

Table 13.1 Features of CTT, DSM-C, DSM-L, and IRT

Feature	CTT	D-scoring method (DSM)		IRT
		DSM-C	DSM-L	
Framework	classical	classical	latent	latent
Type of scores	observed	observed	latent	latent
Type of scale	ordinal	interval	interval	interval
Range of scale	$(0, n)$	$[0, 1]$	$[0,1]$	$(-\infty, +\infty)$
Assumptions	weak	weak	strong	strong
Measurement invariance	No	No	up to nonlinear transformations	up to linear transformations
Rescaling of item parameters	No	nonlinear	nonlinear	linear
Score equating based on rescaled item parameters	No	Yes	Yes	Yes
Model-data fit required	No	No	Yes	Yes
Standard error, SE	same for all examinees	conditional	conditional	conditional
SE towards the ends of the scale	decreases	decreases	decreases	increases
IRF analytic modeling	No	Yes classical	Yes latent	Yes latent
Same scale of person ability and item difficulty	No	Yes	Yes	Yes
Item-person map	No	Yes	Yes	Yes
Potential estimation problems (e.g., local maxima, nonconvergence)	No	No	No	Yes
Person scores based on response vector and item parameters	No	Yes	Yes	Yes

Note: n = number of items in the test; IRF = item response function.

DSM Software

To date, the following DSM-based software packages have been developed by D. V. Atanasov (programming, user interface, and statistical algorithms) and D. M. Dimitrov (psychometric methodology and procedures). In addition to software links provided here, feedback on upgrades and new developments can be obtained from the book author (ddimitro@gmu.edu).

1 **DELTA** (Atanasov & Dimitrov, 2018): Written in MATLAB, DELTA is compiled as a standalone menu-driven computer program for test scoring, equating, testing for item and person fit, and differential item (and test) functioning. The program user can select the DSM framework (DSM-C or DSM-L) and item response function model (RFM1, RFM2, or RFM3). The input data file (.csv format) contains binary (and/or polytomous) items. The results are exported in (.csv) files and graphical depictions of item characteristic curves and differential item functioning (if specified). The operational functions used in the computer program DELTA (written in MATLAB), as well as functions used in a software package for DSM analysis (written in R), are publicly available at GitHub.com (Atanasov, 2022a, 2022b).

2 **TEQ-D** (Atanasov & Dimitrov, 2019): Written in MATLAB, TEQ-D is compiled as a standalone menu-driven computer program for sequential equating of test forms under the NEAT design of test equating. A sequence of k test forms, with common items for any two adjacent forms, are equated: $X_k \rightarrow X_{k-1} \rightarrow \ldots \rightarrow X_2 \rightarrow X_1$, where X_1 is the base test form; that is, person and item parameters of all preceding forms ($X_2 \ldots, X_k$) are mapped onto the scale of test form X_1.

3 **SATA-D** (Atanasov & Dimitrov, 2020): Written in MATLB, SATA-D is a computerized system for automated test assembly and operates via interface with a large item bank that contains precalibrated items

(δ_i values on a common scale). The test assembly algorithm is based on "optimizations under constraints" using the *shadow-test* method (van der Linden, 2010; van der Linden & Diao, 2014). The optimization target is the *minimized standard error of estimate, minSE(D_w)*, over the D-scale (e.g., an application of SATA-D in multistage testing is discussed in Chapter 11).

4 **DELTA-WebApp** (Atanasov, 2022c): DELTA-WebApp is a publicly available web-based demo package for DSM-based library, written in R (https://webapp.ir-statistics.net).

References

Atanasov, D. V. (2022a). Matlab-delta-scoring (https://github.com/amitko/matlab-delta-scoring).

Atanasov, D. V. (2022b). R-delta-scoring (https://github.com/amitko/Dscoring).

Atanasov, D. V. (2022c). *User's guide for DELTA-WebApp: A web-based software for test scoring, equating, and item analysis in the framework of the D-scoring method of measurement (developed in R)*. Riyadh, Saudi Arabia: National Center for Assessment at ETEC.

Atanasov, D. V., & Dimitrov, D. M. (2018). *User's guide for DELTA: A computer program for test scoring, equating, and item analysis in the framework of the D-scoring method of measurement (develop in MATLAB)*. Riyadh, Saudi Arabia: National Center for Assessment at ETEC.

Atanasov, D. V., & Dimitrov, D. M. (2019). *User's guide for TEQ-D: A computer program for sequential test equating in the framework of the D-scoring method of measurement (developed in MATLAB)*. Riyadh, Saudi Arabia: National Center for Assessment at ETEC.

Atanasov, D. V., & Dimitrov, D. M. (2020). *User's guide for SATA-D: A software package for automated test assembly in the framework of the D-scoring method of measurement (developed in MATLAB)*. Riyadh, Saudi Arabia: National Center for Assessment at ETEC.

Brennan, R. L. (1998). Misconceptions at the intersection of measurement theory and practice. *Educational Measurement: Issues and Practice, 17*(1), 5–30.

Dimitrov, D. M. (2018). *Rational function models on the D-scoring scale*. Research Report RR-12-2018. Riyadh, Saudi Arabia: National Center for Assessment at ETEC.

Dimitrov, D. M., Atanasov, D. V., & Luo, Y. (2020). Person-fit assessment under the D-scoring method. *Measurement: Interdisciplinary Research and Perspectives, 18*(3), 111–123.

Drasgow, F., Levin, M. V., & McLaughlin, M. E. (1987). Detecting inappropriate test scores with optimal and practical appropriateness indices. *Applied Psychological Measurement, 11*, 59–79.

Hambleton, R. K., & Swaminathan, H. (1985). *Item response theory: Principles and applications*. Hingham, MA: Kluwer, Nijhoff.

Levine, M. V., & Drasgow, F. (1988). Optimal appropriateness measurement. *Psychometrika, 53*, 161–176.

Raju, N. S., van der Linden, W. J., & Fleer, P. F. (1995). IRT-based internal measures of differential functioning of items and tests. *Applied Psychological Measurement, 19*(4), 353–368.

Ramsay, J. O., & Wilberg, M. (2017). A strategy for replacing sum scoring. *Journal of Educational and Behavioral Statistics, 42*(3), 282–307.

Ramsay, J. O., Wilberg, M., & Li, J. (2020). Full information optimal scoring. *Journal of Educational and Behavioral Statistics, 45*(3), 297–315.

Robitzsch, A. (2021). On the equivalence of the latent D-scoring model and the two-parameter logistic item response theory model. *Mathematics*, DOI: 10.3390/math9131465, https://www.preprints.org/manuscript/202105.0699/v1.

van der Flier, H. (1980). Vergelijkbaarheid van individuele test prestaties [Comparability of individual test performance]. Lisse, the Netherlands: Swets & Zeitlinger.

van der Flier, H. (1982). Deviant response patterns and comparability of test scores. *Journal of Cross Cultural Psychology, 13*, 267–298.

van der Linden, W. J. (2010). Constrained adaptive testing with shadow tests. In W.J. van der Linden and C.A.W. Glas (Eds.), *Elements of computerized adaptive testing*, (pp. 31–55). New York: Springer.

van der Linden, W. J., & Diao, Q. (2014). Using a universal shadow-test assembler with multistage testing. In D. Yan, A.A. von Davier, & C. Lewis (Eds.), *Computerized multistage testing: Theory and applications*, (pp. 101–118). Boca Raton, FL: CRC Press.

Index

Note: **Bold** page numbers refer to tables.

ability scale 16–18, 27, 33
ability score 5–6, 15, 20, 32, 41–42, 51, 61–62, 64–65, 79, 89, 91, 102, 104, 113, 115, 119
absolute model fit 24–25
additive conjoint measurement (ACM) 47, 53, 55
alternate form reliability 7
anchor-test design 31, 34
Angoff method 93–94, 101
automated test assembly (ATA) 104, 106, 108, 124–125

base D-scale 61–64, 99, 114–119, 123
Bayesian 21, 60–63, 123
benchmark method 93, 101
bias 4, 10, 12, 20, 27, 30, 36–37, 69–70, 82
BILOG-MG (software) 24
biserial correlation 5, 42
Bock's 26
body of work method 93
bookmark method 93–95, 99
bootstrapping 38, 46, 54, 99, 118
borderline examinee 93–95, 99

category boundary 87
category response function (CCRF) 87–89, 91–92
chi-square test (for fit) 26
classical D-score 46, 54, 62, 70, 115, 116
classical D-scoring method (DSM-C) 45, 57
coefficient of equivalence 7
compensatory DIF index (CDIF) 30, 78, 123
composite score 9
computer-based test (CBD) 102
computerized adaptive test (CAT) 15, 102, 108–109
conditional standard error 44–45, 51, 57, 59, 114, 122–123
confidence interval 4, 8, 12
confirmatory factor analysis (CFA) 28, 35, 46, 85, 116
constrained model 24, 33
constrained nonlinear optimization (CNO) 65
constructed response item 87, 92
convergence 32, 41, 65, 123–124
Cronbach's coefficient alpha 11
cumulative category response function (CCRF) 87–88, 91

D-scoring method (DSM) 30, 35, 42, 45, 55–58, 64, 67–68, 73, 85, 123–125
degrees of freedom (df) 24–26
DELTA (software) 52–53, 61, 63, 65, 67, 83, 121, 123–125
density transformation theorem 112–113, 119
deterministic Guttman model 75–76
differential item functioning (DIF) 28, 35–38, 78, 85–86, 123–124

domain score 20, 32–33, 41–42
dynamic routing rule 103, 108

effect size (for DIF) 24, 82, 83–85
error function (erf) 42, 46, 120
equal-interval scale 4, 10
equipercentile equating 9–11, 33, 35, 40
equivalent-group design 31
essential unidimensionality 14
essentially tau-equivalent tests 3, 11
expected item difficulty 43, 45–46, 54–55, 61–62, 68, 99, 104–106, 120–122

F-statistic 79
fmincon function 65
focal group 28–29, 30–31, 34, 78–85
full-information bifactor item-response model 14

G^2 statistic 24, 25
gain scores 7, 12
generalized partial credit model 87, 92
goodness-of-fit 15, 24–25, 33, 37–38
Graded response model (GRM) 37, 87, 92
Guttman pattern (GP) 27, 76–77

h-interval 82–84
Hamiltonian Monte Carlo (HMC) algorithm 62–63, 117
H^T statistic 27–28, 75

indeterminacy 19, 20, 33
infit statistic 27
information function 22–23, 27, 33, 40–41, 58, 103–105, 108, 114, 123
inlier-sensitive (infit) 27
internal consistency reliability 3, 7, 11
interval scale 2, 4, 10, 11, 18, 33, 40, 47, 54, 122
intervalness 45, 47, 53
item characteristic curve (ICC) 5, 6, 13, 15, 17–18, 29, 37, 39, 48–49, 50, 57–58, 71, 78, 111, 124
item-descriptor (ID) matching method 93–94, 99, 100
item disordinality 94, 99, 101
item fit 25–27, 33, 35, 37, 55, 66, 74, 77
item information function (IIF) 22–23, 27, 33, 40, 58, 105, 123
item-mapping method 93
item response demands (IRDs) 94
item response function (IRF) 13, 37, 39, 45, 47, 54–55, 57–58, 64, 74, 77, 82, 90, 110, 121–122, 124
item shape parameter 90
item-test biserial correlation 42

joint maximum likelihood (JML) 21, 61, 64–65
JML-CNO method 61–62, 64–65, 115, 123

latent D-score 53–54, 59, 62–65, 70, 72, 89, 114–123
latent D-scoring method (DSM-L) 57, 73, 77
levels of measurement 1
likelihood-ratio test 24
linear equating 9–11
local dependence 14–15, 35–36
local independence 13–15, 24, 33, 39, 40, 43, 89, 103, 123
log-likelihood ratio test 24
log-odds 18–19, 33
logit-normal distribution 113, 119
logit scale 17–19, 20–21, 27, 33, 41, 47, 51, 54, 62, 74, 78, 87–88, 90, 93, 95, 98, 112, 114
logit transformation 111, 113, 119, 123

mapmark method 93, 101
MATLAB (software) 42, 44, 46, 61, 65, 67, 124, 125
maximal reliability 118, 121
maximum likelihood estimation (MLE) 20, 41, 53, 64, 103, 123
mean absolute difference (MAD) 54, 66, 74
mean absolute error (MAE) 74
 criterion 105
minimally proficient (borderline) examinee 93
model fit 24–25, 36, 39, 43, 103, 123
module (in MST) 102–108
Mplus (software) 14, 36, 117, 119, 120–121
multidimensional IRT (MIRT) 13, 115
multiple-choice items (MCI) 3, 17, 41, 48, 50, 58
multistage test (MST) 54, 56, 102–104, 108–109, 121, 123, 125
multistage testing using D-scoring (MST-D) 104–108

National Center for Assessment (NCA) 44, 45, 62, 73, 77, 85, 93, 104, 107, 109, 121, 125
nominal response model 87
nominal scale 1, 11
noncompensatory DIF index (NCDIF) 30
nonequivalent groups with anchor tests (NEAT) design 31, 34, 36, 68, 70, 71, 124
nonuniform DIF 29, 78–79, 80–85
normal distribution 3, 4, 8, 72, 84, 89, 113, 119
normal ogive model 13, 16, 42
normalized scores 3, 4, 11
number-correct score 33, 108
number-correct true score 32–34

odds for success 18=9, 34, 52
odds ratio 18, 34, 53, 111
one-parameter logistic (1PL) model 13, 16–18, 21–23, 26–27, 34, 42, 46
one-parameter rational function model (RFM1) 57
optimal linear combination (OCL) 118
ordered item booklet (OIB) 93–95, 99
ordinal scale 1, 2, 4, 11
outfit statistic 26–27
outlier-sensitive fit (outfit) 27

P-Z method 30, 78, 81–85
panel (in MST) 102–106, 108
parallel tests 2, 11, 39, 43

PARSCALE (software) 24, 36
partial credit model 87, 92
path (in MST) 102–104, 106–108
percentile 3–5, 9–11, 33, 35–36, 76
percentile rank 3, 5, 76
performance level descriptors (PLDs) 94–95, 100
point-biserial correlation 5
polytomous item 45, 87, 88–89, 90–92
pseudo-guessing parameter 17, 31, 42, 46, 48, 50, 53, 58, 76, 102, 110, 119

Rasch model 17, 27–28, 34–38, 111, 119, 123
ratio scale 2, 11, 34
rational function model (RFM) 46–48, 54, 57–58, 64, 110, 121–122, 125
raw score 3–4, 10–11, 21, 26, 41
reference group 28–29, 30, 78–79, 81, 83, 85
relative model fit 25, 36
reliability 3, 6–9, 10–12, 42, 44, 55, 61, 118, 121
rescaling 21, 31, 54, 59, 62–63, 66, 68–69, 71–73, 81, 110, 115–119, 123–124
response pattern 14, 20–21, 24–25, 27, 33, 37, 40, 45–46, 53, 57, 64, 74–77, 122, 125
response probability (RP) 93, 100–101
response vector for mastery (RVM) 55, 93, 95, **96**–98
response vector unit (RVU) 95–96
reversed Guttman pattern (RGP) 76
root-mean-square error (RMSE) 74
routing (in MST) 102–105, 107–109
RP67 93, 95, 100

SATA-D (software) 106–107, 124–125
scale linking 31, 38
score category response function (SCRF) 87–88, 91
shadow test 104, 106, 108–109, 125
shadow-test assembler 104, 108, 109
standard error of estimation (SEE) 9, 59
standard error of measurement (SEM) 8, 40
single-group design 31
SPSS (software) 46, 62, 66, 99, 116, 118
stage (in MST) 102–106, 108
standard normal distribution 3–4, 72, 84, 89, 113
standard setting 54–55, 93, 95, 97–99, 100–101, 123
standardized score 3–4, 11
static routing rule 103, 108
strong true-score theory 1, 12

t-test 81
TEQ-D (software) 124–125
test assembly 102, 104, 106–109
test bias 27, 82
test information function (TIF) 22–23, 40, 58–59, 104, 108, 114, 123
test response function (TRF) 82
test-retest reliability 7, 11
three-parameter logistic (3PL) model 31, 42, 46, 48, 50, 59, 111
three-parameter rational function model (RFM3) 58, 122
threshold 87, 89, **90**, 92, 94–95, 103, 108, 120
threshold region 94–95
Thurstone's method of absolute scaling 10
track (in MST) 54, 102, 106–108
true domain score 20, 32–33, 41–42
true score 1–3, 6, 8–12, 20–21, 32–36, 43, 103
true-score equating 32, 34

two-parameter logistic (2PL) model 13, 15–17, 19, 23, 25, 32, 42, 46, 60, 62, 97–98, 111–112, 114–115, 118–120, 123
two-parameter normal-ogive model 13, 16, 42
two-parameter rational function model (RFM2) 47–48, 57, 62–64, 77, 97, 111–112, 119

$U3$ statistic 75–77, 123
Ud statistic 75–77
unconstrained model 24, 33
unidimensionality 24, 33, 35, 37–40, 43, 123
uniform DIF 29, 78–80, 81–85

virtual item 89–90, 91–92

weak assumptions 2, 39, 43
weak true-score theory 1
Winsteps (software) 27, 36

Yen's Q_1 26

$Z3$ statistic 76–77, 123
Z-scale of normal deviates 66, 68
Zd statistic 75